PRIVATIZATION AND PUBLIC UNIVERSITIES

Privatization and Public Universities

Edited by
Douglas M. Priest and Edward P. St. John

Indiana University Press
Bloomington & Indianapolis

This book is a publication of

Indiana University Press
601 North Morton Street
Bloomington, IN 47404-3797 USA

http://iupress.indiana.edu

Telephone orders   800-842-6796
Fax orders   812-855-7931
Orders by e-mail   iuporder@indiana.edu

The paper used in this publication meets the minimum requirements
of American National Standard for Information Sciences—
Permanence of Paper for Printed Library Materials, ANSI Z39.48-1984.

Manufactured in the United States of America

Library of Congress Cataloging-in-Publication Data

Privatization and public universities / edited by Douglas M. Priest and Edward P.
St. John.
    p. cm.
Includes bibliographical references and index.
ISBN 0-253-34735-1 (cloth : alk. paper)
1. Public universities and colleges—United States—Finance. 2. Privatization in
education—United States. I. Priest, Douglas M., date II. St. John, Edward P.
LB2342.P75 2006
378.1'060973—dc22
2005034288

1 2 3 4 5 11 10 09 08 07 06

Contents

Acknowledgments

It has been our privilege to work with the outstanding scholars that have contributed to this volume. We are indebted to them for their many contributions. We would also like to thank Sarah Martin for her assistance in preparation and review of draft copies, and Robert Sloan for his patience throughout the process.

PRIVATIZATION AND PUBLIC UNIVERSITIES

Introduction

Douglas M. Priest, Edward P. St. John,
and Rachel Dykstra Boon

The days of predictable increases in publicly funded support for higher education—if they ever existed—are long gone. State legislatures are faced with statewide shortfalls. Students are becoming increasingly informed consumers in the college choice process. Local, national, and international events can influence donor income each year as competing interests win out. When the economy shifts, students feel encouraged or discouraged toward receiving postsecondary education. It seems that no public institution from the smallest community college to the largest doctoral-granting university is safe from such fluctuations and uncertainty.

Given this sort of market for postsecondary education, public universities have been pushed further toward private sector methods of revenue generation and cost reduction in an attempt to maintain and increase academic stature. Private not-for-profit institutions have long had to deal with a shifting donor base that pushes them to rely more heavily on tuition and other more creative sources of income. Huge fundraising campaigns have, over the years, created endowments near a billion dollars at several elite private institutions. High tuition has been used to gain income, but high aid packages to those financially unable to pay have been used to maintain access to the institution. Consortia of smaller private institutions have been created to reap the benefits of economies of scale in purchasing. These efforts have largely paid off for private institutions, and a strong cadre of these institutions lead the way on many commonly used indicators of success.

1

To understand the challenges facing public colleges as they adjust to the new financial conditions, we must start with a distinction between privatization of public colleges and commercialization of activities in public and private colleges. We define *privatization* in public higher education as the process of transforming low-tuition institutions that are largely dependent on state funding to provide mass enrollment opportunities at low prices into institutions dependent on tuition revenues and other types of earned income as central sources of operating revenue. In contrast, *commercialization* refers to the process of transforming institutions' teaching, research, and service activities to compete with private enterprises in the larger economic marketplace. Both public and private colleges are confronted with decisions about the commercialization of the educational enterprise, as Bok (2003) correctly argues. Privatization in public colleges has been influenced by changes in state and federal policy in the United States, a pattern that is evident internationally as well (Slaughter and Leslie 1997).

For public colleges and universities, privatization involves becoming more like for-profit corporations and nonprofit colleges, which have functioned for centuries without state subsidies to reduce tuition. By reducing per-student subsidies to public institutions, states have not only influenced tuition increases but have also accelerated market forces, increasing competition between public and private colleges. In the United States this transition began in the 1980s as a consequence of changes in federal student aid programs and reductions in state per-student subsidies to public colleges (St. John 1994). Like private colleges, public colleges now emphasize generating revenue from alternative sources, including philanthropy, patents and royalties, and tuition.

Public colleges are not alone in adapting their technologies to new market forces. Not only are efforts to raise support from philanthropy and other sources common to both public and private colleges, but public colleges are playing catch-up with the private sector on many other fronts, borrowing or adapting methods such as incentive budgeting from private colleges (Priest, Becker, Hossler, and St. John 2002). However, both public and private colleges are confronted with decisions about whether they can use outsourcing of auxiliary services (i.e., food services, book stores, etc.), a special form of privatization within both sectors, as a means of improving quality and/or reducing costs for students. In addition, both public and private colleges face strategic choices about technology integration that are similar to those faced by private corporations. Thus, adaptations to new conditions are common to public and private institutions of higher education, but these adaptations are more complicated in the public sector because they are being made in a period of privatization.

While the topic of privatization has been widely studied in the United States, the specific issue of adaptation and change in the public sector of American higher education has not been examined in relation to the public interest. Historically, the federal and state governments developed and invested in the public sector of higher education to pursue social and economic goals that were thought to be in the public interest. Over a century and a half, from the creation of land grant colleges to the present, arguments for the public good have been used as rationales for public funding. Changes in the public sector give us reason to ponder the public interest and the obligation of public colleges and universities to respond to this interest in the context of pressures to privatize in a more competitive marketplace, where competition for students and faculty are major driving forces in the pursuit of excellence. This volume is organized to address four interrelated issues concerning the privatization of public colleges: public policy, alternative revenue sources, modernization, and the public interest.

Privatization and Public Policy

The privatization of public colleges and universities is inexorably linked to shifts in public policy both in the United States and globally. Declines in state funding and in federal need-based grants, along with the emergence of federal loans, have been the root cause. The chapters in part 1 examine trends in state and federal policy affecting higher education and situate these trends in the context of the globalization process.

In chapter 1, Donald Heller examines the trends in state funding for colleges and for college students, identifying critical issues and suggesting possible remedies. He notes that the trends in state funding have been particularly dismal from 2002 to 2004 and that only a modest recovery should be expected. Meanwhile, increases in demand for higher education and the needs of individual campuses are not expected to abate. The result will be a long-term widening of the gap between state appropriations and overall expenditures at public universities, where institutional financial aid continues to be a priority. Heller's recommendations regarding aid to students and state formulas for future appropriations could help maintain the system and the integrity of institutional missions to provide access to residents.

3

St. John and Ontario Wooden examine, in chapter 2, the trends in federal support for research, postsecondary institutions, and students and consider how federal policy has been a catalyst for the privatization of public higher education. Reflecting on how changes in federal student aid policy—especially the decline in grants and the rise in loans—have influenced pricing in both public and private universities, they untangle reasons for prices becoming more important to public colleges as they have moved toward privatization.

Chapter 3 takes a step back and places the changes in education, public finance and education policies in the global context. Fazal Rizvi explores how globalization in education has emphasized implementation of new forms of accountability schemes along with privatization. Therefore, the U.S. experience with privatization is appropriately viewed in relation to the movement toward the new accountability regime in K–12 education—standards, testing and aligned curriculum, especially in math—used as a means of improving academic preparation and rationalizing limited opportunity to enroll in four-year colleges.

Alternative Revenue Sources

The shift away from public funding has led to increased emphasis on alternative revenue sources as well as an increased emphasis on using strategic enrollment management to improve tuition revenue. The new financial strategies hasten the organizational transformations of public colleges and universities by changing incentives and values within universities. The authors in part 2 examine trends and consider the implications of these new monetary and fiscal management schemes.

A focus on the options for revenue diversification and the implications of each is taken by James Hearn in chapter 4. His categorization of various revenue-stream options for institutions and the consequent strategic and philosophical assessment provide readers a good sense of the questions that university administrators are addressing in the press to identify budgetary sources in line with the missions of their institutions. Based on business models, the options Hearn describes are leading many in higher education to question the path of privatization of public universities, while the allure of additional funding creates an imperative for administrators to closely examine each option available.

As the search for revenue has diversified, the traditional method of raising tuition has not been abandoned. Chapter 5 provides a close look at the use of students and families as a larger revenue source for public institutions. The emphasis on this revenue stream affects prospective and current students as well as the trend to privatization itself. Don Hossler examines the incentives for the institutions, the impacts on equity and access, operational issues for the institutions, and the prognosis for states considering or enacting legislation on new tuition models like those in Colorado and South Carolina.

Joshua Powers examines patents and royalties as revenue sources for universities in chapter 6. The opportunities for returns in this area have been well exploited by a few universities, thus enticing many more to try to get a piece of the pie. Powers outlines the risks involved as well as the ethics and social responsibility of universities to the constituents of their locale. The tendency toward privatization through patents and royalties and the projected path on which it could lead a willing institution deserve careful consideration.

Another funding source as old as universities themselves, but taking on new meaning in the modern age of privatization of public institutions, is philanthropy. Aaron Conley and Eugene Tempel address the critical implications facing public institutions as they attempt to follow the lead of America's private universities in raising philanthropic support. Chapter 7 provides a contextual overview of philanthropy in higher education through the early twentieth century, highlighting those few institutions that established comprehensive development programs before 1950. Dramatic growth is observed through data on campaigns and "mega-gifts" in the last twenty years. The importance of growth in the staff and budget of development offices as well as in the endowments is illustrative of the vital importance of this revenue stream.

Privatization within University Enterprises

The global economy and the information age have also influenced transformations of the university enterprise within both public and private universities. Public institutions, like private colleges, are adopting new budget models that make it easier to respond to the new incentive structures and to face decisions about using private contractors to run services that were formerly operated by the universities. Moreover, universities are adapting to changes in information technology in both the academic and administrative sides of the university enterprise.

Also reflective of the movement of financial trends from public to private institutions is the use of incentive-based budgeting. Such approaches have a reasonably long history in private institutions in this country. As public institutions have begun to adapt this method over the past decade, the goal has been to stimulate specific sorts of activities on campus. In chapter 8, Douglas Priest and Rachel Boon explore how these approaches to budgeting are using incentives previously seen only in businesses and private universities, making adjustments that allow them to handle budget shortfalls in other areas while maintaining the overall mission of the university. Questions of how universities can deal with the vagaries of the marketplace and how they can best use incentives to leverage institutional change are addressed. A better understanding of the ultimate changes in the role of public higher education as institutions deal with financial stresses can be gained by considering these issues.

Chapter 9 examines the recent history of privatization of various support services in higher education. Priest, Bruce Jacobs, and Boon detail several examples of the effects of privatization on certain services to show the issues most salient to institutions considering such a move. Though each service area is different, the most important factor is the difference in each campus culture, mission, and strategic plan. Auxiliaries can support each of these in important and frequently nonfinancial ways, and often that is the most important consideration in an outsourcing decision process.

Like most other corporate enterprises, colleges and universities are faced with increasingly complex and difficult decisions about investment in information systems. The newer comprehensive information systems restructure work processes and interactions with students in admissions, financial aid, and libraries; they also restructure financial systems and personnel systems. Many public universities have made multi-year, multi-million-dollar investments in these new "enterprise" systems, while others have built their own legacy systems. In chapter 10, Don Hossler and William Gorr examine the history of enterprise systems, the risks associated with these investments, the potential benefits, and strategies for building cooperation in their development.

Finally, in chapter 11, James Farmer examines the emergence of e-learning in higher education as a change in the academic side of the university enterprise. It is now evident that changes in publishing, including movement toward electronic dissemination of information, are inexorably linked to change in the educational enterprise. Farmer examines the current process of change in educational delivery in relation to change in the publication and dissemination of information.

Making Privatization Work

It is no longer a question of whether privatization of public higher education will occur, but rather of how well government, universities, and the public will adapt to the changes that are now under way. Given the expected increases in college enrollment during the next few decades as a result in growth in the college-age cohort and improvements in academic preparation, demand for higher education will probably grow, thus increasing pressure to privatize.

Given these shifts, the editors take a step back and review the changes in policy and public funding with an eye on the nature of the public interest in education. Higher education has played an important role in social mobility and economic development in the United States during the past two centuries. In chapter 12 we take a look at the implications for the public interest of the shifts toward privatization. It is abundantly evident, when viewed from this perspective, that privatization has enabled the nation to expand higher education enrollment at lower taxpayer cost than would have been possible had the low-tuition policies of prior decades been maintained. However, there has been growing financial and racial inequality in access, especially relative to the opportunity to enroll in four-year colleges.

Finally, these changes have implications for how public universities are viewed, the roles they are able to play in society, and how administrators respond to the challenges they face. In the final chapter, we re-examine the major themes—the decline in public funding, the efforts to generate revenue from alternative sources, and the modernization process—in relation to strategic decisions facing universities in the next decade.

References

Bok, D. 2003. *Universities in the marketplace: The commercialization of higher education*. Princeton, N.J.: Princeton University Press.

Priest, D. M., W. E. Becker, D. Hossler, and E. P. St. John. 2002. Why incentive-based budgeting systems in the public sector and why now? In *Incentive-based budgeting systems in public universities*, ed. D. M. Priest et al., 1–8. Northampton, Mass.: Edward Elgar.

Slaughter, S., and L. L. Leslie. 1997. *Academic capitalism: Politics, policies, and the entrepreneurial university*. Baltimore, Md.: Johns Hopkins University Press.

St. John, E. P. 1994. *Prices, productivity, and investment*. ASHE/ERIC monograph, No. 3. San Francisco: Jossey-Bass.

I
PUBLIC POLICY AND
PRIVATIZATION

CHAPTER ONE

State Support of Higher Education: Past, Present, and Future

Donald E. Heller

Funding for public higher education today has been described as being in "crisis" (Jenny and Arbak 2004; National Education Association 2004; Trounson 2004). The budget constraints incurred by most states in response to the slowdown in the economy has caused state funding for higher education to be cut for two years in a row (Center for the Study of Education Policy 2004). From fiscal year 2002 to 2004, state funding for higher education declined 4 percent in current dollars, or, when inflation is taken into account, a decline of 8 percent.

Largely because of these funding cuts, tuition prices at public institutions have skyrocketed during this period. The average tuition price nationally among public four-year institutions increased 26 percent from the 2001–2002 to 2003–2004 academic years and 18 percent at community colleges (College Board 2003a) during a two-year period when the Consumer Price Index increased just 4 percent.

These funding cuts and price increases have occurred while demand for higher education is at an all-time high, driven both by demographics and by the preferences of more and more traditional-age (18–24 years old) and adult students to attend college. From a low of 2.5 million in 1994, the number of high school graduates in the nation is projected to peak at 3.2 million in 2009, an increase of 28 percent (Western Interstate Commission for Higher Education 2003). In 1980, half of all high school graduates enrolled in postsecondary education within a year of graduation. By 1997, this had increased to two-thirds of all graduates (National Center for Education Statistics [NCES] 2003a, table 183). From 1980 to 2000, enrollment of adult students (those over the age of 24) increased 32 percent, compared to a 24-percent increase in the enrollment of those under age 24 (NCES 2003a, table 174).

There has also been an important shift in state and institutional financial aid policy in recent years. Throughout most of the nation's history financial aid was awarded to students based on their financial need in order to promote access to college for poor students, but recently both states and higher education institutions have been turning more and more to merit aid, which is disproportionately awarded to students from higher-income families.

In this chapter I critically examine these trends, summarize the research on the consequences of these new patterns of state financing for higher education, and discuss possible new strategies for strengthening state support of this nation's public colleges and the students who attend them.

State Support of Higher Education

The Historical Roots

State support of higher education in the United States began with public allocations to private, largely church-chartered institutions.[1] This support was often in the form of the granting of public lands and authorization for the running of lotteries to benefit the institution. Many state governments in the late eighteenth and early nineteenth centuries began to provide direct financial support from general tax revenues to support a number of private colleges and universities.

The first truly "public" institutions of higher education were initially chartered in the late eighteenth century, primarily in the South and the Midwest. The passage of the Morrill Act in 1862, however, heralded the great expansion in the public system of higher education. The Morrill Act provided federal land grants to states, which could in turn sell the land and use the proceeds for the creation and expansion of public universities. The number of higher education institutions in the country increased from 563 in 1869 to 977 at the end of the nineteenth century. During the same period, the number of students enrolled in these institutions increased more than fourfold, from 52,286 to 237,592 (NCES 2003a, table 3). Public institutions were funded primarily through revenues from the land grants, supplemented by appropriations from state general fund tax revenues.

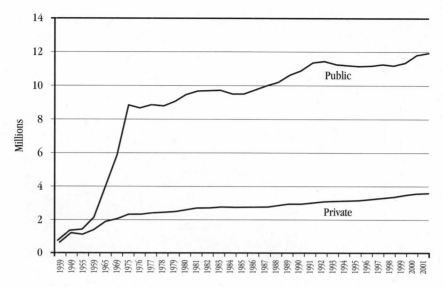

Figure 1.1. Enrollment in public and private higher education institutions.
(National Center for Education Statistics 2003a, table 3.)

The proceeds of land sales and state appropriations were not the only sources of revenues for public colleges, however. These public institutions often charged tuition directly to the individual, though the charges were generally well below the level of those charged by private institutions and were not universal. An early-twentieth-century study on the subject of public tuition charges concluded,

> Yet the idea of fees or tuition was not entirely absent from the state university plan even in the beginning. The Federal Land Grant Act does not make any restriction against fees. . . . However, in the majority of cases no tuition as such was introduced in the new type [public] of institution and such fees as were created were nominal in amount. Probably the boards found then, as now, that other sources of income were not sufficient and that a charge of some kind against the student was a necessity. Probably they felt that the student would appreciate his work more if he paid something for it. (Morey 1928, 185–86)

Another study confirmed the nominal nature of early tuition rates at public institutions, noting mid-nineteenth-century annual tuition and fee rates of $12 at the University of Wisconsin (1855), $10 at the University of Tennessee (1866), $5 at the University of Illinois (1868), $15 at Ohio State (1874), and $5 at the University of Missouri (1874) (Sears 1923).

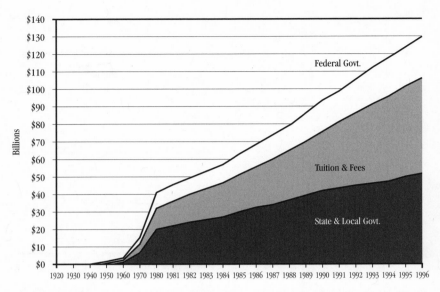

Figure 1.2. Revenues received by public and private higher education institutions from 1920 to 1996. (National Center for Education Statistics 2003a, table 333.)

The passage of the Servicemen's Readjustment Act (more commonly known as the GI Bill) in 1944 helped increase enrollments at both private and public colleges. As recently as just after World War II, enrollments at public and private institutions were roughly equivalent. Beginning in the economic expansion of the 1950s and continuing into the 1960s, however, enrollment at public institutions began to greatly outstrip that of private colleges. Figure 1.1 shows enrollment in each sector from 1939 through 2001.

Both public and private higher education institutions have diverse revenue streams. Public appropriations (from state, local, and the federal governments), tuition and fees, gifts and endowment income, contracts, and sales of educational services all bring revenue into colleges. Historically, however, appropriations from the states had been the largest revenue source for all institutions, public and private, combined.

Since the early part of the twentieth century, the Department of Education and its predecessor agencies have tracked the revenues (and expenditures) of higher education institutions. The three largest sources of revenues have been the federal government, tuition and fees, and state and local governments.[2] Figure 1.2 shows the revenues received by all higher education institutions from these three sources.

14

Table 1.1. Revenues Received by Public and Private Higher Education
Institutions over Three Time Periods (Author's calculations from
National Center for Education Statistics 2003a, tables 333–336)

	Tuition and Fees	Federal Government	State and Local Governments
1940–1960	$956,585,000	$998,130,000	$1,350,577,000
1960–1980	10,772,858,000	7,865,854,000	18,439,660,000
1980–2000	50,568,107,000	20,440,022,000	44,213,574,000

The great expansion in funding for higher education between 1960
and 1980 can be seen in figure 1.2. Total revenues in higher education
increased over $50 billion, or tenfold, during these two decades, from
$5.8 billion to $58 billion. In contrast, the previous two decades (from
1940 to 1960) saw an increase of only $5 billion in revenues.

While all three sources have contributed to the rise in revenues in
colleges and universities, tuition and fees have become the fastest growing revenue source. Table 1.1 shows the changes in revenues from each
of these sources over three time periods. Both from 1940 to 1960, and
from 1960 to 1980, funding from state and local governments was the
largest source of increased revenues, far outstripping the growth in revenues from the other two sources. In the most recent two decades, however, tuition and fees contributed more to revenues than the other two
sources.

While the Department of Education has not yet released revenue
data from the years after 2000, it is very likely that tuition and fees have
continued to be the fastest growing component of university revenues.
From fiscal year 2000 to 2004, state appropriations for higher education
increased only 6.5 percent (Center for the Study of Education Policy
2001, 2004). During the same period, tuition prices increased 27 percent, 40 percent, and 16 percent in private four-year institutions, public
four-year institutions, and community colleges, respectively (College
Board 2003a).[3]

The relative contributions of these three main sources of revenues
can be seen in figure 1.3. In the first half of the twentieth century, support from the states and tuition and fees dwarfed revenues received
from the federal government. World War II, however, spurred the development of federally funded research at the nation's universities.

The period beginning in 1950 and ending in 1980 was an era of
large growth in support for higher education by the states. This three-

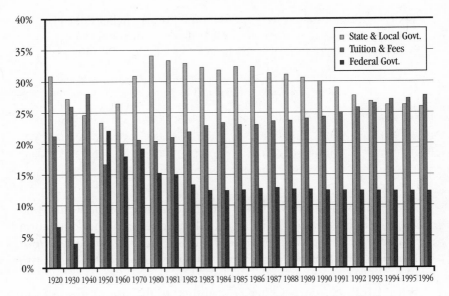

Figure 1.3. Share of total revenues of higher education institutions for three major sources. (Author's calculations from National Center for Education Statistics 2003a, table 333.)

decade period saw state spending on higher education increase almost 40-fold as colleges and universities expanded their enrollments. Since 1980, however, the state (and local community) share of total college and university revenues has declined, from a high of 34 percent to 26 percent in 1996. The federal share of university revenues also declined slightly during this period, from 15 percent to 12 percent. Both of these declines were largely supplanted by the increase in the share of revenues earned from tuition and fees, which rose from 20 percent of total revenues in 1980 to 28 percent in 1996. And this trend has continued in the ensuing years.

Recent Funding of Public Colleges and Universities

Over 97 percent of all state and local appropriations nationally are directed to public institutions (see note 2). Understanding changes in state funding is also complicated by changes in enrollment. Thus, I will focus here on changes in state funding on a per-student basis since 1980. Because of a lag in data available from the National Center for Education Statistics, I have augmented the NCES data with other sources where available. The sources of data used to calculate and esti-

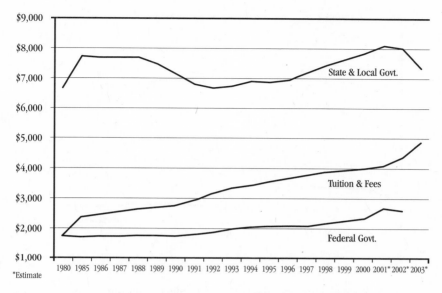

Figure 1.4. Income per full-time-equivalent student in public institutions (2003 $). (Author's calculations; see appendix.)

mate the public college and university revenues and enrollments are detailed in an appendix to this chapter.

Since 1980, enrollments in public institutions have increased from 9.4 million to 12.5 million students in 2003, an increase of 33 percent.[4] Taking into account part-time enrollees, the increase in full-time-equivalent enrollments was from 6.6 to 8.8 million students. During this same period, state and local appropriations to public institutions increased 31 percent in real (2003) dollars, from $48.9 billion to $64.3 billion, almost matching the proportional increase in enrollments.

While at first glance it would appear that the states maintained their real level of support for higher education, what this comparison ignores is that the cost of educating each student has increased significantly. Data on expenditures in public institutions show that overall educational and general expenditures increased 65 percent in real terms from 1980 to 1999 (NCES 2003a, table 347), while enrollment increased only 21 percent. Instruction, which makes up the largest share of expenditures, increased only 46 percent during this period. Research and public service both grew at rates more than double that of instruction.[5]

Thus, the fact that state appropriations kept pace with enrollment growth was not sufficient for public higher education institutions to

17

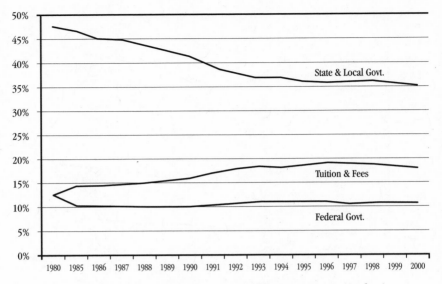

Figure 1.5. Share of current fund revenues in public institutions. (Author's calculations; see appendix.)

maintain their funding base. The primary source that these institutions turned toward to make up the difference was the revenues received from students and their families. Figure 1.4 shows the changes in income per student for the three primary revenue sources of public institutions.

Public college and university revenue per student from state and local governments was slightly higher in 2003 than in 1980, increasing from $6,595 to $7,320 in constant dollars but was still below the 1985 level of $7,715. Revenue from the federal government increased 48 percent from 1980 to 2002. Federal funds are primarily awarded for sponsored research and other contracts and cannot be used for general subsidy of undergraduate instruction. Tuition and fee revenue saw the largest growth of the three primary sources in public institutions during this period, increasing 173 percent, from $1,793 in 1980 to $4,897 in 2003.[6]

These changes can be seen when you examine the share of total current fund revenues received by public institutions, shown in figure 1.5. In 1980, state and local appropriations provided just under half the revenues received by public colleges and universities. By 2000, this had declined to 35 percent. The share of revenues received from the federal government decreased from 13 percent to 11 percent. Tuition and fees

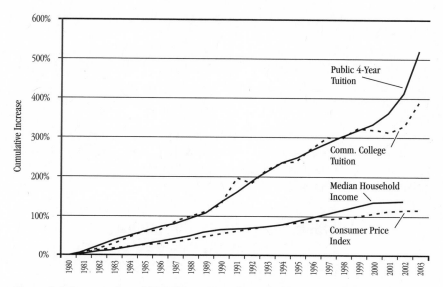

Figure 1.6. Increase in public tuition prices, household incomes, and consumer prices. (Bureau of Labor Statistics 2004; College Board 2003a; and U.S. Bureau of the Census 2004a.)

received from students and their families increased from 13 percent of total revenues in 1980 to 18 percent in 2000. During these two decades, the proportion of total current fund revenues received from these three sources combined decreased from 73 percent to 64 percent.

Total current fund revenues are only available from the NCES through the 2000–2001 academic year, and there are no reliable national-level sources available to estimate them for more recent years. However, given the trends since then noted earlier—overall state appropriations for higher education decreased one-half percent in current dollars from 2000 to 2003 (Center for the Study of Education Policy 2001, 2004), and tuition prices increased 35 percent at public four-year institutions and 16 percent at community colleges (College Board 2003a)—it is very likely that the share of total revenues received from tuition and fees has risen well above the peak level of 19 percent reached in the mid-1990s.

The substitution of tuition and fees paid by students and their families for general appropriations from the state over the last two decades is reflected in the tuition price increases shown in figure 1.6. The cumulative increases since 1980 in tuition prices in public four-year institutions and community colleges nationally are shown along with the in-

19

creases in the Consumer Price Index (for all urban consumers) and median household income in the country.

While incomes and inflation increased less than 150 percent between 1980 and 2003, tuition prices at public four-year institutions rose 517 percent, and community college prices increased 387 percent.[7] Prices in both sectors rose at more than twice the rate of increase in consumer prices as well as the ability of families to pay for higher education. For lower-income students the picture is even bleaker. Because wealthier households have made more gains in income than poorer households over the last two decades, the burden of paying for college for poorer families is greater (Heller 2001).

Shifts in State and Institutional Financial Aid Policies

Trends in the States

Historically, most financial aid was awarded for the purpose of helping to increase access to higher education. Title IV of the Higher Education Act of 1965, which authorizes the federal student financial assistance programs, opens with this statement:

> It is the purpose of this part to provide, through institutions of higher education, educational opportunity grants to assist in making available benefits of higher education to qualified high school graduates of exceptional financial need who, for lack of financial means of their own or of their families, would be unable to obtain such benefits without such aid. (Higher Education Act of 1965, § 401)

In order to meet this statute, federal grants—particularly Pell Grants, the largest federal grant program—have been awarded for the last four decades, using the financial need of the student and her family as the primary criterion.[8]

The 1972 reauthorization of the Higher Education Act created the State Student Incentive Grant (SSIG) program, which provided matching funds from the federal government to states that established or expanded need-based scholarship programs of their own. As I noted in an earlier article,

> This proved to be a critical catalyst to the development and expansion of the state programs. While in 1969, 19 states appropriated just under $200 million for these programs, by 1974 this had expanded to 36 states and $423 million. By 1979 every state (and the District of Columbia) re-

20

ported at least one grant program, and the total appropriated had increased to over $800 million. A 1975 survey conducted by the National Association of State Scholarship Programs commented that "growth represented in '74–75 and '75–76. . . to a large degree, is a response to the new SSIG Program which permits up to a $1,500 annual student award (equal shares of $750 Federal/State) in this new form of State/Federal partnership." (Heller 2002a, 230–31)

While the SSIG program, later renamed Leveraging Educational Assistance Partnership (LEAP), helped spur the initial development of state need-based grant programs, they grew largely through the efforts of the states themselves. Funding for SSIG (and later LEAP) expanded at a much slower pace than the state programs. Even without the federal incentives, however, most states maintained a commitment to financial aid that mirrored that of the federal government:

> Access and choice are two principal themes in student aid that have become familiar through frequent and thorough discussion over the past 20 years as they unfolded first in hortatory statements, then in large and growing funded student aid programs. The expressed goal of such programs has been to benefit young persons in the society by providing wide access to their choice of postsecondary education institutions. . . . The goal of wider access was achieved by changing the nature and purpose of monetary awards, from prizes recognizing accomplishments or potential to assistance granted almost solely to offset financial need. (Fenske and Boyd 1981, 2–3)

The awarding of grants based on financial need has been recognized as being particularly effective in promoting initial college entry and persistence through college to students from lower-income families. Research reviews conducted over three decades have confirmed that lower-income students are the most price sensitive and that they have the largest enrollment response to an offer of a grant that lowers the price of attendance (Heller 1997; Jackson and Weathersby 1975; Leslie and Brinkman 1988). Grants to higher-income students have little impact on their college entry decisions, but they can help influence where a wealthier student attends college.

During the 1980s and early 1990s, the commitment to need-based aid on the part of the states continued. While the total dollars awarded to undergraduates grew from $975 million in fiscal year 1982 to $2.4 billion in 1994, the percentage of dollars awarded without using financial need as a measure fluctuated between 8.9 percent and 11.1 percent of the total (National Association of State Scholarship and Grant Programs, various years).

21

The decade of the 1990s, however, saw major changes in state financial aid policy, with some states moving away from financial need as the primary criterion used for awarding grants. With the development of the Helping Outstanding Students Educationally (HOPE) program in 1993, Georgia became the first state to develop a broad-based merit grant program that functioned as an entitlement (i.e., every student who met the award criteria was guaranteed a grant) and did not use financial need as a criterion for awards.[9] All students in the state who graduated from high school with a B average were awarded a full-tuition scholarship at any public institution in the state or $500 to attend a private institution in Georgia.[10]

From this start, merit scholarship programs, those that award their grants without consideration of financial need, have become the fastest-growing category of financial aid in the states. In 1992, the year before the development of Georgia HOPE, 9 percent of state aid to undergraduate students was awarded without consideration of financial need. This increased to 23 percent in 2002, the most recent year for which data are available (National Association of State Scholarship and Grant Programs, various years). During this period, the total dollars awarded by the states without consideration of the financial need of the student rose 483 percent, while the volume of need-based grant dollars increased 101 percent. Over a dozen states now have programs similar to HOPE. While the merit criteria used to award the grants vary, the programs are similar in that they are structured largely as entitlements and they award the grants without means testing (Heller 2002b).

In contrast to the research cited above on need-based grants, which have been found to be instrumental in promoting access for lower-income students, merit grants have a quite different impact. Because of the strong correlation between socioeconomic status and the academic criteria used for awarding the grants—which generally include high school grades, standardized test scores, or some combination of the two—the benefits of merit grants flow disproportionately to students from more well-off families. A 2002 report that analyzed four of the largest state merit aid programs concluded,

> Overall, the studies in this report make it clear that the students least likely to be awarded a merit scholarship come from populations that have traditionally been underrepresented in higher education. This hinders the potential to increase college access among minority and low-income students, especially if these scholarship programs continue to overshadow need-based programs. (Marin 2002, 112)

Table 1.2. Institutional Grant Awards to Dependent Students in Public Institutions (Author's calculations from National Center for Education Statistics 2004a, 2004b)

	1992–1993	1999–2000	% change
Total dollars (millions)			
Need-based	$423	$678	60
Merit	$677	$1,283	89
Total	$1,100	$1,961	78
Number of grants			
Need-based	$317,000	$448,000	41
Merit	$334,000	$490,000	47
Total*	$621,000	$896,000	44
Average per student**			
Need-based	$1,336	$1,515	13
Merit	$2,024	$2,618	29
Total	$1,773	$2,189	23

*Total does not equal sum of need-based and merit grants because some students receive both types.
**For students who received a grant.

Trends in Institutional Aid

Through most of the history of American higher education, financial aid was largely the province of private institutions. In recent years, however, public institutions have entered the institutional financial aid field, expanding their awarding of grants from their own resources. These grants have been used for two purposes: to promote access for underserved populations, and for enrollment management. While these efforts are modest in comparison to most private institutions, they are increasing.

Like the federal government and states, some public colleges and universities have recognized the importance of financial aid to ensure that poorer students will be able to enroll in college. As tuition prices have risen faster than the ability of lower-income students and their families to pay—even with the assistance of state and federal grants—public institutions have begun to offer their own need-based grants.[11]

Public institutions have also felt the pressure to use financial aid for enrollment management purposes. The tactic of tuition discounting, or offering institutional grants to attractive students—those often perceived to benefit the institution in national college guides and rankings

23

such as those produced by *U.S. News & World Report*—has spread from private colleges into public institutions as well.[12]

Table 1.2 shows the changes in institutional need-based and non-need, or merit grants in public colleges between 1992 and 1999. The analysis uses data from the National Postsecondary Student Aid Study, a nationally representative survey of how college students finance their education.

Between 1992 and 1999 overall spending on institutional grants to dependent undergraduates increased 78 percent, with spending on merit grants outpacing that of need-based grants.[13] The increase in grant spending was the result of both an increase in the number of grants awarded and an increase in the average amount of each grant.

The increase in grant spending is less impressive, however, in the context of change in tuition prices. Tuition prices increased 44 percent at four-year public institutions and 48 percent in community colleges over the same seven years (College Board 2003a). Thus, while more students received both need-based and merit grants (and enrollment was stable during this period), the increase in the average award was considerably less than the tuition price increases.

Another important trend in institutional grant awards—one that mirrors what was happening in state financial aid during this period—was that merit awards increased both in size and in number at a faster pace than did need-based awards. Merit awards, which are used primarily for enrollment management purposes, became a more prominent tactic of financial aid policy in public institutions.

The Implications of Rising Prices and Changing Financial Aid Policies

As described in the previous section, lower-income students are the most sensitive to rising tuition prices when they make decisions to enroll in college and to persist through to a degree or other credential once enrolled. This sensitivity is both to rising tuition prices, which discourage college enrollment and persistence, and financial aid (particularly grants), which encourages enrollment and persistence.

The shifting of the burden of paying for college from the public to students and their families as well as the increasing use of merit aid by the states and public institutions have not occurred in a policy vacuum. Federal financial aid is still the largest single source of assistance for paying for college. According to data from the College Board (2003b),

68 percent of the $105 billion in student aid that was available in the 2002–2003 academic year was from the federal government. Of the $72 billion in aid provided by the federal government, however, 69 percent was in the form of loans, and 8 percent was in the form of educational tax credits. Overall, less than 40 percent of all aid was awarded in the form of grants.

Grants, loans, and tax credits each have a different effect on the college enrollment decisions of youth who are underrepresented in higher education. The research on college choice noted earlier has consistently found that grants are more effective than loans in improving access and persistence for these students. An important reason for this difference is that loans do not function to lower the price of education; instead they are a mechanism to allow students to postpone paying for college until after they have graduated and are presumably benefiting from the higher salaries available to college graduates. Student loans, in fact, *increase* the cost of college going, because of the loan origination fees and interest charged during repayment.[14]

Education tax credits, while still a fairly new college financing policy, have been found to have little impact on college access and choice for lower-income students. The federal HOPE and Lifetime Learning tax credits have important characteristics that work against their usefulness for lower-income students:

- They are nonrefundable and therefore require the student or her parents to have a tax liability, which for the lowest-income students excludes them from eligibility.
- They can only be applied to tuition charges, not to other components of the cost of attendance.
- Any other grants received must first be applied to tuition, and only any remaining tuition charge can be used for the tax credits.
- The credits can only be taken against prior tax year costs, e.g., a student enrolling in college in September in a given year would not receive the credit until January or later of that academic year.

A recent analysis of the impact of the tax credits found that while less than 5 percent of families with incomes below $20,000 took advantage of the credits in 2000, 12 percent of families with incomes above $75,000 and below $100,000 (at which level the credits phase out) took the credits. This analysis concluded, "insufficient tax liability due to low income levels, competing tax credits and deductions, and the interaction with other aid programs prevents many low-income individuals from qualifying for the aid" (Long 2003, 44).

25

The nation has done little to close the gap in college participation between the rich and the poor. While all income groups have increased the rate at which they attend college, a gap of approximately 30 percentage points between students in the top income quartile and those in the bottom has stubbornly persisted over the last three decades (College Board 2003a). Similar gaps between the enrollment of white and underrepresented minority students (African American, Latino, and Native American) have also persisted.

Finances are not the only barrier that low-income and other underrepresented students face when attempting to enroll in college. Academic preparation, family and peer support, and cultural barriers also play a role.[15] But even among students who prepare themselves for college academically and in other ways, finances still play a role in keeping them out of college. The Advisory Committee on Student Financial Assistance, a federal body charged with advising both the Secretary of Education and Congress on financial aid policy, recently conducted an analysis of the impact of unmet financial need, or the difference between college costs and the resources available to students (from their own and family resources, as well as from financial aid) to meet them. It examined a cohort of students who were graduating from high school in 1992 and who were "college-qualified—that is, those having adequate academic course preparation, grades, and aptitude test scores to meet the minimal entrance requirements of most four-year colleges" (Advisory Committee on Student Financial Assistance 2002, 16). It also classified the students based on their level of unmet need when applying for college. Among these students, 93 percent from high-income families (those with little unmet financial need) enrolled in postsecondary education within two years of high school graduation. In contrast, only 64 percent of students with high unmet need enrolled in college within the same period. Even more striking is that 77 percent of all high-income students attended a four-year college, while only 33 percent of the poorer students did. These gaps in college entry led to later gaps in degree attainment. While 62 percent of the higher-income high school graduates went on to complete a bachelor's degree, only 21 percent of their lower-income peers were able to attain this level of education.

Using these analyses, the Advisory Committee estimated the overall national impact of unmet need on the college enrollment of students from low-income families (below $25,000 per year in the 2001–2002 academic year) and those from moderate-income families (between $25,000 and $50,000). It found that these financial barriers prevented more than 400,000 students nationally from enrolling in a four-year in-

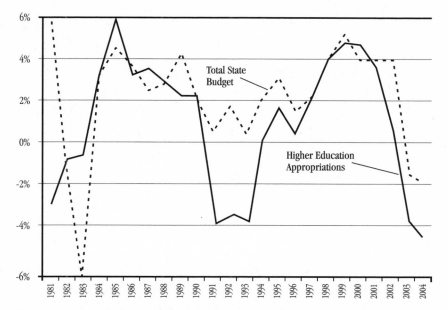

Figure 1.7. Annual changes in higher education appropriations and total state expenditures. (Center for the Study of Education Policy [various years] and National Association of State Budget Officers [various years].)

stitution, and 170,000 students were barred from attending any postsecondary education at all. Over the course of the ensuing decade, financial barriers would keep more than 4 million students out of four-year colleges and 2 million from any college.

Reversing the Trends

The simplistic solution to the issues raised in this chapter could be summarized in two words: more money. But simply throwing more money at higher education is a solution that is (1) unlikely to be accepted anytime in the near future and (2) unlikely to solve the problem if the money is not wisely targeted.

The decline of funding for higher education as a priority for states has been well documented (Breneman and Finney 1997; Hovey 1999; Mumper 2001; Rizzo 2003). Many of these and other observers of the higher education landscape believe that we are unlikely to see a recovery in state funding similar to that seen after the last recession.[16] This pessimism is understandable when one examines the declining priority of higher education in state budgets. Figure 1.7 shows the annual percentage of change in higher education appropriations and total state expenditures across the nation. In every year since 1988, with the exception of 2000, the annual increase in overall expenditures by states was equal to or exceeded that of the change in appropriations for higher education.[17]

"We're on a kind of collision course in the country," says Pat Callan, president of the National Center for Public Policy and Higher Education in San Jose, Calif., noting that along with the higher-ed cuts, many states are seeing big increases in the number of high school grads. "Every generation since the GI Bill has been better educated than the one before it. Now we're living in an economy that really demands better-educated people, and yet that's the very time where our commitment to educate the next generation seems to be more problematic" (quoted in Paulson 2004, 11).

Even given the declining priority of higher education, it is reasonable to assume that there will be *some* recovery in state funding when state budgets begin to turn around from the dismal period experienced in 2002 to 2004, when state appropriations declined in current dollars for two years in a row. In fact, early tabulations of state funding for the 2005 fiscal year indicate that funding will be increased by approximately 2 percent over the 2004 level.[18]

While it appears that higher education institutions and students will benefit from slowly increasing appropriations, it is unlikely that the increasing support will keep up with the demand for higher education. Estimates by the Western Interstate Commission for Higher Education (2003) show that the number of high school graduates in the nation will increase 8 percent from 2004 to a peak in 2009. Thus, demographics alone would require that state appropriations would have to increase $5 billion by 2009 just to keep funding at the 2004 level of $60 billion. And this estimate does not include any additional funding required for

- continuing increases in the cost of providing instruction, a likely condition given the issues described earlier in this chapter;
- increases in the college-going rate of high school graduates, whether driven by higher demand for college-educated workers in the labor markets or by the success of the No Child Left Behind Act, which seeks to increase the academic preparation and achievement of students in K–12 schools.

Continued constraints on state appropriations will likely result in ongoing upward pressure on tuition prices. While public higher education institutions, especially the larger research universities, have become more aggressive in seeking additional sources of support (such as from fund raising), revenues from tuition and fees will continue to grow as a share of the overall revenue received by public colleges and universities. The era of universally low tuition in the public sector, an era that dominated most of the nation's history, is over and will not return.

In order to ensure that states are meeting the access and success needs of all students who are academically prepared for college, the resources available for higher education must be effectively targeted and wisely used. It is imperative that both the states and public higher education institutions maintain a commitment to meeting the needs of those who are most dependent on public funds to attend college and to be successful once there.

Higher education has come to be seen as a discretionary item in state budgets in contrast to areas such as Medicare, corrections, and K–12 education, which have become de facto entitlements. There are a number of steps that states could take to help eliminate the swings of the annual state budget cycle shown in figure 1.7.

First, states should investigate linking funding for higher education to measures of demand, such as the number of high school graduates in the state and the number of adults who desire to return to postsecondary education. While the number of high school graduates is an easily obtainable figure (albeit with somewhat of a time lag), ascertaining the number of adults who want postsecondary training would require more work by most states. But surveys of employers, workforce development programs, and other organizations could help pinpoint this number.

Linking funding for higher education to independent measures of demand is an improvement over the formula-based budgeting approach used in some states. In these states, funding for higher education institutions is generally based on a formula that takes into account a variety of measures, including the enrollment in different postsecondary levels and programs. But linking funding to students already enrolled in the institution leaves the state open to missing opportunities for students who have graduated from high school (or are in the adult working population but in need of postsecondary training) but could not enroll in public institutions because of the financial barriers noted above. By benchmarking higher education funding to some baseline level and then increasing it annually by the rise in the underlying demand population, appropriations are more likely to stay in line with needs.

Second, governors, state legislators, higher education boards, and the leaders of public colleges and universities need to come to agreement on an appropriate mechanism for compensating institutions for increasing costs. Institutional leaders have long argued that the nature of higher education—it is labor intensive and employs a large proportion of highly skilled (and compensated) workers compared to the rest of state government—mandates that costs will rise faster than in most other sectors of the economy. Legislatures and governors, on the other hand, want to ensure that public colleges have incentives to control those costs and that state appropriations do not provide an incentive to increase them further.

A compromise would be to agree upon a measure that could be used to recognize the unique cost structure of higher education yet would not take on the appearance of an open checkbook to those responsible for funding it. A recent effort by the State Higher Education Executive Officers (SHEEO) to develop such a measure appears to hold promise (Lingenfelter, L'Orange, Winter, and Wright 2004). The organization developed the Higher Education Cost Adjustment (HECA) index, which is determined by a blend of two existing federal government indices: (1) the Gross Domestic Product Implicit Price Deflator (25% of the index) and (2) the Employment Cost Index (75% of the index). The latter is a measure of salaries and benefits for white-collar workers in the economy, those judged to be most similar to the skilled professions in colleges and universities. As a basis of comparison, while the Consumer Price Index increased 40 percent between 1990 and 2002, the SHEEO calculation of HECA increased 49 percent.

Third, states should investigate giving public colleges and universities more flexibility in using funds across fiscal years. Most states require public agencies to use all of their budgeted funds within a given fiscal year; any funds unspent at the close of the year have to be returned to the state treasury. This often forces administrators into "spending frenzies" as the end of the year approaches, which may not result in the best use of public resources. Allowing institutions to carry over unspent funds from one year to the next can help smooth the budget swings that occur as a result of state fiscal conditions. In good fiscal times, when state support is relatively strong, colleges and universities could bank funds toward use when the inevitable downturn occurs.

Fourth, public institutions of higher education have an obligation to ensure that the public resources with which they are entrusted are used efficiently and effectively. Accountability of higher education has been

30

at the forefront of state policy in recent times (Zumeta 2001). Colleges and universities must work with state legislative and executive branches and higher education governing or coordinating board leaders to develop a set of measures that all agree measure the performance of the public system of higher education in meeting the needs of the state. These must not be seen as punitive, used solely to punish institutions by withholding funds, but rather as formative tools to help guide institutional goals and objectives in alignment with state interests.

Fifth, both states and higher education institutions must ensure that all financial aid resources are targeted toward students who truly need the aid in order to enroll in college and be successful once there. As described earlier in this chapter, over the last decade the largest growth in both state and institutional aid to undergraduate students has been in the form of merit grants. As shown in table 1.2, between 1992 and 1999 institutional merit aid grant dollars in public institutions increased 89 percent, while need-based awards increased 60 percent. In the state aid programs, growth of merit aid was even more dramatic. Need-based state aid to students in public institutions increased 75 percent between 1992 and 1999, while merit aid from the state increased 460 percent during the period (author's calculations from NCES 2004a, 2004b).

The research on the effectiveness of grants has consistently shown that they are most effective when targeted at meeting the college access needs of low- and moderate-income students. The research on state merit aid programs has demonstrated that merit aid is used primarily to subsidize the college going of students who would have attended college even without the assistance of public funds. Thomas Mortenson, a long-time observer of higher education policy issues, has summed up the situation very cogently:

> In the economic world of highly constrained social welfare maximization, giving scarce financial aid resources to people who do not need them is wasteful, unnecessary, unproductive, and comes at the price of adequate and appropriate student financial aid for others who could not afford to attend college without such assistance. (Mortenson 1997, 2)

While there is no "silver bullet" that will resolve the problem of shrinking support for public higher education, these recommendations can help set the stage for a renewed compact among states, public institutions of higher education, and students and their families.

Appendix

DATA SOURCES FOR ESTIMATES OF REVENUES
AND ENROLLMENT THROUGH 2003

Public college enrollments

1980–2000:   National Center for Education Statistics 2003a, tables 173 and 200.

2001:   Knapp et al. 2003.

2002–2003:   National Center for Education Statistics 2003b, table 10, middle projection.

Tuition and fees revenues

1980–1999:   NCES, *Digest of Education Statistics* (various years), current fund revenues of public degree-granting institutions of higher education.

2000:   Knapp et al. 2003.

2001–2003:   Increased by the estimated annual increase in public college enrollments (from above) and annual increase in prices in public four-year and community colleges as reported by the College Board (2003a).

State and local appropriations

1980–1999:   NCES, *Digest of Education Statistics* (various years), current fund revenues of public degree-granting institutions of higher education.

2000:   Knapp et al. 2003.

2001–2003:   Lingenfelter et al. 2004.

Federal government revenues

1980–1999:   NCES, *Digest of Education Statistics* (various years), current fund revenues of public degree-granting institutions of higher education.

2000:   Knapp et al. 2003.

2001–2002:   Increased by the change in federal research funding reported in United States Census Bureau 2004b, table 220.

Consumer Price Index

1980–2001:   National Center for Education Statistics 2003a, table 35.

2002–2003:   Bureau of Labor Statistics 2004.

Notes

1. For a more detailed history of the state support of higher education, see Heller (2002a).

2. Tuition and fees here are calculated before student aid is deducted. Local governments are included with state governments because some states have relatively large levels of appropriations to community colleges from municipal or county tax revenues. In fiscal year 1996 approximately 11 percent of the $51 billion contributed by state and local governments combined originated from local governments (NCES 2003a, table 333). While some states do provide direct appropriations to private institutions, the great majority of these funds are allocated to public institutions. Over 97 percent of state and local appropriations in 1999–2000 were directed to public institutions (author's calculations from NCES 2003a, tables 334–336).

3. Again, it is important to note here that the tuition and fee revenues described here do *not* include the portion that is covered by student financial aid. A portion of these increases in tuition is offset by increases in grants, loans, and work-study aid. The role of financial aid is described later in this chapter.

4. Unless otherwise specified, all years used here refer to the fall of the academic year, e.g., "2003" is the 2003–2004 academic year.

5. The reasons for these cost increases are complex and are beyond the scope of this chapter. Two recent books (Clotfelter 1996; Ehrenberg 2000) have focused on the explanation for increasing costs (as opposed to prices) in higher education. While both primarily discuss private higher education, their accounts are still relevant for public institutions. In addition, a recent study conducted for the NCES (Cunningham, Wellman, Clinedinst, and Merisotis 2001) examined the reasons behind both cost and price increases in the public and private sectors.

6. The NCES does not require institutions to break out tuition and fees received from undergraduate versus graduate students. Thus, the figures reported in this section include both enrollments and tuition revenues for all students in public institutions. In 2000, 90 percent of the students enrolled in public institutions were undergraduates (NCES 2003a, table 177). It should also be noted that the tuition and fee revenues reported to NCES are gross of financial aid received. Because institutions are not required to break out spending on institutional grants by level of students (undergraduate versus graduate), it is impossible to calculate how much public institutions are discounting the gross tuition revenue for undergraduate students.

7. Household income data are available only through 2002, at which point median household income in the nation was 139 percent higher than in 1980.

8. Pell Grants, and all federal aid, do have a merit component. In order to be awarded federal aid, students have to be a high-school graduate (or GED recipient), be accepted into an accredited institution of higher education, and once enrolled, maintain satisfactory progress toward a degree or certificate as determined by the institution.

9. When first implemented in 1993, a family income eligibility cap of $66,000, or approximately twice the median family income in the state, was imposed. This was increased to $100,000 the following year, and the cap was eliminated entirely in 1995.

10. See Cornwell and Mustard (2002), Dynarski (2000), and Mumper (1999) for history and analyses of the Georgia HOPE scholarship program.

11. See Ferreri (2003) and Hebel (2004) for description of recent efforts by public universities to use institutional aid to ensure access for low-income students.

12. See Heller and Nelson Laird (1999), Lapovsky and Hubbell (2000, 2003), Redd (2000), and Reindl and Redd (1999) for recent analyses of the practice of tuition discounting by colleges and universities.

13. Dependent students are often described as "traditional" college students, that is, under age 25, unmarried, and still claimed as dependents on their parents' tax returns.

14. There are also many different kinds of student loans. Federal subsidized loans provide both a below-market, government-subsidized interest rate to the borrower as well as deferment of the interest on the loan while the student is enrolled in college. Unsubsidized loans are still guaranteed by the federal government but charge a higher interest rate and provide no in-school deferral of interest charges. Private loans, offered by many banks and other lenders outside of the federal loan programs, generally charge a market interest rate, with the interest accruing throughout the life of the loan.

15. See for example Hossler, Schmit, and Vesper (1999) and McDonough (1997) for analyses of the effect of these factors on college participation.

16. In figure 1.4, it can be seen that state and local appropriations per student increased by $1,000 in constant dollars between 1995 and 2001.

17. In 1990 and 1998 the increase in higher education expenditures exceeded that of total state budgets by one-tenth of a percentage point.

18. This estimate was prepared in August 2004 by the State Higher Education Executive Officers (2004) and included data from 44 states.

References

Advisory Committee on Student Financial Assistance. 2002. *Empty promises: The myth of college access in America*. Washington, D.C.: U.S. Department of Education.

Breneman, D. W., and J. E. Finney. 1997. The changing landscape: Higher education finance in the 1990s. In *Public and private financing of higher education*, ed. P. M. Callan and J. E. Finney, 30–59. Phoenix, Ariz.: Oryx Press.

Bureau of Labor Statistics. 2004. *Consumer price index: All urban consumers* [on-line data file]. U.S. Department of Commerce. Retrieved at http://www.bls.gov/cpi/home.htm.

Center for the Study of Education Policy. 2001. *State tax appropriations to higher education, fiscal year 2001*. Normal: Illinois State University.

———. 2004. *Appropriations of state tax funds for operating expenses of higher education*. Normal: Illinois State University.

———. (various years). *Appropriations of state tax funds for operating expenses of higher education*. Normal: Illinois State University.

Clotfelter, C. T. 1996. *Buying the best: Cost escalation in elite higher education*. Princeton, N.J.: Princeton University Press.

College Board. 2003a. *Trends in college pricing, 2003*. Washington, D.C.: College Board.

———. 2003b. *Trends in student aid, 2003*. Washington, D.C.: College Board.

Cornwell, C., and D. Mustard. 2002. Race and the effects of Georgia's HOPE scholarship. In *Who should we help? The negative social consequences of merit scholarships*, ed. D. E. Heller and P. Marin, 57–72. Cambridge, Mass.: Harvard Civil Rights Project.

Cunningham, A. F., J. V. Wellman, M. E. Clinedinst, and J. P. Merisotis. 2001. *Study of college costs and prices, 1988–89 to 1997–98*, Vol. 1. NCES 2002–157. Washington, D.C.: U.S. Department of Education, National Center for Education Statistics.

Dynarski, S. 2000. Hope for whom? Financial aid for the middle class and its impact on college attendance. *National Tax Journal* 53 (3 [Part 2]): 629–61.

Ehrenberg, R. G. 2000. *Tuition rising: Why college costs so much*. Cambridge, Mass.: Harvard University Press.

Fenske, R. H., and J. D. Boyd. 1981. *State need-based college scholarship and grant programs: A study of their development, 1969–1980*. New York: College Entrance Examination Board.

Ferreri, E. 2003. UNC to boost aid for low-income students. *The* (Durham, N.C.) *Herald-Sun*, 2 October, A1.

Hebel, S. 2004. U. of Virginia announces new student-aid policy. *Chronicle of Higher Education*, 20 February, A24.

Heller, D. E. 1997. Student price response in higher education: An update to Leslie and Brinkman. *Journal of Higher Education* 68(6): 624–59.

———. 2001. Trends in the affordability of public colleges and universities: The contradiction of increasing prices and increasing enrollment. In *The states and public higher education policy: Affordability, access, and accountability*, ed. D. E. Heller, 11–38. Baltimore, Md.: Johns Hopkins University Press.

———. 2002a. The policy shift in state financial aid programs. In *Higher education: Handbook of theory and research*, ed. J. C. Smart, 17:221–61. New York: Agathon Press.

———. 2002b. State merit scholarship programs: An introduction. In *Who should we help? The negative social consequences of merit scholarships*, ed. D. E. Heller and P. Marin 15–23. Cambridge, Mass.: Harvard Civil Rights Project.

Heller, D. E., and T. F. Nelson Laird. 1999. Institutional need-based and non-need grants: Trends and differences among college and university sectors. *Journal of Student Financial Aid* 29(3): 7–24.

Higher Education Act of 1965, Pub. L., No. 89–329 (1965).

Hossler, D., J. Schmit, and N. Vesper. 1999. *Going to college: How social, economic, and educational factors influence the decisions students make*. Baltimore, Md.: Johns Hopkins University Press.

Hovey, H. A. 1999. *State spending for higher education in the next decade: The battle to sustain current support*. San Jose, Calif.: National Center for Public Policy and Higher Education.

Jackson, G. A., and G. B. Weathersby. 1975. Individual demand for higher education. *Journal of Higher Education* 46(6): 623–52.

Jenny, N. W., and E. Arbak. 2004. Challenges for financing public higher education. *The Rockefeller Institute State Fiscal News* 4 (March).

Knapp, L. G., J. E. Kelly, R. W. Whitmore, S. Wu, B. Levine, and S. Huh. 2003. *Enrollment in postsecondary institutions, fall 2001 and financial statistics, fiscal year 2001* (NCES 2004–155). Washington, D.C.: U.S. Department of Education, National Center for Education Statistics.

Lapovsky, L., and L. L. Hubbell. 2000. Positioning for competition. *NACUBO Business Officer* 33(9): 22–30.

———. (2003). Tuition discounting continues to grow. *Business Officer* 36(9): 20–27.

Leslie, L. L., and P. T. Brinkman. 1988. *The economic value of higher education*. New York: American Council on Education/Macmillan Publishing.

Lingenfelter, P. E., H. P. L'Orange, S. B. Winter, and D. L. Wright. 2004. *State higher education finance FY 2003*. Denver, Colo.: State Higher Education Executive Officers.

Long, B. T. 2003. *The impact of federal tax credits for higher education expenses* (Working Paper 9553). Cambridge, Mass.: National Bureau of Economic Research.

Marin, P. 2002. Merit scholarships and the outlook for equal opportunity in higher education. In *Who should we help? The negative social consequences of merit scholarships*, ed. D. E. Heller and P. Marin, 109–14. Cambridge, Mass.: Harvard Civil Rights Project.

McDonough, P. M. 1997. *Choosing colleges: How social class and schools structure opportunity*. Albany: State University of New York Press.

Morey, L. 1928. Student fees in state universities and colleges. *School and Society* 28(712): 185–92.

Mortenson, T. G. 1997. Georgia's HOPE Scholarship Program: Good intentions, strong funding, bad design. *Postsecondary Education OPPORTUNITY* 56 (February): 1–3.

Mumper, M. 1999 (November). *HOPE and its critics: Sorting out the competing claims about Georgia's HOPE scholarship.* Paper presented at the annual meeting of the Association for the Study of Higher Education, San Antonio, Tex.

———. 2001. The paradox of college prices: Five stories with no clear lesson. In *The states and public higher education policy: Affordability, access, and accountability,* ed. D. E. Heller, 39–63. Baltimore, Md.: Johns Hopkins University Press.

National Association of State Budget Officers. (various years). *State expenditure report.* Washington, D.C.: Author.

National Association of State Scholarship and Grant Programs. (various years). *NASSGP/ NASSGAP annual survey report.* Deerfield, Ill.; Harrisburg, Pa.; and Albany, N.Y.: Illinois State Scholarship Commission; Pennsylvania Higher Education Assistance Agency; and New York State Higher Education Services Corporation.

National Center for Education Statistics. 2003a. *Digest of education statistics, 2002* (NCES 2003–060). Washington, D.C.: U.S. Department of Education.

———. 2003b. *Projections of education statistics to 2013* (NCES 2004–013). Washington, D.C.: U.S. Department of Education.

———. (2004a). *National Postsecondary Student Aid Study 1992–1993 data analysis system.* Washington, D.C.: U.S. Department of Education. Retrieved at http://nces.ed.gov/das/.

———. 2004b. *National Postsecondary Student Aid Study 1999–2000 data analysis system.* U.S. Department of Education. Retrieved at http://nces.ed.gov/das/.

National Education Association. 2004. *Financing higher education: A crisis in state funding.* Washington, D.C.: Author. Retrieved at http://www.nea.org/he/fiscalcrisis/.

Paulson, A. 2004. Colleges face spare changes. *Christian Science Monitor,* 16 March, 11.

Redd, K. E. 2000. *Discounting toward disaster: Tuition discounting, college finances, and enrollments of low-income undergraduates.* Indianapolis, Ind.: USA Group Foundation.

Reindl, T., and K. Redd. 1999 (May). *Institutional aid in the 1990s: The consequences of policy connections.* Paper presented at the NASSGAP/NCHELP Research Network Conference, Savannah, Georgia.

Rizzo, M. J. 2003. *A (less than) zero sum game? State funding for public education: How public higher education institutions have lost* (WP42). Ithaca, N.Y.: Cornell University Higher Education Research Institute.

Sears, J. B. (1923). Our theory of free higher education. *Educational Review* 65 (January): 27–34.

State Higher Education Executive Officers. 2004. *State tax appropriations for higher education operating expenses, fiscal years 2004 and 2005.* Denver, Colo.: Author.

Trounson, R. 2004. Colleges' budget crunch growing; State funding cuts are "chipping away" at a long-admired system of campuses, and fee hikes are making higher education less accessible. *Los Angeles Times,* 4 April, A1.

United States Census Bureau. 2004a. *Race and Hispanic origin of householder—households by median and mean income: 1967 to 2002* [on-line data file]. Washington, D.C.: United States Census Bureau. Retrieved at http://www.census.gov/hhes/income/histinc/h05.html.

———. 2004b. *Statistical abstract of the United States: 2003.* Washington, D.C.: United States Census Bureau.

Western Interstate Commission for Higher Education. 2003. *Knocking at the college door: Projections of high school graduates by state, income, and race/ethnicity 1988–2018.* Boulder, Colo.: Western Interstate Commission for Higher Education.

Zumeta, W. 2001. Public policy and accountability in higher education: Lessons from the past and present for the new millennium. In *The states and public higher education policy: Affordability, access, and accountability,* ed. D. E. Heller, 155–97. Baltimore, Md.: Johns Hopkins University Press.

CHAPTER TWO

Privatization and Federal Funding
for Higher Education

Edward P. St. John and Ontario S. Wooden

Changes in the federal role in higher education have been widely discussed over the past few decades (Finn 1978; Hearn 1993, 2003; McPherson and Schapiro 1991; Mumper 1996; Slaughter and Leslie 1997; St. John and Byce 1982; Thelin 2004). While Thelin (2004) aptly points out that colleges and universities have lobbied governments for funding since before the nation was founded, there have been very substantial shifts in the federal role in higher education over time. To build an understanding of why the federal role has changed and the consequences of these changes, we first provide a general historical overview of changes in federal policy in U.S. higher education. Next, we examine trends of funding since 1970 and consider research on the impact of these shifts. Finally, we offer a perspective on the future of the federal role and institutional strategy during the current period of globalization.

Shifting Policy Rationales

Discussions of the history of the federal role have often centered narrowly on higher education (Finn 1978; Slaughter and Leslie 1997; Thelin 2004), rather than on a broader view of the federal role in the economy and society. While it is crucial that distinctions be made between education and social programs, it is appropriate to view the federal government's interest in higher education as being related to the underlying approach used to promote the nation's economic and social development. From a historical perspective on the United States, it is appropriate to distinguish three periods in the federal role: the institutional founding period, the federal progressive period, and the global economy period.

The Institutional Founding Period

The historical literature on higher education has shown that the practice of appealing to governments for funding goes back as far as the time of the founding of American colleges (Herbst 1976; Lucas 1994; Rudolph 1990). This practice continues through to this day (Thelin 2004). When the Founding Fathers wrote the Constitution, they left responsibility for education to the states (Thelin 2004). The federal government did get into the business of founding a few educational institutions, like the military academy at West Point, but it resisted appeals to found a national university (Jencks and Reisman 1968).

The federal government had a more substantial influence on the development of higher education as uniquely American through the courts than it did through funding during this early period. In *Dartmouth College v. Woodward*, the Supreme Court decided in favor of the college's claim that its charter was independent of the state (Lucas 1994; Rudolph 1990). Not only is this decision credited with stimulating the private sector of higher education in the United States earlier than in other countries, but it was part of a larger set of policy decisions that shaped the early evolution of the American economy, if not the evolution of American society.

In the early American period, there was a great deal of conflict about the role of private capital and private banks as well as about state interests. The federal system evolved through a long history of well-documented tension between northern progressive interests and southern interests promoting states' rights. Different strategies for economic development included federal and local taxation, but the federal role was limited, especially in education. Even the states were slow to develop state systems of education, as local governments retained responsibility for taxing to support local schools. Furthermore, the pattern of educational development was variable both within and across states. Opportunities to obtain a basic education were better in urban communities than in rural ones and in northern states than in southern ones. However, colleges were founded by local communities, including rural communities, across the country. Many of these early colleges offered a curriculum that was more like a modern high school than the collegiate-level education of the past century.

The federal government played a more direct role in educational development in the Northwest Territories, now known as the Midwest, providing allotments of land for education as well as for homes. This strategy helped build schools along with communities, creating a direct and vital link between social and economic development. It is little wonder that the social progressive movements evolved in the Midwest, where the linkages between social and economic development have been explicit since westward expansion. However, settlement patterns varied, and there was not a clear pattern of educational development in communities across the country. Just as the Northwest Territories Acts proved that the federal government could intervene to promote social and economic development, the absence of such strategies in other regions created contrasting patterns of community building and educational development, resulting in wide variation in educational attainment across regions of the country.

The Federal Progressive Period

After the Civil War the federal government took a more active interest in national social and economic development. Abraham Lincoln is credited with starting the national railroads (Fogel 2000) and land grant universities (Johnson 1981/1989), two developments that fostered economic and social progress nationally. With the ability to move products and people, railroads transformed both commercial enterprises and social mobility. Railroads opened new markets for what became national industries and created communities in their wake. The land grant universities focused on agricultural and economic development in rural America, becoming one of the catalysts for the industrial revolution.

The federal strategy used to build railroads and universities was through grants of land. Engaged in a war against the southern states, the federal government lacked the revenue to build railroads and universities; however, it could claim the rights to land within its borders, which had expanded after the Louisiana Purchase, and it used that land strategically to encourage development. These new strategies did not, however, coordinate the economic and social aspects of development as did the strategies used in the Northwest Territories Acts. The first Land Grant Acts created universities that provided both social and economic benefits to states and placed states in control of their development

(Johnson 1981/1989), an appropriate tactic, given the states' legal authority over education. In contrast, the plan for building the railroads used large national corporations that not only built railroads but were given portions of land along their routes, creating railroad towns across the country. While there is plenty of room to criticize this policy because it concentrated wealth rather than promoting social development (Fogel 2000), it may have been the only feasible approach to take, given the economic status of the United States during and after the Civil War.

A social progressive period was born in the post–Civil War period, with the federal government playing an increasing role in social, economic, and educational development. Progressivism in the late 1800s and early 1900s led to regulation of monopolies like the railroads and utilities. After World War I, there was more emphasis on manpower development, which funded education programs in health and other fields thought to be in the federal interest (Finn 1988a, 1988b). And during the Great Depression, social welfare programs became a focal point for the federal government (Selznick 1969). Before, during, and after World War II, the federal government increased spending on research and development, including many projects in universities. And finally, after World War II, the GI Bill provided educational grants to returning veterans, stimulating the federal role in student financial aid.

The Great Society programs, envisioned by the Kennedy administration and put into legislation during Johnson's administration, expanded the federal role in elementary and secondary education, higher education, civil rights, health, and social welfare. This socially progressive agenda was carried forward through the 1970s in spite of the high cost of the Vietnam War and an extended period of Republican administrations (under Nixon and Ford). The rationale that fueled public investment in education and social welfare was held together by arguments that education and other social programs promoted social mobility and economic development.

The social mobility argument appealed to liberals, and the economic argument appealed to conservatives. The *extent* of investment was the issue, not whether society should make these investments. The logic of human capital theory (Becker 1964) and social attainment theory (Blau and Duncan 1967) supported these arguments, as did liberal social philosophy (Rawls 1971). While there was not a consensus on any single program or strategy, most social and economic development programs evolved without critical examination. Once they were created and funds started flowing to state and local entities, these programs had their own constituents. The progressive ethos had evolved over a century and had taken hold in Western democracies (Huber and Stephens 2001), stimulated in part by the rebuilding of Europe after World War II and modeled after the U.S. social progressive model. In retrospect, the Cold War had much to do with the evolution of social welfare states, for social democratic governance was in an ideological war with communism.

The U.S. federal government had firmly established its role in higher education finance by the middle 1970s, providing support for education programs in the federal interest (agriculture, health, and so forth); for research and development, stimulating growth of the major research universities; and for student financial aid. By the middle 1970s, student aid had become the major federal role (Finn 1978; Gladieux and Wolanin 1976), with an extensive array of grant, loan, and work-study programs. In 1980 the student financial aid programs were moved to the new U.S. Department of Education, along with many other federal education programs. However, much of the funding for research and education programs remained in other agencies, like the National Science Foundation and the U.S. Department of Agriculture.

The Global Economy Period and Reform of the Federal Role

While there were hints of new conservative rationales in the late 1970s, the pace of regressive change was rapid in the 1980s. Ronald Reagan entered office with a belief in self-help (loans and work-study), a belief that challenged the political lobby community that argued for funding of student aid (Hearn 1993). However, change in higher education funding was only the tip of the iceberg. The Reagan agenda included tax cuts, downsizing social programs, and rebuilding the nation's defense. Prior to the Reagan era, analysts in the U.S. Department of Education mapped out strategies for reducing the costs of higher education while maintaining social equity (St. John and Byce 1982), but analyses of the social and educational efficacy of spending plans were not a high priority. Instead, there was a substantial investment of research efforts to reduce waste, fraud, and abuse in federal student aid systems (Advanced Technology 1983).

But the change in federal strategies leading to reductions in student financial aid paled in comparison to the cuts in other social programs. Cuts in social welfare and privatization of services were occurring across Western democracies as a new pattern of global economics fell into place. With the end of the Cold War, capitalism was thought to be the cause for victory, not the massive investments in education that had promoted social mobility. As multinational corporations moved manufacturing offshore, the tax base eroded (Tabb 2001). Furthermore, cuts in tax rates became an ideological position of the right in the United States, and Western democracies adjusted to the new pattern of economic development, a period when corporations ruled. Indeed, the new period had similarities to earlier periods when there had been insufficient regulation of industry. The education and social programs in the United States were being heavily regulated and controlled through the new accountability movement, but the private sector had fewer regulatory hurdles in the new global environment.

In the United States, educational improvement entered the domain of roles the federal government assumed in education. After publication of *A Nation at Risk* (National Commission on Excellence in Education 1983), the federal government took on the role of comparing states on test scores and other indicators of success (First 1992) as well as promoting accountability systems in education. Even the one Democratic president during the period carried forward the new "excellence" agenda, including greater accountability in K–12 and higher education. The initial effort to impose state reporting and accountability failed during the Clinton years (St. John 1994), but the "new liberal" reform agenda continued mostly unabated.

A new pattern of public finance had developed in U.S. higher education. By 1990 loans had replaced grants as the primary form of federal student financial aid (Hearn 1993; St. John 1994), and cuts in state support for public higher education, stimulated by the new conservative rationale of the 1980s, had influenced a rapid rise of tuition charges (St. John 1993). Soon this form of privatization of higher education—higher tuition and higher loans—was being promoted by the World Bank and became an international pattern (Henry, Ligard, Rizvi, and Taylor 2001). Privatization of education became integral to higher education finance because it reduced taxpayer costs, but it had little observable effect on enrollment (Stiglitz 2003).

In the United States these changes had been stimulated in part by the new federal role of leadership in education. In the second Reagan administration, federal officials severely criticized education for being unproductive and wasteful (Finn 1988a, 1988b), making the claim that higher education increased tuition as means of capturing more student aid dollars (Bennett 1987; Carnes 1987). The popular press carried stories about excess, simply assuming these claims were true (Brimelow

1987; Putka 1987), and universities were ill equipped to respond (St. John 1994). The U.S. Department of Education published reports advocating that colleges implement cost control mechanisms (Carnes 1987; Finn 1988a, 1988b). The pervasive notion that higher education was excessive and wasteful made it easier for states to further reduce spending on higher education. Institutions continued to use the old progressive rationale to argue for public funding (e.g., Honeyman and Bruhn 1996; McKeown 1996), but without much success. Federal and state spending per FTE fell in both the 1980s and 1990s in the U.S. (St. John 2003).

During the past two decades, the federal government has developed an extensive research program focusing on the academic pipeline to college (Adelman 1995, 1999; Choy 2002; NCES 1997a, 1997b, 2001a, 2001b, 2002a, 2002b; Pelavin and Kane 1988). This research has focused on the correlations between high school courses, especially in math, and college success. While actively encouraging states to adopt education reform policies, this research has failed to evaluate the impact of these policies or of the reductions in federal grants (St. John 2003). Recently, several analysts reexamined the NCES research, documenting that millions of college-qualified, low-income students had been left behind in the 1990s and early 2000s as a consequence of the reductions in student aid (Advisory Committee on Student Financial Assistance 2002; Fitzgerald 2004; Lee 2004). Rather than providing leadership, the U.S. Department of Education had become a bully pulpit to push states into new policies in both K–12 and higher education that went largely unexamined.

Federal Funding for Higher Education

While the social progressive period of American history has given way to the new global period, the basic roles of the federal government have remained largely intact. These include:

- Support of institutions through programs thought to be in the federal interest;
- Research and development, which provides funding for universities and private corporations;
- Support for college students in the form of grants, loans, and work-study;
- Leadership and the power of the bully pulpit, promoting state and federal action through research tailored to a federal agenda.

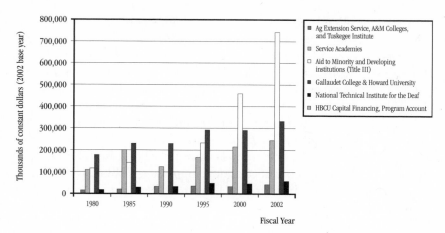

Figure 2.1. Direct federal appropriations to institutions of higher learning.
(*Digest of Education Statistics* 2002, table 365, p. 424, and table 367, p. 430.
NCES 2003–060. National Center for Education Statistics 2003a.)
Note: 2002 dollar amounts are estimates.

In the United States, as is the case internationally, the privatization process of higher education has been promoted through shifts in policies within each of these domains of federal responsibility. Therefore, it is important to examine how these roles and funding have changed and to consider research that has studied the consequences of these changes.

Funding for Colleges

Although the original federal role was to fund agricultural colleges, direct funding of institutions has been modest compared to funding for research and college students. The most substantial federal program funded Historically Black Colleges and Universities (HBCUs), Hispanic Serving Institutions (HSIs) and other developing institutions through the Title III and Title V programs of the Higher Education Act (HEA). Funding for these programs more than tripled in the past decade, from slightly more than $200 million in 1995 to more than $700 million in 2002. Changes in other programs that directly support colleges and universities were more modest after 1980 (see figure 2.1).

The Title III program had been an integral part of the HEA in 1965. At the time there was a dedicated federal commitment to supporting HBCUs, community colleges, and liberal arts colleges that had been outside of the "educational mainstream." However, by the late 1970s the federal government was reconsidering its investment in Title III, because the developmental goals of Title III had become elusive (St. John 1981). The federal government also began to push the goal of funding development of HBCUs to states as part of the settlement process in *Adams v. Richardson* (1973) (Williams 1988). While federal aid to developing colleges was not a priority in the 1980s, it emerged again in the 1990s.

A shift toward the funding of Title III after the 1990s came at a time of a shift in the legal basis for desegregation. The Supreme Count's *Fordice* decision (*United States v. Fordice* [1992]) shifted the focus of settlement away from institutional development of HBCUs and toward desegregation of these institutions (Brown, Butler, and Donahoo 2004; Conrad and Weerts 2004). As a consequence, HBCUs successfully lobbied the federal government once again for support of their development goals. Funds from the government for the HBCU Capital Financing Program only include costs for administering the program, which ranged from $150,000 in 2000 to $197,000 in 2002. However, funding to institutions comes in the form of loans instead of grants. According to the Department of Education's website,

> the goal of the HBCU Capital Financing Program is to provide low cost capital to finance improvements to the infrastructure of the nation's HBCUs. Specifically, the program provides HBCUs with access to capital financing or refinancing for the repair, renovation, and construction of classrooms, libraries, laboratories, dormitories, instructional equipment, and research instrumentation. (U.S. Department of Education 2004)

These loans average about eight and a half million dollars annually.

While funding for Hispanic higher education was included in Title III, the major vehicle for funding for HSIs was moved to Title V. In order for institutions to receive funding from Title V, they must have an undergraduate FTE enrollment that is at least 25 percent Hispanic students. Also, 50 percent of their Hispanic students must be low-income individuals, and the institutions must be not-for-profit (NCES 2002c). They must also apply for the funds. Programs aimed at providing greater financial support for Hispanics are of increasing importance, given the fact that their numbers as a percentage of the U.S. population are increasing dramatically. Moreover, the percentage of Hispanics who are participating in higher education is at record levels. According to NCES, "enrollment in HSIs in the United States grew rapidly between 1990 and 1999. During this period, the number of students enrolled increased by 14%, exceeding the 7% growth for all institutions" (2002c, 2). While the funding for HSIs may not have increased to meet

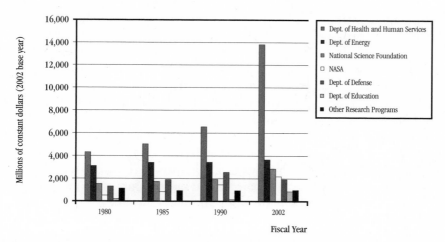

Figure 2.2. Research appropriations by level or educational purpose.
(*Federal Support for Education, Fiscal Years 1980 to 2002*, table 4, p. 10.
NCES 2003–006. National Center for Education Statistics 2003b.)
Note: In 1985, Department of Education research appropriations were
less than $50 million. Dollar amounts for 2002 are estimates.

the needs of these unique institutions, the funding has grown significantly over a relatively short period of time.

The second most substantial area of funding is for national colleges: Howard University, Gallaudet College, National Technical Institute for the Deaf, and educational programs at the service academies. All of these funding programs have shown modest increases since 1980. In addition to funding for education programs, the service academies (e.g., West Point) receive funding for the military bases and programs that are not visible as separate line items in the federal budget.

It is also noticeable that funding for agricultural extension and other agricultural programs remains a modest allocation compared even to other federal programs. While support for agriculture was the original federal initiative, it now represents a relatively minor part of the federal investment in higher education.

Federal Appropriations for Research

With one exception, federal funding for research has not increased substantially since 1980 (see figure 2.2). Funding for research on health grew from slightly more than $4 billion in 1980 to nearly $14 billion in 2002. This growth in research funding for health has not only

47

stimulated breakthroughs in medicine but has also influenced priority and power shifts within research universities.

The policy literature on higher education now includes extensive critiques of the new priorities. In *Universities in the Marketplace*, Bok (2003) addresses the complex issues related to commercialization of research, especially in the sciences, with the rising costs of equipping scientific laboratories, along with growing pressure to generate revenue from nongovernmental sources. In *Academic Capitalism*, Slaughter and Leslie (1997) argue that these patterns of federal investment increase the costs of attracting leading scientists to research universities and stimulate investment in patents and partnerships with industry as means of generating revenue from alternative sources. These forces have a substantial influence on budgeting in research universities, especially relative to the costs of funding labs. In *Tuition Rising*, Ehrenberg (2002) argues that the costs of laboratories and scientists shift power relations among faculties in research universities as well as budget priorities.

These critiques are consonant with trends in funding. No area of research other than health has reached the $14 billion funding threshold. Research in the Department of Energy and NASA has had incremental increases. However, other areas of funding have oscillated, reflecting shifting federal priorities. Funding for research through the U.S. Department of Education, as an example, fell to less than $50 million in 1985, but rose by 2002, reflecting the new science priorities for education research as defined by the No Child Left Behind Act (2001). To the extent that political power in the academy follows external funding, health and related fields, like chemistry and biology, are the tails that wag the university dog. The historic values of community-based governance in academe are seldom even discussed in the budget development process in many research institutions. Rather, strategies for leveraging institutional positions for external funding have taken priority over other values (Bok 2003; Ehrenberg 2002; Slaughter and Leslie 1997).

Funds for Students through Federal Programs

The shift in funding students, especially through the development of loan programs that use private capital, continues to be a major stimulus for privatization. To deconstruct the underlying issues in this shift, we examine trends in funds for students through loans programs, funds through federal grants, and the purchasing power of Pell Grants (award maximums in relation to costs of attending four-year colleges).

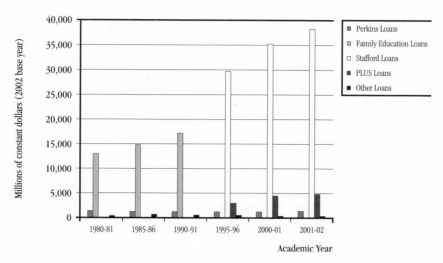

Figure 2.3. Federal loan aid for postsecondary education expenses. (*Trends in Student Aid 2002*, table 2, p. 7, appendix B, p. 19. College Board 2002.) Note: Dollar amounts for 2001–2002 are estimates.

Loans for College Students

The growth in private capital for college students and parents (figure 2.3) is remarkable. The federal government guarantees loans for college students who borrow from private lenders. These guaranteed loan programs—called Federal Family Education Loans (FFELP) in the 1980s and early 1990s and renamed Stafford Loans in the late 1990s—provided about $13 billion in loan capital in 1980, before new conservative rationales reshaped federal financing of higher education, and rose to about $38 billion in 2001–2002. In addition, the second biggest federal program, Parent Loans for Undergraduates Students (PLUS), uses the private capital market to provide loans for parents. Started with the 1992 reauthorization of the Higher Education Act, PLUS loans reached nearly $5 billion in 2001–2002.

The costs to the taxpayers associated with federally guaranteed loans are not reflected in these funding trends. Service costs for state agencies and lenders create some administrative costs. However, as loans have been extended to more students who are likely to repay, the default rates have dropped—and default rates are the primary reason for loans to have costs. Upper- and middle-income students have a high probability of paying back their loans (Flint 1997). In the 1990s borrowing grew at about the same rate as tuition in public four-year colleges (St. John, Hu, and Weber 2000, 2001).

The major alternative to using private capital for loans—using federal capital in revolving accounts maintained by campuses (e.g., Perkins Loans)—has not grown since 1980. The use of private capital for loans—a key component of privatization internationally—is the dominant way of funding higher education. The more than $40 billion in private capital for loans from Stafford and PLUS overwhelms the direct investment in research in life sciences, a trifling $14 billion in comparison. Private capital for students saves tax dollars as compared to higher education grants because of the substantially lower cost of lending money.

The political issue now for policy makers and economists is whether lower-cost strategies for stimulating capital investment can be found. For example, Lleras (2004) has argued for human capital contracts, private loans that would be repaid on an income-contingent basis. If the federal government brokers such a program, as is now the case in Australia, then government costs can be eliminated. However, given the substantial lobbying power of private lenders in the United States, the critical issue will be how to set the interest rates in new loan schemes to ensure profitability for lenders. This is not idle critique; rather, it is recognition of the power of lobbyists for loan programs (Hearn and Holdsworth 2004; Parsons 2004).

The critical issue underlying this debate is whether the use of private capital is a fair and equitable approach to finance. If we accept John Rawls' second principle of justice, which proposes that the least advantaged should be the first to benefit from basic liberties, and if we regard funding for within-generation equity a priority (Rawls 2001), then the shift from grants to loans raises a troubling issue. When responsibility for funding equity shifts from taxpayers to low-income students, the penalty of being from a low-income family then extends across a lifetime. In such a scheme, education no longer remedies inequality.

Federal Funding of Grant Programs

The Pell Grant program has been the major federal need-based grant program since it was implemented, as Basic Educational Opportunity Grants, in 1973. Pell Grants provide a need-based, voucher-like grant awarded directly to students by the federal government. The college disburses funds, but the amount of funds colleges receive and disburse through Pell is dependent on the number of low-income students who enroll.

Other than Pell, the federal government funds Leveraging Educational Assistance Partnerships (LEAP), Supplemental Educational Opportunity Grants (SEOGs), and other grants. SEOG is an artifact of an

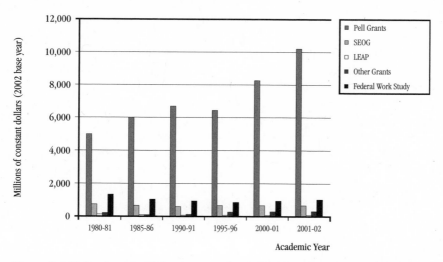

Figure 2.4. Federal grant aid for postsecondary education expenses. (*Trends in Student Aid* 2002, table 2, p. 7, appendix B, p. 19. College Board 2002.) Note: Dollar amounts for 2001–2002 are estimates.

earlier period when the federal government gave block grants to colleges as a means of funding students. LEAP is funded at one-third by the federal government and two-thirds by states. It is woefully underfunded, given its potential for improving unequal opportunity. If LEAP had been appropriately reconstructed, almost two million more students could have gone to college in the 1990s (St. John et al. 2004).

The story of federal funding for Pell (figure 2.4) is far from compelling. Funding rose slightly during the 1980s, from about $5 billion in 1980 to nearly $7 billion in 1990–1991, as the Reagan administration retargeted the program on low-income students. One of the ironies of this period was that it was possible to redirect funds from middle-income to low-income students by lowering the maximum award (St. John and Byce 1982). Reductions in the award maximum did not hurt low-income students who enrolled in four-year colleges in the early 1980s because there was a half-cost provision: it was not possible to secure a grant of more that half the cost of attendance, and during this time public colleges still had low tuition. However, as tuition rose, the half-cost provision was dropped (St. John 2003).

Funding for Pell actually dropped during the early Clinton years as the federal government, sadly, allowed inequalities in enrollment opportunities to grow (Ellwood and Kane 2000; St. John 2003). There has been some increase in funding for Pell in recent years, growing to more than $10 billion in 2001–2002, indicating that the G. W. Bush administration has been more responsive to the equity issue than the Clinton administration was. However, the increase in funding for Pell does not mean that low-income students have been better able to pay the costs of attending, as noted below in the discussion of the purchasing power of Pell.

The federal government faces a number of complex issues that must be resolved before it is possible to address the new inequality in the opportunity to enroll. However, it is necessary to consider the funding level of Pell first, since Pell's funding problems illustrate the severity of the equity challenge facing higher education in the United States.

THE PURCHASING POWER OF PELL

While the renewed funding for the Pell Grant program has created an impression of reinvestment, the new spending level has done little to reduce the funding problem for low-income students. Trends in the purchasing power of Pell Grants (figure 2.5) reveal a growing gap between the maximum Pell award and the average cost of attending a public four-year college in the United States. In 1980 the maximum Pell award was about $4,000, below the 1975 inflation-adjusted maximum but higher than the Pell maximum in subsequent years. The maximum Pell award—the amount the lowest-income students can receive—was only modestly lower than the average cost of attending a public four-year college. However, at the time, low-income students in public four-year colleges did not receive the maximum Pell because of the half-cost limit: their Pell award was capped at half the cost of attendance. By 1990–1991 the half-cost provision had been removed, but the net cost of attending public four-year colleges was much higher. The maximum Pell award was less than $3,000, while the net cost after Pell was more than $5,000. There were modest increases in the maximum Pell award after 1995, rising to $4,000 once again, but the gap after Pell was nearly $6,000 in public colleges.

The cost of attending the average public four-year college nearly doubled, from $5,000+ in 1980–1981 to nearly $10,000 in 2002–2003. The rise in tuition charges in public colleges was also related to privatization—the shift from tax dollars to tuition dollars (St. John 2003; see also Heller, chapter 2 of this volume). These changes fundamentally shifted the pattern of public finance: from using tax dollars to support access across generations (i.e., funding colleges) and reduce inequality (i.e., federal need-based grants) to using private capital (i.e., loans) to mitigate the negative effects of rising costs on expanding access. But the shift simply did not maintain equal opportunity.

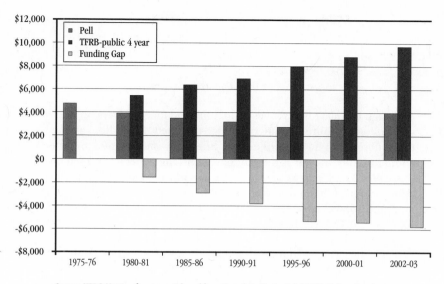

Source: TFRB-Tuition, fees, room & board from *Trends in Student Aid 2003*, College Board, 2003; Pell data from *Digest of Education Statistics*, NCES, 1989, 2004.

Figure 2.5. Financial trends: the growing gap between declining federal Pell Grants and rising university attendance costs (tuition, fees, room, and board).

Misinformation about Access

In addition to funding education to achieve federal policy goals, the federal government is responsible for evaluating whether their policies have the intended effects. If federal policy induces privatization and improves access, then it is conceivable that these policies improve financial efficiencies. The legislative intent of the federal student aid programs has been to equalize educational opportunity, as measured by access, college choice, and persistence (Gladieux and Wolanin 1976; National Commission on the Financing of Postsecondary Education 1973). Therefore, it is crucial for the federal government to have reliable information on these measures, especially in relation to federal public finance strategies. Below we briefly review the official information on college access, as promoted in research publications by NCES, and then examine evidence from trends related to these policy reports.

Official Information on Access

Through its role in collecting information on education and reporting on conditions of education, the National Center for Education Statistics (NCES) is the government's official agency for reporting on college access. The primary theme of the official reports released by the agency with NCES as recommended author has been: *There is equal access for students who prepare for college.* An executive summary from one of the early reports heralding this theme claims,

> Although there are differences by income and race-ethnicity in the four-year college enrollment rates of college-qualified high school graduates, the difference between college-qualified low-income and middle-income students, as well as the differences among college-qualified black, Hispanic, Asian, and White students, are eliminated among those students who have taken the college entrance examinations and completed an application for admission, the two steps necessary to attend a four-year college. (NCES 1997a, iii)

Among the criteria that NCES used to select a sample of students for evaluation of equal access was application to college, a variable measured during the senior year of high school. Open admission colleges, including most two-year and some four-year colleges, do not require advance admission as assumed in this criterion. Most students who apply for admission six months in advance probably believe they can afford to attend a public or private four-year college. Thus, this is not a fair measure of access. In the same report, NCES described their interpretation of this criterion as follows:

> If the financial aid system is providing equal educational opportunities and access to postsecondary schooling, one would expect no substantial differences by family income in the four-year college enrollment rates of students whose academic records show they are likely to be admitted to a four-year college and who have taken the necessary steps to be considered for admission. The findings of this study indicate that this is indeed generally the case: there were no substantial differences by family income in the four-year college enrollment rates of college-qualified high school graduates who apply to and are accepted for admission at four-year colleges. (NCES 1997a, 1–2)

According to this criterion, students who were qualified to attend a four-year college but did not apply due to family income reasons would have been excluded from the analysis, creating an unfair standard for judging the efficacy of federal student aid.

Recently the Advisory Committee on Student Financial Assistance (ACSFA), a congressional advisory panel with responsibility for reviewing federal research on student financial aid, commissioned reviews of

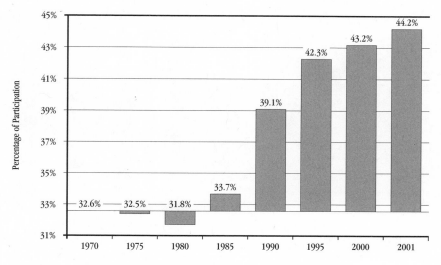

Source: St. John, Tuttle, & Musoba, in press; data from NCES Digest 2002, Table 188.

Figure 2.6. Trends in participation rate of traditional college-age high school graduates by year, 1970–2001.

the NCES reports (Fitzgerald 2004). These reviews found a recurrent pattern of statistical errors in the NCES reports on access and persistence (Becker 2004; Heller 2004). The reviews revealed consistent patterns of selection bias (i.e., selecting students in ways that made inappropriate comparisons), misspecification (i.e., including inappropriate variables in multivariable analyses), and statistical errors. A reanalysis of the NCES data indicated that regardless of the measures of preparation, more low-income students than middle- or upper-income students lacked the opportunity to enroll in four-year colleges (Lee 2004). Clearly, NCES had used flawed research to promote the false belief that there was equal access.

Trends in Access

When evaluating the federal role in financing college access, it is important to think about opportunity for all (i.e., whether enrollment rates improve) and whether there is equal opportunity for the financially disadvantaged. A more reasonable approach than that cleverly crafted in the NCES reports involves looking at trends in enrollment rate and equity in opportunity in relation to federal policy (St. John 2003).

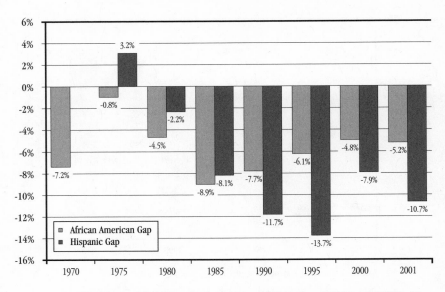

Source: Adapted from St. John, 2003; updated with 2000 and 2001 data from NCES Digest 2002, Table 187.

Figure 2.7. Difference gaps in the college enrollment rates of Hispanic and African American 18- to 24-year-old high school graduates compared to white.

An examination of trends in enrollment rates for high school graduates (figure 2.6) illustrates that the percentage of high school graduates who enrolled in college was relatively flat in the 1970s, a period when enrollment expanded due to growth in the number of students of college age. An enrollment decline was predicted for the 1980s (Carnegie Commission 1973), but instead the percentage of traditional-age high school graduates who enrolled in college increased, helping to stabilize enrollment. The enrollment rate for high school graduates was 44.2 percent in 2001 compared to 31.8 percent in 1980, indicating substantial growth in opportunity.

If we examine these trends in relation to federal financing policy, then it is apparent that the expansion of loans corresponded with the improvement in enrollment rates. From these trends, one could hypothesize that the availability of private capital improved access. In fact, in some studies, there is evidence that loans, as a part of packages with need-based and merit aid, are associated with enrollment and persistence (St. John 2003). However, it is not possible to evaluate the efficacy of federal policies without considering equal opportunity, which is related to the federal intent of student aid.

When trends in enrollment by diverse racial/ethnic groups (figure 2.7) or income (Ellwood and Kane 2000) are examined, there is evidence of a growing gap in the opportunity to enroll in college. In this analysis we use racial/ethnic groups because information on ethnicity is more consistently available than information on income. In this analysis it is evident that an inequality in opportunity for college enrollment opened after 1980. Reviews of the research on the impact of financial aid reveal that grant amount is associated with enrollment, especially for low-income students (Heller 1997; St. John 2003).

Rethinking Misinformation

There is no doubt now that the NCES reports on access and persistence made serious statistical errors as well as consistently demonstrating research bias. In an effort to build a new rationale for academic preparation as a rationale for promoting college access, they not only made serious errors, but they failed to examine how the privatization process influenced access. As a society concerned about equal opportunity, we also need to evaluate the efficacy of federal policy in promoting access. While the trends alone do not provide sufficient information to provide an empirically sound evaluation, they do provide a basis for making informed judgments that could be further tested in future studies.

It is reasonable to hypothesize that privatization is a more economical way for the United States to promote college access. Expansion in loans corresponded with expansion in enrollment rates, indicating that the change in policy did not reduce opportunity overall. Arguments for reducing government costs of loans could be rationalized based on efficiency arguments. However, typically these rationales also argue for equal access (e.g., Lleras 2004), similar to the argument for federal student aid.

Since the federal student aid programs are not rationalized or based on equalizing the opportunity for low-income students who qualify, it is important to think through the role of financial aid in equalizing opportunity. The rising gap between the Pell maximum and the cost of attendance appears to explain the growing gap in enrollment rates. However, there are a number of intervening variables, including issues related to the maximum limit for borrowing for the federal guaranteed loan programs and the burden of repayment. If income-contingent repayment schemes did reduce the repayment burden, then they might also equalize opportunity.

The issues facing federal policy makers as they debate policies on student aid and privatization of higher education are quite complex. The major contribution of NCES research on access has been to build understandings about the role of preparation (Adelman 1995, 2004). However, since access to quality K–12 education is also related to the financial means of families, even this issue is not as simple as it is usually portrayed. Therefore, there is a fundamental need to rethink federal policy on the financing of higher education.

Implications

Ultimately, the debate about federal policy on higher education finance has direct implications for state policy on higher education and indirect implications for both public and private colleges. The strategies states use to fund colleges and students represent the core public role in higher education, a domain of policy that is inherently a federal responsibility. However, federal policy has a shaping influence on both public and private colleges. Four domains of public policy affecting public and private colleges merit consideration.

First, the federal role in funding institutions is modest but relatively stable. The agricultural colleges, military colleges, and colleges for students with special needs continue along with incremental improvement in their base funding. The one area of federal spending that has increased is Title III, especially support for HBCUs. The federal role in providing supplemental support for minority-serving institutions remains appropriate, given the long history of race discrimination in the United States (Brown, Butler, and Donahoo 2004; Williams 1997). This is a domain of federal policy that merits further attention (Conrad and Weerts 2004).

Second, the federal role in funding research has a shaping influence on the privatizations of public and private universities. The commercialization of science within academe is evident in both public and private research universities (Bok 2003; Ehrenberg 2002; Slaughter and Leslie 1997). In their efforts to position themselves to compete for funds, research universities shift the priorities within, valuing some disciplines over others. The new internal inequality within academe runs counter to traditional academic values in the academy, including notions of shared governance and public service (St. John, in press). This domain of policy also merits consideration by states as well as by research universities.

Third, the federal government enables massive investment of private capital in guaranteed loan programs. The structure of federal loans may be inefficient, but it is difficult to debate alternatives such as income-contingent loans (Lleras 2004) in the United States because of the strong lobbying position of the lending industry (Hearn and Holdsworth 2004; Parsons 2004). The trends in federal programs and college enrollment rates indicate loans have enabled more students to enroll. These policies have benefited both public and private colleges. In fact, the shares of total enrollments in private colleges and two-year colleges increased during the 1990s (St. John 2003) largely because of the decline in the purchasing power of Pell in public four-year colleges.

Finally, the decline in federal grant aid, coupled with shifts in state funding for higher education, have fueled a new period of unequal opportunity. There is substantial evidence that low-income, college-qualified students have been left behind in large numbers (Fitzgerald 2004; Lee 2004). The official reports released by the National Center for Education Statistics not only made serious statistical errors and demonstrated interpretive bias (Becker 2004; Fitzgerald 2004; Heller 2004; St. John 2003) but also misled public officials about the nature of the access challenge. Low-income students have unequal opportunity even when they qualify academically. There is a need for public and private colleges of all types to adjust admissions policies to make sure that they are fair and equitable, given the inequalities in the K–12 system (Musoba 2004; St. John and Musoba 2002). But the inequalities that result from the failure to fully fund Pell grants merit wider attention as well.

References

Adams v. Richardson, Civ. A. No. 3095–70, U.S. Dist., 356 F. Supp. 92 (16 February 1973).

Adelman, C. 1995. *The new college course map and transcript files: Changes in course-taking and achievement, 1972–1993*. Washington, D.C.: National Center for Education Statistics.

———. 1999. *Answers in the tool box: Academic intensity, attendance patterns, and bachelor's degree attainment*. Washington, D.C.: National Center for Education Statistics.

———. 2004. *Principle indicators of student academic histories in postsecondary education, 1972–2000*. Washington, D.C.: U.S. Department of Education, Institute of Education Sciences.

Advanced Technology, Inc., and Westat, Inc. 1983. *Quality control study: Final report*. Reston, Va.: Author.

Advisory Committee on Student Financial Assistance. 2002. *Empty promises: The myth of college access in America*. Washington, D.C.: Author.

59

Becker, G. S. 1964. *Human capital: A theoretical and empirical analysis with special reference to education.* New York: Columbia University Press.

Becker, W. E. 2004. Omitted variables and sample selection in studies of college-going decisions. In *Readings on equal education: Vol. 19. Public policy and college access: Investigating the federal and state roles in equalizing postsecondary opportunity,* ed. E. P. St. John, 65–86. New York: AMS Press.

Bennett, W. J. 1987. Our greedy colleges. *New York Times,* 18 February, I 31.

Blau, P., and O. D. Duncan. 1967. *The American occupational structure.* New York: Wiley.

Bok, D. 2003. *Universities in the marketplace: The commercialization of higher education.* Princeton, N.J.: Princeton University Press.

Brimelow, P. 1987. The untouchables. *Forbes,* 30 November, 141–50.

Brown, M. C., II, J. Butler, and S. Donahoo. 2004. Desegregation and diversity: Finding new ways to meet the challenge. In *Public funding of higher education: Changing contexts and new rationales,* ed. E. P. St. John and M. D. Parsons, 108–23. Baltimore, Md.: Johns Hopkins University Press.

Carnegie Commission on Higher Education. 1973. *Priorities for action: Final report.* New York: McGraw-Hill.

Carnes, B. M. 1987. The campus cost explosion: College tuitions are unnecessarily high. *Policy Review* 40: 68–71.

Choy, S. P. 2002. *Access and persistence: Findings from 10 years of longitudinal research on students.* Washington, D.C.: American Council on Education.

College Board. 2002. *Trends in student aid 2002.* Washington, D.C.: Author.

———. 2003. *Trends in student aid 2003.* Washington, D.C.: Author.

Conrad, C. F., and D. J. Weerts. 2004. Federal involvement in higher education desegregation: An unfinished agenda. In *Public funding of higher education: Changing contexts and new rationales,* ed. E. P. St. John and M. D. Parsons, 60–73. Baltimore, Md.: Johns Hopkins University Press.

Dartmouth College v. Woodward, 17 U.S. 518 (1819).

Ehrenberg, R. G. 2002. *Tuition rising: Why college costs so much.* Cambridge, Mass.: Harvard University Press.

Ellwood, D., and T. J. Kane. 2000. Who is getting a college education: Family background and the growing gaps in enrollment. In *Securing the future: Investing in children from birth to college,* ed. S. Danziger and J. Waldfogel, 264–82. New York: Russell Sage Foundation.

Finn, C. E., Jr. 1978. *Scholars, dollars, and bureaucrats: Federal policy toward higher education.* Washington, D.C.: The Brookings Institution Press.

———. 1988a. Judgment time for higher education in the court of public opinion. *Change* 20 (July/August): 35–38.

———. 1988b. Prepared statement and attachments. Hearing before the Subcommittee on Postsecondary Education, Committee on Education and Labor, House of Representatives, 100th Congress, 1st Session, No. 100–47, September 25. Washington, D.C.: U.S. Government Printing Office.

First, P. F. 1992. *Educational policy for school administrators.* Boston: Allyn and Bacon.

Fitzgerald, B. 2004. Federal financial aid and college access. In *Readings on equal education: Vol. 19. Public policy and college access: Investigating the federal and state roles in equalizing postsecondary opportunity,* ed. E. P. St. John, 1–28. New York: AMS Press.

Flint, T. 1997. Predicting student loan defaults. *Journal of Higher Education* 68: 322–54.

Fogel, R. W. 2000. *The fourth great awakening and the future of egalitarianism.* Chicago: University of Chicago Press.

Gladieux, L. E., and T. Wolanin. 1976. *Congress and the colleges: The national politics of higher education.* Lexington, Mass.: Lexington Books.

Hearn, J. C. 1993. The paradox of growth in federal aid for college students, 1965–1990. In *Higher education: Handbook of theory and research, Vol. 9,* ed. J. C. Smart, 94–153. New York: Agathon Press.

———. 2003. *Diversifying campus revenue streams: Opportunities and risks.* Washington, D.C.: American Council on Education. Available at http://www.acenet.edu/bookstore/pdf/2003_diversify_campus.pdf.

Hearn, J. C., and J. M. Holdsworth. 2004. Federal student aid: The shift from grants to loans. In *Public funding of higher education: Changing contexts and new rationales,* ed. E. P. St. John and M. P. Parsons, 40–59. Baltimore, Md.: Johns Hopkins University Press.

Heller, D. E. 1997. Student price response in higher education: An update of Leslie and Brinkman. *Journal of Higher Education* 68(6): 624–59.

———. 2004. NCES research on college participation: A critical analysis. In *Readings on equal education: Vol. 19, Public policy and college access: Investigating the federal and state roles in equalizing postsecondary opportunity,* ed. E. P. St. John, 29–64. New York: AMS Press.

Henry, M., B. Ligard, F. Rizvi, and S. Taylor. 2001. *The OECD, globalization and education policy.* Amsterdam: Pergamon.

Herbst, J. 1976. From religion to politics: Debates and confrontations over American college governance in mid-eighteenth century America. *Harvard Educational Review* 46: 397–424.

Honeyman, D. S., and M. Bruhn. 1996. The financing of higher education. In *A struggle to survive: Funding higher education in the next century,* ed. D. S. Honeyman, J. L. Wattenbarger, and K. C. Westbrook, 1–28. Thousand Oaks, Calif.: Corwin.

Huber, E., and J. D. Stephens. 2001. *Development and crisis of the welfare state: Parties and policies in global markets.* Chicago: University of Chicago Press.

Jencks, C., and D. Reisman. 1968. *The academic revolution.* Chicago: Doubleday Press.

Johnson, E. L. 1981/1989. Misconceptions about the early land-grant colleges. In *The history of higher education,* ed. L. F. Goodchild and H. S. Wechsler, 222–33. Needham Heights, Mass.: Ginn. (Reprinted from *Journal of Higher Education* 52(4): 333–57.)

Lee, J. B. 2004. Access revisited: A preliminary reanalysis of NELS. In *Readings on equal education: Vol. 19. Public policy and college access: Investigating the federal and state roles in equalizing postsecondary opportunity,* ed. E. P. St. John, 87–96. New York: AMS Press.

Lleras, M. P. 2004. *Investing in human capital: A capital markets approach to student funding.* Cambridge, UK: Cambridge University Press.

Lucas, C. J. 1994. *American higher education: A history.* New York: St. Martin's Press.

McKeown, M. P. 1996. State funding formulas: Promise fulfilled? In *A struggle to survive: Funding higher education in the next century,* ed. D. S. Honeyman, J. L. Wattenbarger, and K. C. Westbrook. Thousand Oaks, Calif.: Corwin Press.

McPherson, M. S., and M. O. Schapiro. 1991. *Keeping college affordable: Government and educational opportunity.* Washington, D.C.: The Brookings Institution.

Mumper, M. 1996. *Removing college price barriers: What government has done and why it hasn't worked.* Albany: State University of New York Press.

Musoba, G. D. 2004. Postsecondary encouragement for diverse students: A reexamination of the Twenty-first Century Scholars Program. In *Readings on equal education: Vol. 19. Public policy and college access: Investigating the federal and state roles in equalizing postsecondary opportunity,* ed. E. P. St. John, 153–80. New York: AMS Press.

National Center for Education Statistics. 1997a. *Access to higher postsecondary education for the 1992 high school graduates.* NCES 98–105. By L. Berkner and L. Chavez. Washington, D.C.: National Center for Education Statistics.

———. 1997b. *Confronting the odds: Students at risk and the pipeline to higher education.* NCES 98–094. By L. J. Horn. Washington, D.C.: National Center for Education Statistics.

———. 2001a. *Bridging the gap: Academic preparation and postsecondary success of first-generation students.* NCES 2001–153. By E. C. Warburton and R. Bugarin. Washington, D.C.: National Center for Education Statistics.

———. 2001b. *Students whose parents did not go to college: Postsecondary access, persistence, and attainment.* By S. Choy. Washington, D.C.: National Center for Education Statistics.

———. 2002a. *The condition of education 2002.* NCES 2002–025. Washington, D.C.: National Center for Education Statistics.

———. 2002b. *Digest of education statistics 2001.* NCES 2002–130. Washington, D.C.: National Center for Education Statistics.

———. 2002c. *Hispanic serving institutions: Statistical trends from 1990–1999.* NCES 2002–051. Washington, D.C.: National Center for Education Statistics.

———. 2003a. *Digest of education statistics 2002.* NCES 2003–060. Washington, D.C.: National Center for Education Statistics.

———. 2003b. *Federal support for education, fiscal years 1980 to 2002.* NCES 2003–006. Washington, D.C.: National Center for Education Statistics.

———. 2004. *Digest of education statistics 2003.* NCES 2005–025. Washington, D.C.: National Center for Education Statistics.

National Commission on Excellence in Education. 1983. *A nation at risk: The imperative for educational reform.* Washington, D.C.: U.S. Government Printing Office.

National Commission on the Financing of Postsecondary Education. 1973. *Financing postsecondary education in the United States.* Washington, D.C.: Government Printing Office.

No Child Left Behind Act of 2001. Public Law 107–110.

Parsons, M. D. 2004. Lobbying in higher education: Theory and practice. In *Public funding of higher education: Changing contexts and new rationales,* ed. E. P. St. John and M. D. Parsons, 215–30. Baltimore, Md.: Johns Hopkins University Press.

Pelavin, S. H., and M. B. Kane. 1988. *Minority participation in higher education.* Prepared for the U.S. Department of Education, Office of Planning, Budget and Evaluation. Washington, D.C.: Pelavin Associates.

Putka, G. 1987. Tracking tuition: Why college fees are rising so sharply. *Wall Street Journal,* 11 December, 1.

Rawls, J. 1971. *A theory of justice.* Cambridge, Mass.: Belknap Press of Harvard University Press.

Rawls, J. 2001. *Justice as fairness: A restatement.* Cambridge, Mass.: Belknap Press of Harvard University Press.

Rudolph, F. 1990. *The American college and university: A history.* Athens: University of Georgia Press.

Selznick, P. 1969. *Law, society, and industrial justice.* New York: Russell Sage Foundation.

Slaughter, S., and L. L. Leslie. 1997. *Academic capitalism: Politics, policies, and the entrepreneurial university.* Baltimore, Md.: Johns Hopkins University Press.

Stiglitz, J. E. 2003. *Globalization and its discontents.* New York: Norton.

St. John, E. P. 1981. *Public policy and college management: Title III of the Higher Education Act.* New York: Praeger Press.

———. 1993. Untangling the web: Using price-response measures in enrollment projections. *Journal of Higher Education* 64(6): 676–95.

———. 1994. *Prices, productivity, and investment.* ASHE/ERIC monograph, No. 3. San Francisco: Jossey-Bass.

———. 2003. *Refinancing the college dream: Access, equal opportunity, and justice for taxpayers.* Baltimore, Md.: Johns Hopkins University Press.

———. (in press). Commercialization, privatization, and the professorate: Implications for teaching, research, and service. *Academe.*

St. John, E. P., and C. Byce. 1982. The changing federal role in student financial aid. In *New directions for higher education, Volume 40: Meeting student aid needs in a period of retrenchment,* ed. M. Kramer, 21–40. San Francisco: Jossey-Bass.

St. John, E. P., C. G. Chung, G. D. Musoba, A. B. Simmons, O. S. Wooden, and J. Mendez. 2004. *Expanding college access: The impact of state finance strategies.* Indianapolis, Ind.: The Lumina Foundation for Education.

St. John, E. P., S. Hu, and J. Weber. 2000. Keeping public colleges affordable: A study of persistence in Indiana's public colleges and universities. *Journal of Student Financial Aid* 30(1): 21–32.

———. 2001. State policy and the affordability of public higher education: The influence of state grants on persistence in Indiana. *Research in Higher Education* 42: 401–28.

St. John, E. P., and G. D. Musoba. 2002. Academic access and equal opportunity: Rethinking the foundations for policy on diversity. In *Readings on equal education: Vol. 18. Equity and access in higher education: Changing the definition of educational opportunity,* ed. M. C. Brown and C. Freeman, 171–92. New York: AMS Press.

St. John, E. P., T. Tuttle, and G. D. Musoba. (in press). *Access and equal opportunity in U.S. higher education: A balanced assessment of the effects of federal policy.*

Tabb, W. K. 2001. *The amoral elephant: Globalization and social justice in the twenty-first century.* New York: Monthly Review Press.

Thelin, J. R. 2004. *A history of American higher education.* Baltimore, Md.: Johns Hopkins University Press.

U.S. Department of Education. 1990. *Tough choices: A guide to administrative cost management in colleges and universities.* Washington, D.C.: U.S. Department of Education.

———. 2004. Historically Black Colleges and Universities Capital Financing Program, basic information. Available online at http://web99.ed.gov/GTEP/Program2.nsf/0/f0316a80a8192303852563bc0054052c.

United States v. Fordice, 505 U.S. 717; 112 S. Ct. 2727; 120 L. Ed. 2d 575 (26 June 1992).

Williams, J. B. 1988. Title VI regulation of higher education. In *Desegregating America's colleges and universities: Title VI regulation of higher education,* ed. J. B. Williams, 33–53. New York: Teachers College Press.

———. 1997. *Race discrimination in higher education.* New York: Praeger.

CHAPTER THREE

The Ideology of Privatization in Higher Education: A Global Perspective

Fazal Rizvi

Over the past two decades, the ideology of privatization has been embraced by most higher education systems around the world. Privatization has become a major plank within a broader set of reforms that have transformed the governance of higher education. These reforms are linked to the globalization of economy and have deepened the shift from Keynesianism to neoliberalism. Public institutions in most parts of the world have been encouraged, if not compelled, to adopt the principles of market dynamics in the management of their key functions. These developments have resulted in a new discourse in higher education that is constituted by such concepts as strategic planning, cost-efficiency, human resource allocation, competition and choice, optimizing information technology, performance management, and accountability. They provide the basis for a new managerialist approach to public administration that redefines the relationship between the state and its institutions, and individuals and civil society. Universities are implored to restructure the way in which they make decisions and to reimagine the manner in which they are funded, relate to their clients, and manage their resources.

Schugurensky (1999) has noted that when viewed from a global and comparative perspective "what is most striking about the current higher education restructuring is the unprecedented scope and depth of changes taking place as well as the similarity of changes occurring in a wide variety of nations having different social, political, historical, and economic characteristics" (284). Indeed, any international review of recent policy initiatives in higher education shows the direction of change implemented by nations around the world to be remarkably similar, with similar sets of government directives and plans that demand that public universities become more responsive to the external market pressures and restructure their priorities in line with the requirements of global economy. There is an almost universal belief that the state should no longer be asked to fund the growth of the higher education sector but that there should be greater reliance on private sources of revenue to meet even the existing commitments. Even nation-states not faced with fiscal crisis, such as Singapore (see Gopinathan 2001), appear to have embraced this worldview, setting in place mechanisms for their universities to generate funds from a variety of sources and allowing a number of private operators to enter the higher education market.

A number of recent scholars of higher education have spoken of "global convergence" toward a neoliberal discourse, within the framework of which the idea of privatization is located. For example, Samoff (1999) has argued that, either through borrowing or imposition, systems of higher education around the world are converging around a set of ideas about technology, knowledge, economy, and management. For Foucault (1991), these ideas represent a new form of governance, understood as a response to economic globalization and a shift from Fordist to flexible forms of production. This neoliberal governmentality, as he calls it, involves a redefinition of the relationship between state and society in which primacy is accorded to economic factors in addressing the totality of human behavior. Foucault highlights the specificity of contemporary forms of governance, premised on the active consent and subjugation of subjects rather than their oppression, domination, or external control. Neoliberalism requires governments to reform the conduct of individuals to make them more competitive and efficient as a way of ensuring global economic advantage. As Hoogvelt (1997) maintains, an awareness of global competition "constrains individuals and groups, and even national governments, to conform to international standards of price and quality" (124). Governments that fail to so conform are not only marginalized within the global economy but can also be subjected to various forms of direct and indirect sanctions, such as those imposed by the International Monetary Fund (IMF) and the World Bank. This development has led numerous scholars to suggest that we may indeed be witnessing the emergence of "a new regime of discipline in which governmentality is un-hitched from the nation-state to be instituted anew on a global scale" (Gupta 1998, 321).

In this essay, I attempt to understand privatization as a global ideol-ogy, constituted as a new regime of discipline that seems to be increas-ingly shaping the management style and strategies of public universities around the world in both developed and developing countries. I ex-plore some of the processes through which this ideology circulates around the world, compelling nations to accept its main tenets. I argue, however, that like all ideologies, the global trend toward privatization of higher education is far from complete and that while the influence of neoliberal governmentality is strong, its requirements for public higher education are interpreted in a wide variety of different ways. Using the contrasting examples of higher education in Australia and China, I at-tempt to show how different motivations and different political and his-torical factors produce major variations in strategies pursued to imple-ment privatization, as governments struggle to negotiate neoliberal pressures with local demands for autonomy, democracy, and justice.

The Ideology of Privatization

In very broad terms, the idea of privatization refers to the transfer of services provided by the public sector to a range of private sector inter-ests. As a political construct, the idea of privatization emerged in the 1970s as an attempt by a number of Western countries, like the United States, to separate decision making in the areas of public policy from the execution of service provision. Three decades later, it has become globally pervasive, increasingly assumed to be the only way to ensure that public services, including education, are delivered efficiently and effectively. It has come to symbolize a new way of looking at public in-stitutions and at the role of the state in managing the affairs of its citi-zens. Under this broad philosophical orientation, many possible activi-ties are construed as privatization, ranging from selling state-owned enterprises to contracting out public services to private contractors, be they individuals or corporations. According to Bray (1996), privatiza-tion of education takes at least three forms: transferring ownership of public institutions, shifting sectoral balance without redesignating ex-isting institutions, and increasing government funding and support for private institutions. Bray might have added a fourth to this list: con-tracting out functions and services. Indeed, contracting out and enterprise sales may perhaps be the most influential modalities of privatization in the contemporary public sector.

Just as privatization appears in several forms, so do the reasons governments give in favor of privatization. Most of the reasons are couched in economic terms. It is argued that privatization leads to cost-effective delivery of public services and that it enhances the productivity of government agencies. Governments also suggest that the power of private property rights, market forces, and competition brings out the best in public sector employees. When the public sector is forced to compete against private contractors, the service delivery is necessarily more efficient. When public institutions are thrust into market environments, they become much more organizationally agile and innovative, with greater commitment to reform. Economic arguments in favor of privatization also view it as necessary for growth and for meeting increasing levels of demand for particular services, including higher education. Such arguments necessarily assume the welfare state to be a thing of the past, withering away, no longer capable of meeting the requirements both of society and individuals who are increasingly interested in managing their own affairs and do not trust the state to look after them.

Many of these arguments have become commonplace, even if most cannot be substantiated with any hard data. So, for example, that private contractors are more efficient and cost-effective in delivering services without compromising on quality is a contention that has repeatedly been shown to be both groundless and perhaps even unverifiable (Boyer and Drache 1996), yet this does not seem to stop advocates of privatization from asserting it like a mantra. The fact is that economic arguments, on their own, cannot justify privatization. To try to do so is to grossly underestimate the political nature of the privatization agenda and also to misunderstand the role of ideology in promoting it. In the end, the political context in which privatization is promoted is inherently ideological. It is based on an almost ontological assumption that the private sector is intrinsically more productive than the public sector.

Such an assumption is based on a philosophical conception of society as constituted by self-maximizing individuals as well as a conception of government as necessarily inimical to individual interests. Accordingly, public institutions are regarded as distant and unresponsive organs of government that pose serious threats to individual property rights and freedom. According to this neoliberal view, individual freedom is not the only value that is endangered by government institutions; justice is threatened as well. Justice, it is assumed, is compromised because of the perennial desire of governments to redistribute wealth that is never theirs and to seek to control human affairs that are best left to individual discretion. While neoliberalism accepts that some redistribution and control may be necessary, it suggests that the Keynesian welfare state exceeded its democratic authority and is no longer relevant to contemporary economic and social life, especially under the cultural conditions of globalization.

Freedom, justice, and efficiency are thus key ingredients underpinning neoliberal ideology and have increasingly been redefined in the self-image of that perspective. These social concepts, developed with particular meaning and significance within social democratic traditions, have been systematically rearticulated. Within the neoliberal discourse, the idea of freedom has, for example, become tied to a negative view of freedom as "freedom from," rather than a positive view of freedom as "freedom to," in terms, for example, articulated by Amartya Sen (1999), who has defined freedom in terms of the capabilities that people have to exercise choices and live decent lives, free from poverty and exploitation.

Similarly, the idea of justice has been reduced to property rights rather than personal rights (Bowles and Gintis 1987). A property right vests in individuals the power to enter into social relationships on the basis and extent of their property, whereas personal rights are based on simple membership in their social collectivity. Personal rights involve equal treatment of citizens, capacity to enjoy autonomy, equal access to participation in decision making in social institutions, and reciprocity in relations of power and authority. The neoliberal view of justice, on the other hand, is located in the processes of acquisition and production rather than in the need to build community and social lives that are characterized by human dignity for all. Such a conception of freedom necessarily privileges the ruling capitalist class, who are able to access property rights within a system of asymmetrical power relations and labor exploitation.

The neoliberal notion of efficiency is equally problematic because it cannot be interpreted neutrally, as neoliberal theorists often do, without reference to the more fundamental moral and political criteria against which it might be measured. Nothing is efficient in its own right. We need to ask the more basic question, "Efficiency in terms of what?" As the philosopher Alasdair MacIntyre (1981) points out, there are strong grounds for rejecting the claim that efficiency is a morally neutral concept. Rather, it is "inseparable from a mode of existence in which the contrivance of means is in central part the manipulation of human beings into compliant patterns of behavior" (71). In an organizational setting, efficiency drives always involve control over people, achieved through either sanctions or hegemonic compliance. What this brief discussion shows, then, is that to embrace the interpretation of the concepts of freedom, justice, and efficiency in neoliberal terms is to accept a certain preferred mode of existence, to become drawn into processes of governmentality described by Foucault.

Philosophical assumptions relating to this preferred mode of existence underpin most theories of privatization. Chief among these are the public choice theory, the agency theory, the theory of transaction cost analysis, the new public management theory, and the property rights theory. Each of these theories assumes the key rationale for privatization to be the need to increase economic efficiency through better organizational performance and control as a means of increasing the well-being of citizens. The *public choice theory* is based on the fundamental notion that self-interest dominates human behavior and that human beings are essentially "rational utility maximizers"; that individuals can express their personal preferences much more effectively through market exchanges than, say, political participation; and that the role of government should therefore be restricted to establishing high-level policy objectives rather than delivering the services per se. *Agency theory* views the delivery of services through an organization as a series of contracts which, if optimally established and operated, can generate significant levels of efficiency. The theory of *transaction cost analysis* suggests that organizational costs of transacting business can be minimized and made more efficient through vertical integration, best achieved through the privatization of all functions of an organization except those that are regarded as absolutely central to organizational mission.

The idea of *new public management* shares its assumptions with theories of agency and transactional cost analysis, and applies them to the public sector. It emphasizes a range of concepts that have become commonplace in higher education around the world. Collectively, these concepts amount to what Waters (1995) refers to as "organizational ecumenism," a single idealization of appropriate organizational behavior. These concepts include generic management skills; quantified performance targets; devolution; the separation of policy, commercial, and noncommercial functions; the use of private sector practices such as corporate plans and flexible labor practices; just-in-time inventory; monetary incentives; cost-cutting; and above all, the privatization of the so-called noncore functions and services. It thus emphasizes a prefer-

70

ence for private ownership and prescribes, wherever possible, the use of contracting out and competition in the provision of public services.

Aligned to these concepts is the theory of *property rights*, which argues that private ownership of the assets of an organization results in superior profitability and effectiveness. In each of these theories, the emphasis on the principles of efficiency, effectiveness, productivity, and profitability is paramount. These theories moreover assume that these principles are generic and apply equally to all kinds of organizations, be they commercial or service-oriented, be they private or public. As organizations increasingly work in the international sphere, these theories seek to universalize these principles, eschewing those organizational practices that are situated within local and national cultural traditions.

However, what these theories mask is a range of philosophic assumptions about how society and its institutions are best organized. Insofar as they provide empirical justification for their various claims about efficiency and productivity, they do so within a self-referential framework in which its principles are assumed to be self-evidently good, even when they might conflict with other equally important goals. Public agencies like universities have multiple and complex goals, yet these theories focus only on a narrow range of goals, making it difficult, if not impossible, to measure the justificatory claims that are made by their proponents. For unlike commercial businesses, performance in the public sector cannot be aggregated up to a single valid measurement of an agency's effectiveness. Yet most advocates of privatization try to do precisely this, often treating efficiency as a foundational principle, an end in its own right. In so doing, they clearly show how ideologically driven arguments in favor of privatization really are. Since no one can really object to efficiency and profitability, the neoliberal emphasis on these principles appears as self-evident and hence highly persuasive. Yet it is only when they are juxtaposed with other equally worthy service-related goals that they become contestable. And insofar as these contests are obscured by a narrowly defined language of freedom and justice, as we have already noted, the emphasis on efficiency and effectiveness obscures the powerful elite capitalist interests that privatization serves. The idea of privatization thus functions as an ideology.

Ideology is a highly contested theoretical construct. In popular parlance, it often refers to a set of ideas to which one is totally committed, even if those ideas have no basis in fact. Ideology is often also associated with theories that are impractical, abstract, and even fanatically held. In the classical Marxist tradition, it is viewed as a misrepresentation of reality, nothing more than the ideal expression of the dominant material relationships designed to obscure historical truths, encouraging subordinate groups to give assent to ruling ideas—in short, "false consciousness." I use the term *ideology* in a neo-Marxist sense, stripped of its association with historical determinism but highlighting the material interests of the ruling classes it serves by obscuring their real interests. In this sense, I regard ideology as a contingent phenomenon employed by people to make sense of the world in ways that are never neutral but always interest-relative. Ideology thus has both discursive and material dimensions: it names "mental frameworks—the languages, the concepts, categories, imagery of thought, and the systems of representation—which different classes and social groups deploy in order to make sense of, define, figure out, and render intelligible the way society works" (Hall 1996, 26).

If privatization is an ideology in this sense, then we need to ask how it has become global. How have the languages, concepts, categories, imagery of thought, and systems of representation associated with privatization become globally ubiquitous? To address this issue, we need to examine the ways in which ideologies travel through time and space under the conditions of contemporary globalization; and we need to identify some of the processes through which privatization has become a dominant ideology in ways that are globally converging and politically hegemonic.

Global Drivers of Privatization

Some of the processes of this ideological shift, of course, lie within the political dynamics of a particular nation-state, as neoliberal ideologies are promoted in that country by local systems of communication, political parties, and corporate interests. This promotion takes place against the political and historical backdrop relevant to that nation-state and can therefore be expected to lead to particular meaning and significance becoming attached to the ideology of privatization. However, this observation about the processes internal to the nation-state begs the question of how these processes are affected by the broader global processes and how these processes are articulated and refracted through the local specificities of the nation-state. This is an important question that needs to tackled if we are to determine the extent to which resistance to the neoliberal agenda in higher education is possible and how a political space opposed to it might be created in search of alternatives that neither romanticize a social democratic past nor accept as inevitable the basic tenets of neoliberalism.

To suggest that the privatization ideology in higher education has become dominant worldwide because of globalization—as a consequence of the imperatives of the emerging global knowledge economy, leading to the convergence of certain modes of educational governance around neoliberal notions of global interconnectivity and interdependence—is not particularly helpful. It is far too general and presupposes a broader discourse of capitalist triumphalism, and it is suggestive of Fukuyama's (1992) flawed vision of "the end of history." It assumes, as Currie and Newsom (1998) do, that recent neoliberal higher education reforms are a necessary outcome of the structural conditions under which they are developed and that these conditions are anchored in a global economy that shape, in some functional way, the educational policy options nation-states have. This line of thinking is based on an assumption that globalization is unstoppable and represents a tidal wave force.

The main problem with this view, however, is that it draws our attention "disproportionately upon the global economy, reified as a pre-given 'thing,' existing outside of thought," the logic of which not only explains the development of policies but even determines the subjectivity of people "without ever interrogating them about what they are up to" (Smith 2000, 6). Moreover, it privileges the economic over the sociocultural and political processes. And, as Smith adds, it gives "scant attention to the discursive and material practices by which people create the regularized patterns that enable and constrain them; these discourses lack an effective theory of political agency, or any other kind of agency" (6).

If, on the other hand, we take political agency seriously, then the global acceptance of the ideology of privatization needs to be understood in terms of a set of historically specific processes articulated through various power configurations. These processes are inherently political and work in various locally contingent and historically specific ways. In what follows, I discuss four sets of such processes. The first relates to the global circulation of ideas and ideologies, increasingly powered by developments in transportation, information, and communication technologies. With these developments in transportation technologies, the international mobility of people has never been greater. This mobility has enabled ideas to be exchanged among policy makers and researchers coming together from different countries, even if this exchange is not symmetrical in its power configurations. So, for example, the ideas emanating from the West have a greater chance of becoming accepted, even if these ideas are self-serving. A new policy space has thus emerged that allows ideas and ideologies to be produced and distributed instantaneously. This space has often been sponsored by inter-governmental organizations such as the OECD, UNESCO, and the European Union. While these organizations often insist that they seek to provide forums for open and free exploration of educational ideas, they find it hard to hide their own positions committed to neoliberal reforms in higher education. For example, in recent years the OECD, which views itself as a forum of the free exchange of ideas, has become a major carrier of neoliberal policy thinking about higher education: it has become a policy actor in its own right (Henry et al. 2001).

Appadurai (1996) has written of "ideoscapes" that are constituted as "concatenations of images" that circulate throughout the world in an explicitly political fashion. This circulation is frequently affected by the ideologies of states and the counter-ideologies of movements opposed to them. In the contemporary period, educational policies seem to be converging toward a particular concatenation of neoliberal ideas that we have discussed above, despite opposition from a wide variety of sources. The concatenation Appadurai speaks of is produced by policy borrowing, modeling transfer, diffusion, appropriation, and copying, which occur across the boundaries of nation-states and which, as Halpin (1994) has argued, "lead to universalizing tendencies in educational reform" (204). At conferences and in journals where educational ideas circulate, it is often difficult to determine the extent to which there has been free exchange of ideas—or indeed, where policy debates have already been constructed within the framework of the dominant neoliberal ideology. But the point that needs to be emphasized here is that the circulation of educational ideologies is not a function of globalization per se but involves actual historical processes, human agents, organizations, and governments—with capacity to accept, resist, or reject them. Acceptance of ideas and ideologies is thus a consequence of political processes located within particular configurations of power and hegemonic relations.

The second set of processes through which the ideology of privatization has been globally accepted relates to international conventions, embodying consensus between parties. These conventions have invariably led developing countries in particular to accept neoliberal ideologies, even if there has been political opposition to them. Examples of such conventions include not only human rights and democratic elections but also modes of governance. The idea of "good governance," for example, has become a major policy agenda around the world. Many of these conventions involve formal agreements and commitments that have exposed the domestic policy practices of nation-states to external scrutiny, thus reducing their autonomy. While conventions are supposedly entered into voluntarily, there is often a great deal of pressure on countries to conform to particular ideologies.

Perhaps the best-known recent example of neoliberal consensus is the Washington Consensus. The term *Washington Consensus* refers to "the lowest common denominator of policy advice addressed by the Washington-based institutions to Latin American countries" (Williamson 1990, 9–19). According to Williamson, the Washington Consensus is a product of "the intellectual convergence," which is designed to get most of Latin America and elsewhere to accept a set of common assumptions about economic reform and institutional governance. George Soros (1998) calls these assumptions "market fundamentalism" and suggests that much of their acceptance worldwide is in no small measure due to the persuasive rhetoric of right-wing think tanks in the United States. And even though the principles of the Washington Consensus no longer enjoy the appeal they once had (Gore 2000), most Washington-based development institutions, such as the U.S. Agency for International Development (USAID) and the World Bank, have continued to sing from the same song sheet, preaching relentlessly the values of macroeconomic discipline, trade openness, market-friendly microeconomic policies, and the new public sector management. In the field of education, this has implied fiscal discipline about educational funding, a redirection of public expenditure policies toward fields offering both high economic returns and the potential to improve income distribution, such as primary education, as well as privatization and deregulation.

A third set of processes relates not so much to the covert pressures of consensus and conventions but much more explicitly to coercive strategies such as those represented by Structural Adjustment Programs (SAP). These programs are ostensibly created because developing countries are unable to meet the payment schedules on their debts to international banks such as the World Bank and the International Monetary Fund (IMF). But before these countries are permitted to renegotiate schedules of debt repayment, they are forced to meet a range of conditions—in order to "better manage their economy" and "get their house in order." And while these conditions are often assumed to have the status of contracts, they are often negotiated under coercive demands of the banks and require debtor nations to pursue privatization as a condition of loans.

According to Faraclas (1997), "far from being mechanisms of debt reduction and economic recovery, SAPs have often resulted in the consolidation of neocolonial power" (147), and the institutionalization of a series of new enclosures. These enclosures have a transparently global character, involving a common set of ideological beliefs about the capitalist path of accumulation and appropriation of new resources and new labor power. To the policy makers in the developing countries, such as Papua New Guinea, from where Faraclas writes, the coercive SAP contracts represent a major dilemma. On the one hand, it is almost impossible for them to reject the offer of help, yet on the other hand, the conditions attached to the offer of help often involve implementing alienating and exploitative policies. Ultimately, SAPs require developing countries to concede some of their autonomy and pursue policies designed to create conditions more conducive to international investment than to the improvement of social conditions and educational opportunities.

Of course, it is not only the international lending agencies that demand neoliberal restructuring of the educational systems of the developing countries as a condition of loans to them; the transnational corporations (TNCs) offering to invest do as well. The relationship between TNCs and governments is a complex one, involving dynamics of both conflict and cooperation. Dicken (1998) argues that sometimes governments and TNCs may be rivals, but they may collude with one another at the same time. In the global economy, the governments need TNCs to help them in the process of material wealth creation, while TNCs require the nation-states to "provide the necessary supportive infrastructures, both physical and institutional, on the basis of which they can pursue their strategic objectives" (276). TNCs and governments are often involved in a bargaining process as each tries to get maximum advantage from the other. As Dicken observes, "states have become increasingly locked into a cut-throat competitive bidding process for investments, a process which provides TNCs with the opportunity to play off one bidder against another" (276). Some of this bargaining involves the demand by TNCs that education be restructured along market lines, with policies conducive to the creation of a human resource pool to better meet their labor needs.

And finally, a fourth set of processes involves cooperation among nations. Perhaps the best example of such cooperation is the Bologna Declaration (Council of Europe 1999). Signed by twenty-nine European countries in 1999, it pledges to reform their higher education systems in a convergent way. The declaration insists that the reform process it prescribes is not a path toward standardization or uniformization of European higher education but "reflects a search for a common European answer to common European problems" (Van der Wende 2000, 305). Its action program is designed to enhance the employability and mobility of citizens, conditioned by globalization. It builds upon highly successful European Union programs such as ERASMUS and SOCRATES and views itself as an important strategy toward the process of European integration. The Bologna process involves the development of a common framework of readable and comparable degrees, the introduction of undergraduate and postgraduate levels in all countries, comparable credit systems of courses and learning activities, a Europe-wide system of quality assurance, and the elimination of all remaining barriers to student mobility.

While appearing to be entirely transparent, as a consensus document, however, the Bologna Declaration masks a number of assumptions. Despite its insistence on the principles of diversity and national autonomy, it nonetheless assumes the importance of Europe-wide commitment to neoliberal reforms in higher education, weakening national control and unlinking education from powerful political sentiments in the field of national culture, language, and social emancipation. But more importantly, the Bologna process barely hides its more fundamental economic rationale: its preference for the marketization of higher education. While it does not completely support liberalization and deregulation of higher education, its main objectives are informed by a market logic—the need for the European system to become a more effective and efficient player in the highly competitive global market in higher education. The course of the Bologna process is thus heavily influenced by dominant neoliberal readings of globalization, issues of trade in higher education, and more specifically the World Trade Organization's General Agreement on Trade in Services (GATS) negotiations (Robertson and Dale 2004).

One of the main ambitions of the Bologna process is to strengthen the competitiveness of European higher education in the global marketplace so it can more effectively compete with American and Australian universities, which have been more active and successful in the export of higher education. Convergence in degree structures, the development of a credit transfer system, and a comprehensive quality assurance system are moves considered to be essential in the international trade of higher education. But in accepting this commercial logic, the Bologna Declaration in effect embraces the global trends toward commodification, privatization, and commercialization of higher education, sidelining higher education's traditional commitment to the "public good." So despite recent policy discourses in Europe that highlight ideas of social inclusion, neoliberal assumptions about higher education remain embedded in the Bologna Declaration.

Dilemmas of Privatization
in Higher Education

So far in this essay, I have discussed some of the processes through which privatization has become a dominant ideology around the world. I have argued that globalization has been given impetus through greater *circulation* of neoliberal ideas and ideologies; *consensus* among nations around conventions on, among other things, appropriate modes of governance; a range of *coercive* practices of international agencies directing nation-states toward particular neoliberal policy positions; and self-interested *cooperation* among nations so that they are better able to compete within the emerging global markets in higher education. I am not arguing, however, that these processes determine the behavior of governments. Rather, I am suggesting that these global processes represent pressures that governments have to negotiate, against their own particular histories and political conditions. Each of these processes thus involves a different pattern of political activity and power play and has varied consequences for particular educational systems as they attempt to interpret, negotiate, and translate into practice external global pressures driving the ideology of privatization in higher education.

In so doing, governments and higher education systems confront major dilemmas relating not only to the reasons for accepting privatization as a policy solution to their problems but also relating to the consequences of privatization for academic traditions as well as for access, equity, and organizational democracy. Indeed, the very nature and purposes of higher education are affected, since privatization involves much more than simply shifting public sector services to private contractors. The things shifted are themselves transformed into something else. As Brodie (1996) points out, "as things are shifted from the public to the private, they become differently encoded, constructed, and regulated" (389). Citizens with rights to higher education become consumers of alternative educational delivery systems capable of purchasing choice. This affects curriculum and pedagogy, as well as research,

78

in ways more dramatic than is often realized. So, for instance, peda-gogic approaches are evaluated in terms of cost-effectiveness, efficiency, and marketability rather than in terms of the academic mission of uni-versities. Research is judged more in terms of its market-use value than of its academic contribution (Slaughter and Rhoades 2004).

Perhaps the most dramatic example of this cultural shift as a result of privatization can be found in Australian higher education. The origins of privatization in Australian higher education go back to the mid-1980s, with the decision by the government to allow universities to charge international students full cost-recovery tuition fees. This policy was embraced by the cash-starved universities with great enthusiasm, unleashing a culture of entrepreneurialism that had been inconceiv-able earlier in the decade. The policy shift established mechanisms for growth in Australian higher education that had hitherto been managed by the federal bureaucracy of education. The next fifteen years wit-nessed a dramatic increase in the number of international students en-rolled in Australian universities, from just over 26,000 in 1989 to over 210,000 in 2004. International activity now constitutes almost 20 per-cent of the total student enrollment, generating almost 30 percent of the revenue for some of the leading universities, bringing in more than $4 billion to the Australian economy.

Now, while this form of privatization was to apply only to interna-tional activity, it has in fact transformed the organizational culture of Australian universities. Australian higher education has thus not only witnessed a new discourse of internationalization, defining the ways in which universities engage with the emerging issues of globalization — pointing to the commercial opportunities offered by the increasing movement of people, capital, and ideas — but a new, more general knowledge system has emerged in the process, stipulating preferred modes of governance and academic programs along neoliberal princi-ples (Rizvi 2005). A new administrative technology for managing higher education has emerged, with its own rules of operation based on knowl-edge of market segments and specificities, as well as a language about the distinctive benefits of educational products and services. This is a neoliberal language, which, in Australia, has effectively privatized high-er education not only for international students but for the rest of the system as well. The government, of course, has not been slow to recog-nize this, and is now encouraging universities to extend their commer-cial orientation to every aspect of their activities, for example, in mar-ket-based tuition fees for domestic students and contracting out of many university services, including some teaching and research.

This transformation has, of course, not been without its problems, which some university leaders are now beginning to recognize. Serious issues of capacity, volume, faculty commitment, balance, knowledge orientation, and quality have emerged. More significantly, however, the academic mission of universities has now begun to be defined largely in commercial terms. There has been a steady decline in the number of students in traditional disciplines and a disproportionately large growth in just three disciplinary areas: business studies, engineering, and computer science. Student attitudes toward education have become increasingly instrumental, with economic returns in mind. As consumers of higher education, students now demand an appropriate level of support and expect grades that will position them highly within the labor market. All this has seriously compromised the traditional academic mission of higher education, which Australian universities will not find easy to recover, given their heavy dependence on private sources of income. Privatization has been a virus that has affected the whole university body. The Australian case indicates, moreover, that once various aspects of the public system of higher education are privatized, it is very difficult to make a U-turn, for the faculty to regain control over the public mission of the universities, and to recover traditions of organizational democracy.

If internationalization has been a force driving the privatization of Australian universities, the Chinese system has been driven toward privatization by the incapacity of its public universities to meet fast-growing demand for higher education. This growth in demand is due to a range of factors, including China's spectacular economic growth, which has averaged more than 8 percent since China accepted some of the principles of market economy in 1979; the need for skilled workers in the Chinese economy; the growth of new professions linked to the expansion of the service sector and knowledge economy; increasing employment opportunities for young people; one-child family planning policies, resulting in higher levels of disposal income; and traditional cultural beliefs in China about the importance of education. According to Pretorius and Xue (2003), the growth in student demand for higher education in China has averaged 7.7 percent per year over the past twenty years, transforming the Chinese system of higher education from elite to mass (Trow 1974).

On the supply side, Chinese public universities were never capable of meeting this growth in demand, hence the government's decision to allow private sector investment in education, resulting in a rapid rise in the development of private colleges from almost none in 1979 to 1,277 in 1999, serving some 1.23 million students (Qu 2000). Most of these colleges remain certificate-awarding bodies and do not generally enjoy high status. Yet the very existence of private colleges has transformed the higher education system in China, requiring the government to develop policies that not only allow the establishment of non-state-run (*minban*) education with "active encouragement, strong support, proper guidelines, and sound management" but also enable state universities to privatize some of its services and collaborate with private providers, including international universities, motivated more by profit than educational access and equality (Hu 1999, 6).

Demand, however, is not the only factor driving privatization in Chinese higher education; external global pressures are also relevant. These pressures relate to China's decision in 1979 to "open up" its economy to the world, to become globally integrated. This policy desire for global integration eventually led China to achieve membership in the World Trade Organization in 2001. However, the membership has placed a range of specific requirements on China, not only in relation to issues of trade in commodities but also trade in services, including higher education. Under the provisions of the GATS that is being negotiated, China is required to open up its higher education system to private operators and to embrace a number of market principles. China has used the WTO rhetoric to initiate far-reaching reforms in the governance structure of its system of higher education, against the recognition that demand for higher education exceeds the capacity of its public sector higher education to meet it. China has recognized that global economic integration demands human resources capable of understanding and engaging the requirements of global economy. It has acknowledged, furthermore, that these policy objectives cannot be realized without input from outside China, hence its commitment to internationalize its higher education by developing cooperative links with universities around the world as a way of reforming its curriculum and pedagogy and introducing to its governance practices some of the principles of new public sector management.

China has proceeded with higher education reform with grave caution and reservations. For example, while it has permitted its universities to "cooperate" with international partners, it has developed a strict regulatory regime that embodies its attempt to reconcile market principles with its political ideologies. Such a regime involves numerous regulations (for example, Article 6, Chapter 1: *Regulations on the Social Forces Running Educational Establishments*) that prohibit Chinese public universities from entering into private contracts not approved by the local communist party committee (see Hu 1999, 7). In this way, while China has accepted some of the principles of market economy, it nonetheless remains committed to a communist ideology in social and cultural matters. It is one thing for China to join the WTO; its interpretation and use of WTO principles to reshape its economic and social institutions for its own benefit is quite another. There is thus a ubiquitous policy tension within its higher education system, which China has exploited creatively at one level but which also threatens to overwhelm universities and pressure them into submitting to the global dictates of neoliberal ideologies.

Conclusion

While the Australian case shows enthusiastic acceptance of privatization of public universities, the Chinese example is illustrative of a more cautious approach. Whereas the Australian government has embraced privatization unequivocally, China has interpreted it in more strategic terms, preferring to use it as a way of creating more educational opportunities to meet the emerging market needs, restructuring its public system of higher education, and introducing much-needed reforms to its curriculum, research practices, and administrative systems.

As privatization becomes increasingly pervasive in higher education systems around the world, its pitfalls are becoming increasingly apparent. There is little evidence, for example, to show that privatization has contributed to greater organizational efficiency and effectiveness or to improvements in the quality of higher education or has led to greater educational opportunities and equality beyond formal access to universities, which does not in itself guarantee a more educated citizenry. Furthermore, as Petras and Vetmeyer (2001) have shown, privatization has major negative effects on democracy, social mobility, and economic development. There is therefore an urgent need to imagine alternatives to privatization.

The Chinese example above has shown the need for caution and also that there is room for resistance to the global neoliberal pressures toward the privatization of higher education. Such resistance clearly needs to take place at local, national, and global levels—holding neoliberal managers of universities and higher education systems accountable for the patently false ideological claims they make in support of privatization and reimagining collectively how to create a democratic, rather than privatized, future for higher education.

References

Appadurai, A. 1996. *Modernity at large: Cultural dimensions of globalization.* Minneapolis: University of Minnesota Press.

Bowles, S., and H. Gintis. 1987. *Democracy and capitalism.* New York: Basic Books.

Boyer, R., and D. Drache, eds. 1996. *States against markets: The limits of globalization.* London: Routledge.

Bray, M. 1996. *Education and political transition: Themes and experiences in East Asia.* Hong Kong: Comparative Education Research Centre, University of Hong Kong.

Brodie, J. 1995. New state forms, new political spaces. In *States against markets: The limits of globalization,* ed. R. Boyer and D. Drache, 383–98. London: Routledge.

Council of Europe. 1999. *Bologna declaration on the European space for higher education.* Available at http://www.coe.int/T/E/Cultural_Co-operation/education/Higher_education/Activities/Bologna_Process/default.asp

Currie, J., and J. Newsom, eds. 1998. *Universities and globalization: Critical perspectives.* Thousands Oaks, Calif.: Sage.

Dicken, P. 1998. *Global shift: Transforming the world economy.* London: Paul Chapman.

Faraclas, N. 1997. Critical literacy and control in the new world order. In *Constructing critical literacies: Teaching and learning textual practices,* ed. S. Muspratt, A. Luke, and P. Freebody. Sydney: Allen and Unwin.

Foucault, M. 1991. Governmentality. In *The Foucault effect: Studies in governmentality,* ed. G. Burchell, C. Gordon, and P. Miller, 87–104. Chicago: University of Chicago Press.

Fukuyama, F. 1992. *The end of history and the last man.* New York: Free Press.

Gopinathan, S. 2001. Globalization, the state, and education policy in Singapore. In *Education and political transition: Themes and experiences in East Asia,* ed. M. Bray and W. O. Lee, 21–36. Hong Kong: Comparative Education Research Centre, University of Hong Kong.

Gore, C. 2000. The rise and fall of the Washington Consensus as paradigm for the developing countries. *World Development* 28(5): 789–803.

Gupta, A. 1998. *Postcolonial developments: Agriculture in the making of modern India.* London: Duke University Press.

Hall, S. 1996. The problem of ideology: Marxism without guarantees. In *Stuart Hall: Critical dialogues in cultural studies,* ed. D. Morley and K. Chen, 25–46. London: Routledge.

Halpin, D. 1994. Practice and prospects in educational policy research. In *Researching educational policy: Ethical and methodological issues,* ed. D. Halpin and B. Troyna. London: Falmer Press.

Held, D., and A. McGrew, eds. 2000. *The global transformation reader: An introduction to the globalization debate.* Cambridge: Polity Press.

Henry, M., R. Lingard, F. Rizvi, and S. Taylor. 2001. *The OECD, globalization and education policy.* Oxford: Pergamon Press.

Hoogvelt, A. 1997. *Globalization and the postcolonial world: The new political economy of development.* Basingstoke, UK: Macmillan.

Hu, W. 1999. China's non-governmental education development and the strategic framework. Translated from Chinese. *Zhongguo Jiaoyu Rexian* (China Education Online).

MacIntyre, A. 1981. *After virtue: A study in moral theology.* London: Duckworth.

Petras, J., and H. Vetmeyer. 2001. *Globalization unmasked.* London: Zed Books.

Pretorius, S. G., and Y. Q. Xue. 2003. The transition from elite to mass higher education: A Chinese perspective. *Prospects* 33(1): 89–101.

Qu, Y. 2000. National scenario and private education. *China Education Daily,* October 18. Translated from Chinese.

Rizvi, F. 1993. Williams on democracy and the governance of education. In *Views beyond the border country: Raymond Williams and cultural politics,* ed. D. Dworkin and L. G. Roman, 133–57. London and New York: Routledge.

———. 2005. Globalization and the dilemmas of internationalization of Australian higher education. *Access: Critical Perspectives on Communication, Cultural, and Policy Studies* 24(1): 35–48.

Robertson, S., and R. Dale. 2004. Introduction to the special issue on WTO-GATS. *Globalization, Societies and Education* 2(1): 3–9.

Samoff, J. (1999). Institutionalizing international influence. In *Comparative education: The dialectic of the global and the local,* ed. R. Arnove and C. Torres, 51–90. Lanham, Md.: Rowman and Littlefield.

Schugurensky, D. 1999. Higher education restructuring in the era of globalization: Toward a heteronomous model? In *Comparative education: The dialectic of the global and the local,* ed. R. Arnove and C. Torres, 283–304. Lanham, Md.: Rowman and Littlefield.

Sen, A. 1997. *Development as freedom.* Oxford, UK: University of Oxford Press.

Slaughter, S., and G. Rhoades. 2004. *Academic capitalism and the new economy: Markets, state, and higher education.* Baltimore, Md.: Johns Hopkins University.

Smith, M. P. 2000. *Transnational urbanism: Locating globalism.* Malden, Mass.: Blackwell.

Soros, G. 1998. *The crisis of global capitalism.* Boston: Little, Brown.

Trow, M. 1974. Problems in the transition from elite to mass higher education. In *Policies for higher education, general report on the conference on future structures of postsecondary education,* 55–101. Paris: OECD.

Van der Wende, M. C. 2000. The Bologna Declaration: Enhancing the transparency and competitiveness of European higher education. In *Higher Education in Europe* 25(3): 305–10.

Waters, M. 1995. *Globalization.* London: Routledge.

Williamson, J. 1990. What Washington means by policy reform. In *Latin American adjustment: How much has happened,* ed. J. Williamson, 7–20. Washington, D.C.: Institute for International Economics.

II

GENERATING REVENUE
FROM ALTERNATIVE SOURCES

CHAPTER FOUR

Alternative Revenue Sources

James C. Hearn

The idea that institutions should seek to diversify their revenue streams is not new. In 1980, economist and college president Howard Bowen (1980) observed that leaders continually seek funding growth because they operate under a "revenue theory of cost": new revenues are always being sought in order to pursue excellence, prestige, and influence. Because there is no limit to what might be spent in pursuit of those goals, institutions will always raise and spend all the money they can. Bowen's analysis echoed that of two of his contemporaries: "A workable 20th-century definition of institutional autonomy [is] the absence of dependence upon a single or narrow base of support" (Babbidge and Rosezweig 1962, 158).

For public institutions in the twenty-first century, the point rings truer than ever. Economic downturn and political change have squeezed revenues from governmental funding (Hovey 1999; Toutkoushian 2001).[1] Students' acceptance of rising prices has somewhat offset this trend, but not entirely, and legislators and the public resist sustained, significant rises. Sometimes policy makers seem to be asking the impossible, expecting improvements and expansion of instructional and analytic services when only maintenance of effort and, perhaps, preservation of quality seem financially in reach (Clark 1998). Making matters worse, new providers of academic programming have begun to compete more credibly with traditionally organized institutions; and labor, construction, plant maintenance, and health-care costs have risen dramatically, lessening the likelihood of significant overall cost containment. These daunting challenges threaten to place public colleges and universities at an increasing quality and competitive disadvantage relative to private institutions (Alexander 2003; Immerwahr 2002).

Clearly, the context demands new funding sources, and institutions appear to be responding. By the fall of 2000, endowment income, hospitals, auxiliary enterprises, educational activities, and independent operations were accounting for over a quarter of all revenues in public four-year institutions, a proportion notably higher than in the past (Knapp et al. 2002). Public institutions are beginning to resemble private institutions in their revenue mixes, and it is becoming appropriate to label much of public higher education as state-assisted rather than state-supported. Thus, institutions increasingly appear to be accepting the potential benefits of diversifying revenues (Breneman 1997; Clark 2002; Ehrenberg 2000). The more difficult issue is when and how to diversify. In the best case, institutional leaders can develop revenue-generating activities that are educationally valuable and integral to service missions on campus. Less edifying but still necessary are defensible pursuits that simply help valued institutions survive under austere conditions. Most questionable, of course, are new activities that threaten core academic values.

This chapter focuses on the nature and implications of institutions' revenue-diversification opportunities. Unfortunately, the literature on this topic is rather sparse and uneven. After presenting a taxonomy of new revenue sources, the chapter reviews critical decision-making factors, then concludes with consideration of the strategic and philosophical issues embedded in choices concerning new institutional revenues.

New Revenue Streams

Among the many ways institutions are diversifying their revenue streams are instructional initiatives; research and analysis initiatives; pricing initiatives; reforms in financial decision making and management; human-resource initiatives; franchising, licensing, sponsorship, and partnering arrangements with third parties; initiatives in auxiliary enterprises, facilities, and real estate; and development-office initiatives. These approaches will be explored in turn.

Instructional Initiatives

New providers, new markets, and new technologies are calling into question the financial resilience of institutions' core academic programming and, in some cases, changing the grounds on which faculty and institutions make academic decisions (Eckel 2003). Of course, not all recent external developments should be cast as threats. Davies (2001) has noted that the lifelong-learning movement and the globalization of higher education may destabilize cultures and niches at established institutions, but they may also present opportunities for those same institutions. Whether casting new developments as threats or as opportunities, many institutions have been responding aggressively, targeting such new markets as corporate learners, professional enhancement learners, degree-completion adult learners, pre-college (K–12) learners, remediation and test-preparation learners, and recreational learners (Kerr 2002; Levine 2000a; Oblinger et al. 2001).

Sometimes creative governmental policies have facilitated these revenue-diversification efforts. In workforce training and development, for example, several states (including Iowa, Missouri, and Georgia) have encouraged desired instructional offerings by creating policies that divert state taxes into colleges providing appropriately targeted instructional programs (see Sekera et al. 1999).

Many institutions have moved toward offering special versions of high-demand courses at high tuition levels. Such efforts can include summer courses, short courses, online courses, credentialing programs in areas demanded by the labor force (e.g., information technology, education, nursing), and offerings abroad (e.g., see Hinchcliff 2000; Primary Research Group 1997). Often, and especially in the community college sector, instructional offerings are provided through corporate partnerships or by for-profit subsidiaries. Such efforts usually are designed to attract non-degree-seeking students who may be employed or externally funded and thus more able to pay higher tuitions than students in the midst of a lengthy degree program.[2]

New technologies can be important in the pursuit of new instructional revenues.[3] In this uncertain marketplace, Levine (2000a) argues that three kinds of providers are emerging: "brick" (i.e., traditional campus-based institutions), "click" (i.e., institutions existing solely in cyberspace), and "brick and click" (i.e., campus-based institutions also offering online learning opportunities). Of these, Levine argues, the "sweet spot" for mainstream higher education's financial survival is brick and click: having both an electronic and a physical presence. Collis (2002) predicts that sweet spot will be illusive. His analysis suggests that online corporate training will be a larger and more profitable market than online academic education and that, for nonelite institutions without superior "brands," online education may in fact be a losing proposition.

The difficulties of several major, highly touted distributed learning initiatives suggest that *how* institutions incorporate new technologies into their instructional offerings is critical to their fortunes (Hitt and Hartman 2002; Oblinger et al. 2001). Partnerships can be an especially effective way to balance the inevitable risks. In distributed education, early outlays for content development, technical infrastructure, and marketing can be substantial, and partnerships can provide needed capital for generating revenues quickly (Katz et al. 2002). Collis (2002) notes that many leading public institutions have followed this path because it leverages a university's brand name and existing course content with the least risk, with minimal expenditure of time and money, and likely with minimal objection from faculty, all while preserving the exclusivity of the institution's own degree. When such efforts are aimed at the corporate and lifelong-learning markets, as is typical, effects on (and risks to) core undergraduate offerings can be minimal.

Research and Analysis Initiatives

Many public universities are repackaging and reorganizing their research and analysis capabilities. Increasingly, the core rationales appear to be financial (Feller 1997; Karr and Kelley 1996; Kozeracki 1998; Lewis and Hearn 2003).

With strong support from the federal government, patents and licenses based in university research have increased markedly since the 1980s (Geiger 2002; Press and Washburn 2000). Many campuses have profited from discoveries in such areas as computer technology, medicine, and biotechnology (Wellman and Phipps 2001). Noting such trends, Etkowitz et al. (1998) have called the rise of technology transfer a "second academic revolution" in this country.

Some institutions are creating new organizations to generate revenues from research, including for-profit subsidiaries as well as units to nurture start-up firms via consulting and financial support (Johnstone 2002; Leslie and Slaughter 1997; Levine 2000b). The business-incubator approach has been a frequent part of these initiatives and often takes advantage of available low-cost real estate to provide affordable rentals to aspiring science-related commercial enterprises (Geiger 2002). Short of developing separate new organizations, some colleges and universities have developed fee-for-service offerings for off-campus parties and even entered the treacherous waters of e-commerce (Wellman and Phipps 2001).

Overall, the evidence is mixed for new revenue-generation efforts relating to research and analysis (Blumenstyk 2003a). Such initiatives can raise significant mission, governance, and cost-effectiveness questions. Experiences at Stanford, Berkeley, and a few other elite institutions suggest technology-transfer initiatives can pay off spectacularly when core expertise and energy are present (Clark 1998; Geiger 2002), but holding these efforts to stiff financial expectations may be risky; many initiatives fail to break even, much less return net revenue to their home institutions. This realization has prompted reconsideration, redirection, and retrenchment of technology-transfer efforts on some campuses (Feller 1997; Press and Washburn 2000; Geiger 2002).[4] Similarly, early campus-connected research parks in the Boston area, in the Research Triangle area in North Carolina, and in the Palo Alto area in California were great successes, but they are as yet unreplicated (Hebel 2003). Viewed as a whole, academic research activity unquestionably provides public and institutional returns, but often those returns are ambiguous and nonfinancial (Nicklin 1992a). The optimal organizational arrangements for generating new, positive net revenues from those activities remain quite unclear (Mansfield 1995).

Pricing Initiatives

Institutions price their analytic services and auxiliary enterprises, but most importantly, they price their instruction. Tuition and fees have changed in two important ways in recent years: they have risen remarkably and have become increasingly differentiated. Tuition increases have been documented extensively (McPherson and Schapiro 1998), but differentiation has been less considered.

Institutions can differentiate tuition by the offering unit, by the instructional or facilities costs associated with a particular course offering, by the timing of the offering, by the course level, by the physical location of the course, by the student's major field and degree level, by the number of credits being taken or previously accumulated by the student, and by student residency status (see Yanikoski and Wilson 1984; Wetzel 1995). Tuition has long been differentiated on some of these dimensions (out-of-state tuition has long been higher, as has tuition in medicine and law). Now, however, institutions are beginning to experiment with finer distinctions.

The emerging online education and distance education markets are prime grounds for that experimentation in that such areas are less institutionalized and institutions consequently have greater staffing, curricular, and pricing flexibility. Collis (2002) has noted that pricing structures in the online arena are reasonably favorable for institutions: "Extensive price competition is unlikely to occur immediately" (190).

Of course, there is no guarantee that tuition differentiation will generate additional revenues, and in particular additional *net* revenues, for any given institution. Here the critical analytic concept is net price to students, which is produced via formal tuition variations but also via offsetting student-aid awards and tuition discounts, an indirect form of tuition differentiation (McPherson and Schapiro 1998; Johnstone 2002). Econometric analysis of the responses of students and families to different prospective pricing and aid configurations can aid in projecting revenue effects of tuition-differentiation initiatives.

Beyond tuition pricing lies fees pricing. In recent years, the pricing of undergraduate education has increasingly been unbundled from a single overall charge into tuition plus specific "user fees" for technology, athletics, and other services (Wellman and Phipps 2001). This development has allowed some institutions to increase revenues while restraining highly visible tuition rises. In theory, the user-fee approach makes pricing and costing more transparent to students and families. Tying pricing to discrete "objects" can also make institutional decision making more informed and effective. As with other pricing reforms, however, expanding user fees may or may not raise total or net revenues for an individual institution.

Reforms in Financial Decision Making and Management

Many institutions have made financial improvements in both operations and capital spending, bringing new revenues. Judicious investment of various kinds of operating revenues, along with intelligent cash-flow management, can contribute to improved institutional revenue flows. Helpful in this regard are unitized investment pools, that is, pools of funds drawn from multiple sources and managed under a consistent investment approach.

Relative to other major investors, postsecondary institutions remain rather conservative, an approach that has worked reasonably well (Morrell 1997; Spitz 1999). Still, some institutional financial managers have productively adopted more adventurous approaches, including program trading and participation in foreign, arbitrage, and options markets. Investing intelligently in these alternative assets requires specialized expertise. Also, legal charters, regulatory contexts, and leaders' risk tolerance may prohibit such efforts in some settings (Geiger 2002).

For new major revenue-seeking initiatives, institutions typically rely on debt financing. When the acquisition of new revenue streams requires significant front-end investments and public or private seed funding is unavailable, revenue bonds (which are repaid out of future returns) are more appropriate than general-obligation bonds. The risk, however, is that revenue streams for some new initiatives can be less assured than for the traditional objects of revenue financing such as dormitories (Wellman and Phipps 2001). A similar concern applies to shorter-term approaches to financing, such as issuing certificates of participation or revenue-anticipation instruments. Absent reasonable assurances about future revenues, pursuing such funding may be unrealistic.

Several other financing innovations can facilitate new revenue generation. Some institutions set up revolving and incentive funds to support teaching, research, and improvements in physical plant (Wellman and Phipps 2001). Institutions also can encourage entrepreneurial faculty behavior by adopting decentralized budgeting systems that distribute revenues directly to units that are providing lucrative returns for the institution (Priest et al. 2002).

Human-Resource Initiatives

Some institutions employ human resources in new ways to provide revenues. For example, tightening institutional regulations concerning faculty consulting can run more of such work through institutions and thus help capture new revenues. Such moves may alienate faculty, however, especially in units (e.g., business schools) whose faculty salaries are at a market disadvantage. Institutions can also refine compensation and promotion processes to provide more explicit incentives for revenue-generating activities by faculty. Some institutions have begun experimenting not only with providing salary bonuses for revenue-generating faculty but also with breaking faculty salaries into a fixed core component (guaranteed for tenured faculty) and a variable revenue-related component (Hearn 1999).

Franchising, Licensing, Sponsorship, and Partnering Arrangements with Third Parties

Whether event-driven or long-term, collaborations with externally based partners can be fruitful (NASULGC 1997). For example, tours and camps undertaken with closely associated groups like alumni organizations and athletic booster clubs can often generate additional revenues, as can scholarly conferences, concert series, museum showings, and athletic competitions. Partnering with vendors for such activities can potentially bring expert staffing as well as useful discounts and incentives, thus directly or indirectly raising net revenues (Wellman and Phipps 2001).

The instructional arena is a primary focus of third-party collaborations. Partnerships in distributed learning can take many forms, including online applications, campus-based portals, online procurement, online course delivery, supplemental content provision, online library services, online textbooks, and advising and tutoring (see Katz et al. 2002). We may be entering a period of decreasing distinctions and increasing combinations among the various institutional and noninstitutional providers of education and related services (Levine 2000a), but the early evidence on such efforts is mixed.

Sometimes new revenues may be generated simply by paying attention to ways in which third parties are using university resources (including the "brand" itself). Grassmuck (1990), for example, details how colleges and universities were slow to realize the revenues potentially generated by enforcing legal rights over distinctive logos and emblems. Most institutions now closely monitor sales of institutionally themed merchandise in the pursuit of potential revenues from sales or, if necessary, from damages awarded under legal settlements.

Ideally, there is a close relationship between revenues and the use of university assets by others. For example, soft-drink companies, athletic-gear manufacturers, and others provide payments to institutions in exchange for exclusive rights to vend on campus, sell themed items, or have their names and logos displayed prominently at university athletic events or on university facilities.[5] Such arrangements have raised IRS concerns over reporting and taxability (Arnone 2003) but are quite attractive to corporations and can generate substantial additional revenues (Wertz 1997).[6] A newer idea, just beginning to surface, is the sale of ads on institutional websites (Carnevale 2003)—the proliferation of that approach could provide substantial new revenues at the risk of further blurring the lines between public and private enterprise.

Initiatives in Auxiliary Enterprises, Facilities, and Real Estate

Revenues from auxiliary units such as hospitals, athletics departments, bookstores, and dining facilities do not always exceed costs (Arnone 2003; Geiger 2002; Kirp and Roberts 2002; Nicklin 1996; Zimbalist

1999). Sometimes, though, pursuing such efforts as upgrading athletic or dining facilities can increase corporate and consumer support and thus revenues (Koger 2001; Swanquist 1999).

Many institutions are marketing new auxiliary services that bring revenues. Debit cards for purchasing on-campus products and services are increasingly familiar (see Nicklin 1993). Such programs encourage spending on campus while also providing institutions interest income from funds deposited into debit-card accounts. Taking those initiatives a step further, some institutions are expanding revenues by extending use of the cards to off-campus businesses willing to pay a fee for greater access to the spending power of the institution's students, faculty, and staff.

Sometimes revenues are raised simply by imposing new price structures for highly popular products. In major-revenue sports like football and basketball, many NCAA Division I institutions are raising prices for season tickets and "priority seating," confident that the demand for such seating is inelastic with respect to price. Sometimes such price rises are overt, but sometimes they are indirect, tying the promise of tickets to requirements for booster-club contributions at certain dollar levels.[7]

Alumni can also provide new revenues to institutions. Many formerly free alumni magazines are now sent free only to those who have purchased alumni-society memberships or provided gifts in the past. Many alumni magazines are now accepting paying advertisers and, in the interest of generating paying subscribers and gifts, are beginning to feature colorful covers, impressive photography, and engaging, sometimes controversial articles. The move to alumni as sources of revenue has also included such non-education-related enterprises as banking services and home and health insurance (Leder 2002).

Classrooms, residence halls, recreational areas, and undeveloped land potentially can provide additional revenues as well (Biddison and Hier 1998; Kienle 1997). These real estate assets can be put to use for educational or recreational offerings, retirement communities, or cooperative revenue-generating efforts with third parties. They can also be leased or rented to third parties, sold, or used as collateral to secure financing for new entrepreneurial initiatives (e.g., see Horwitz and Rolett 1991; Nicklin 1996).[8]

Development-Office Initiatives

Johnstone (2002, 32) has noted wryly that "no source of revenue is quite as benign and reliable as revenue from unrestricted endowment, once the institution has it." It is the getting of such funding that poses the challenge, of course. Many institutions are aggressively expanding their pursuit of individual and organizational donations (Hirsch 1999). Giving to colleges has ceased its dramatic growth, however (Blumen-styk, 2003b), and few institutions have alumni willing and able to con-tribute sizable unrestricted funds. Most institutions have to work hard to build a self-sustaining development effort. The pursuit of donations must constantly be evaluated as to cost-effectiveness, because many gifts may be revealed upon analysis to be costing more than they return to the institution.

Hirsch (1999) has warned that an emphasis on private giving can un-balance institutions because it may tend to favor certain fields and cer-tain aspects of institutional mission over others. Creating the conditions for institutional success in garnering donations is an undeniable part of strong institutional leadership, but also undeniable is the importance of keeping such efforts in context.

Making Decisions about New Revenue Streams

The generation of new *net returns* should be the ultimate goal of any revenue-diversification effort, not simply the generation of new rev-enues. Potential returns can be nonfinancial as well as financial and can come in the short or long term. The production of new institutional funding that is fully offset or even dwarfed by new associated costs is ac-ceptable only if there are nonfinancial returns of note *and* the new net costs are viewed as acceptable from an individual, institutional, or pub-lic perspective. New revenues should be pursued only with the under-standing that new initiatives will be undertaken only after rigorous con-sideration of the associated costs, including the opportunity costs of forgoing other initiatives.

Thus, effective decision making should be institution-specific and should consider factors not easily monetized. Because each college or university faces a distinctive context, there is no one best approach to decision making about revenue initiatives. Nevertheless, the literature suggests a number of general considerations and guidelines relating to mission and culture, strategic analysis, implementation, and finances and cost-effectiveness.

Mission and Culture

Significant disjunctions of any new revenue-seeking initiative from existing institutional mission and culture must be addressed (Tierney

1999). For example, struggling liberal arts institutions may face dramatic internal strains if their best revenue opportunities emerge out of programming for working adults. Is the prospective activity effectively required by difficult conditions, or does it simply promise bonus revenues for the institution? If the latter logic is a propos, then the acceptability of threats to the institution's organizational culture and core mission must be seriously considered.

Strategic Analysis

In a classic study of the mature, threatened tobacco industry, Miles and Cameron (1982) identified three potentially effective organizational responses to difficult conditions: aggressively maintaining existing markets (domain defense), extending existing activities into new arenas (domain offense), and developing new businesses (domain creation). Like the tobacco industry, traditional higher education in this country may be considered both mature and threatened, so campuses may need to try each of these approaches: finding new ways to protect their current services, expanding the reach of their existing "portfolios," and exploring new ideas.

Taking a strategic perspective requires systematic analysis. Institutions considering new initiatives need to ascertain mission appropriateness, cultural fit, substantive quality, short- and long-term financial prospects, comparative advantage over other existing and potential providers, the risk tolerance of all involved parties, the potential for collaboration with other organizations, the odds that high levels of potential demand may not translate into additional revenues at the margin, and organizational sustainability (Blustain et al. 1998; Katz et al. 2002; Oblinger et al. 2001; Zemsky et al. 2001).

Importantly, institutions need to forgo simplistic reasoning about "the" market for new services. Levine (2000a) conducted interviews with a variety of adult students on what they seek in postsecondary education and found that older students today are resistant to fees assessed across the board on all students and often seek access to a scaled-back, tailored (unbundled) product. The adult student market is clearly distinctive from that for "traditional" students, highlighting the need for understanding the particulars of whatever marketplace being entered.

Implementation

Beyond strategic analysis lies a set of questions regarding implementation of new revenue-seeking initiatives. First, is restructuring necessary to success? Entrepreneurially oriented institutional leaders often choose to restructure (Davies 2001), but doing so raises a number of questions. Are spin-offs or new buffering organizations advisable?[9] Should new partnerships be designed? How are relationships among existing stakeholders and constituents (e.g., funders, government leaders, faculty, staff, students, families, the press) likely to be affected, and are additional structural changes necessary to address these transitions?

Effective implementation requires cultural and organizational conditions necessary to fuel and support entrepreneurial spirit. Work by Leslie et al. (2002) suggests that departments in the life sciences have especially entrepreneurial cultures, but units' entrepreneurialism is not always predictable from their academic emphases or locations (Clark 1998). Davies (2001) found a philosophy department on one European campus bringing in greater new revenues than the engineering unit on the same campus.

Obviously, success in revenue seeking depends in good part on opportunistic, talented individuals with good ideas. Savvy leaders can improve the odds, however. Blustain et al. (1998) identify barriers and frequent mistakes institutions make in implementing new revenue-seeking efforts in the instructional arena: program cannibalization, failure to identify wants and needs of customers, failure to establish guidelines for program development, remaining committed to old-style pedagogy and curricular organization, and assuming that simply providing the program will be enough, absent efforts to market it. They also identify some barriers to new marketplace initiatives that may effectively preclude success: strong faculty and staff resistance on philosophical or other grounds, pressing needs to utilize existing physical plant, and untenable financial demands for new technology commitments (Blustain et al. 1998). In the end, both calculation and daring seem essential to success (Matkin 1997; Newman and Couturier 2001).

Top administrators can establish what Clark (2002) calls the "steering core" for entrepreneurial efforts. Developing and sustaining a culture supportive of change requires leaders who are oriented to problem solving and operate on trust and with openness; who are self-critical, internally responsive, and flexible; who are thoughtful about staff-development priorities and budgets; and who provide expert attention (Clark 2002; Davies 2001). Leaders need to consult actively with all key stakeholders, often including governing boards, governments, and the public as well as insiders (Hirsch 1999).

Also, leaders need to put appropriate incentives in place. Incentives for departments, colleges, staff, and line administrative units are all important, but the financial, professional, and personal incentives for individual faculty merit special attention.[10] Leaders should provide faculty in-kind support, development funds, structured time for entrepreneurial activity, and targeted salary and promotion criteria reflective of the entrepreneurial agenda (Davies 2001).

Johnstone (2002) has observed that leaders must deal effectively with the fact that revenue seeking can divert time and attention from core missions and activities, bring conflict with scholarly canons, and bring uneven reward distributions. Of particular concern is what Clark (2002) has termed the "academic heartland," that is, the humanities and social sciences. Those are usually mission-central areas, but faculty in those areas tend to be less well positioned for substantial revenue generation and may be marginalized and disadvantaged by such efforts. Faculty in the "heartland" may be especially concerned about the details, appropriateness, and value of university/industry relationships (Campbell and Slaughter 1999). Ignoring those concerns may imperil prospects for successful adaptation and revenue gains.

New technologies may very well require a rethinking of faculty roles. For example, continuing and distance-education units are increasingly being integrated into core units (Barbulies and Callister 2000). Similarly, valued new revenues are being generated in many professional schools through the work of non-tenure-track faculty (Hearn and Anderson 2001). Such adaptations can raise internal tensions around faculty activity and reward systems (Baldwin and Chronister 2001; Tierney 1999).

The pursuit of new revenue sources can also raise difficult legal issues (Teitel 1989). Realistically, any new revenue-generating activity poses legal issues, since institutions must consider potential liabilities in court (see Hearn, Clugston, and Heydinger 1993, and Hearn 1996). Colleges and universities need to ensure that clear, enforceable, appropriately structured contracts and control mechanisms are in place for all new revenue-seeking activities (Johnstone 2002).

Finances and Cost-effectiveness

Before implementation, systematic forecasting and analysis of prospective revenue flows from an initiative are essential (Caruthers and Wentworth 1997; Day 1997). After implementation, institutions should regularly employ appropriate benchmarks for cost-effectiveness (Institute for Higher Education Policy and the National Education Association 2000). Leaders should be clear from the start in their commitment to withdraw from failing enterprises. Sunk costs, pride of creation, and public "face" all pale in importance relative to the costs of maintaining a losing operation, especially in arenas not central to institutional mission. Fortunately, it seems that cutting losses in revenue-seeking initiatives may not be posing a major problem for institutions. For example, at the time of the this analysis (2004), there was no current evidence of the existence of a number of campus e-learning initiatives reported upon glowingly in press releases and articles in the mid- and late 1990s.

Financial analysis requires a valid analytic time horizon. Short-term gains may be offset by longer-term costs, and vice versa. For example, licensing certain strategic assets may offer short-term financial gain but may undercut longer-term prospects by diminishing the value of the institution's "brand" among funders or students (Kaludis and Stine 2000). Conversely, in technology-based initiatives, development costs on the front end are usually daunting, but prospects may be strong for net positive returns years after undertaking the initial investment.

There are many stories of financial failure in revenue-seeking initiatives.[11] In this context, leaders told Nicklin (1992b) that those contemplating new initiatives may wish to "overestimate expenses and underestimate revenues." Katz and Associates (1998) observed certain characteristics in successful, cost-effective distance-based instructional programs: (1) market demand is carefully studied in advance; (2) location and scheduling decisions are treated as market factors because those decisions have revenue implications; (3) instructional cost is required operationally to be a variable rather than fixed cost (suggesting a need for a flexible teaching workforce); and (4) each class is required to produce marginal revenues exceeding or equal to marginal cost. Inevitably, institutional context can shape the applicability of any "rules" in this domain, of course, but the suggestions provide some heuristics for success.

It is essential that institutions take into account potential costs and returns of a less easily monetized nature. Feller (1997) notes that technology-transfer offices can serve faculty and promote regional economic development as well as generate additional revenues. Similarly, Tornatzky et al. (2002) found that business-university partnerships provide jobs for graduates and geographically marooned spouses of faculty and staff members, stimulate local research partnerships, and encourage lifestyle amenities associated with the technology industry. None of these benefits is easily quantified, but each nonetheless merits attention.

Campus attitudes regarding money also merit analytic attention. Davies (2001) notes that success in diversifying revenues requires new ways of dealing financially with partners, clients, and stakeholders. In particular, he stresses the need for institutions to develop a "surplus-oriented mentality" in the costing and pricing of contracts and services (34). That is, instead of seeking mainly not to lose money on transactions, institutions should seek to recover more than their costs on transactions whenever possible. When surpluses are generated, leaders need to consider how they should be deployed. Importantly, should surplus funds at the unit level be allowed to be carried forward from year to year, or should these be remanded to central leaders? In essence, to what extent should individual departments be empowered to choose entrepreneurial initiatives and spend money on them?

A final set of financial questions relates to internal incentive systems for faculty. How should faculty salaries and resource contexts be structured to create incentives for new revenue generation?[12] For example, can creating internal "start-up" or venture-capital pools aid in fostering unit and faculty efforts in revenue generation? Thoughtfully designed, such mechanisms may encourage faculty and staff to be appropriately entrepreneurial (Newman and Couturier 2001).

Conclusion

There are no simple answers for institutions seeking new revenues. Local context (including mission, students, faculty, and curriculum as well as the immediate economic, political, technological, and social conditions facing the institution) is central to decisions in this arena, but varies immensely by institution. Still, some issues are pervasive. Most importantly, all institutions must ultimately confront the question of why they are pursuing new revenues. Is the effort required or optional? Is the intent minor adaptation or fundamental institutional change? Is the diversification to occur at the organizational periphery or at the academic/technological core? Many prospective methods for acquiring new revenues can take place outside the core instructional and research operations of the institution with few repercussions. For example, the licensing of logos or the use of residence halls for summer camps raises few academic questions. But when fundamental change is on the table, the stakes become formidable.

One needs to ask, for example, whether faculty across all disciplines should be expected to seek new revenues. Such an expectation may be organizationally unrealistic.[13] While institutions are being asked by external sponsors, prodded by their boards, and pressed by financial circumstances to pursue new ways of operating, faculty at the heart of the academic enterprise are, for the most part, still being trained, hired, and rewarded in traditional ways. For fundamental change to occur, the impulse to do business differently must be communicated and institutionalized throughout the organization. That poses important human-resource challenges.

Those ready to pursue significant new revenues must also consider two dangers. The first is immediate and pressing. Institutions must beware of having public authorities come to believe that higher education can obtain enough new revenue to take care of itself without substantial additional societal investment (Johnstone 2002). In their pursuit of revenue diversification, leaders of public institutions need to bear in mind the parallel need for them to do all they can to maintain the historic and essential commitment of governments to the enterprise. A second danger is just as important but less directly pressing. Unreflective movement toward diversified revenue streams can threaten core institutional identities and missions (Bok 2003; Johnstone 2002). The push for more reliance on grants and contracts from external organizations, for example, can raise costs on campus, redistribute academic power, shift academic priorities, and reduce the sense of community (Leslie et al. 2002; Slaughter and Leslie 1997).

Even changes that seem minor and necessary rather than fundamental and radical require close attention, because dangers to essential traditions may lie in their cumulative effects (Breneman 2002; Clark 2002). Frank Newman (2000) has worried that the push for new business models and revenues is threatening the "soul of higher education" and its place as a home for disinterested scholarship and open and unfettered discussion of important issues. Increasing marketization is probably inevitable in U.S. higher education, but that inevitability does not warrant abandoning vigilance over imperiled core values.

At its worst, the pursuit of new revenues can be mindless and dispiriting. When ideas for new revenue streams are promising in a business sense but threatening in a cultural and organizational sense, and perhaps disserving of the public good, the best choice for institutions may well be to ignore the financial appeal and walk away. But for those rare ideas that are not only promising but also inspired and inspiring, wisdom almost certainly lies in moving forward.

Notes

This chapter builds upon earlier work conducted under contract for the American Council of Education. The author gratefully acknowledges suggestions and feedback from Jacqueline King, Melanie Corrigan, Grady Bogue, Tim Caboni, John Davies, David Longanecker, Michael McLendon, Betty Price, Ed St. John, and John Yeager, as well as research assistance by Kathryn Balink, Edmund Ford, and Ying Liu.

1. The problem is compounded by the fact that many state governments are desperately seeking revenue diversification themselves (Boyd 2002; Arnone, Hebel, and Schmidt 2003).

2. For example, Duke University has been offering for some time a partly online "Global Executive" MBA program at a substantial tuition and fee level (as of this writing, the charge for the entire program totals $100,500), and the program is apparently financially successful. See http://www.fuqua.duke.edu/admin/gemba.

3. Special public funding is available for some instructional initiatives using new technologies (Wellman and Phipps 2001), but often institutions must choose a path without substantial external support.

4. Traditionally, technology transfer provides returns only when patents and licenses are activated and successful (Geiger 2002). Therefore, some institutions accept equity holdings in return for their technology transfers to industry (Feller 1997). Because such holdings may be sold, they can represent institutions' only hope for shorter-term returns on frontier technology.

5. A striking recent example: the indoor stadium at Boise State University was recently renamed "Taco Bell Arena," prompting a local observer to question whether the university was "thinking outside the bun or inside the wallet" (Karlin-Resnick 2004, A7).

6. Outsourcing, covered elsewhere in this book, may also be viewed as a way to seek new revenues, in that such arrangements can trade one form of revenue gathering (the term-by-term garnering of funds from individual students, for example) in favor of another form of revenue gathering (term-by-term payments from third parties).

7. As an example, consider this text from the "Frequently Asked Questions" page of the University of Wisconsin's athletics website: "*Will a gift to the Badger Fund guarantee season tickets?* All donors to Wisconsin Athletics receive first priority for season tickets in football, men's basketball, men's hockey, women's basketball and volleyball. Based on prior experience, we are confident that most donors who make their contribution prior to the deadlines will have an opportunity to purchase season tickets" (http://www.uwbadgers.com/badger_fund/priority_points/faq.aspx).

8. The history of Stanford University (see http://www.stanford.edu/home/stanford/history/lands.html) is often cited as a model use of real estate, but there are numerous other success stories.

9. For example, a separate full-service technology corporation might take responsibility for business aspects of the commercialization of intellectual property, while a university-owned investment company might manage funds generated by nontraditional activities and giving campaigns.

10. Regarding tax status, for example, tax-favored enterprises at some institutions have been challenged as to their right to compete with community-based bookstores and suppliers of office supplies, computer hardware, and software.

11. E.g., see Coal-mining revenues prove insufficient to finance scholarship program at U. of Kentucky, *Chronicle of Higher Education* 48(28), 22 March 2002, A28.

12. For example, Oblinger et al. (2001) stress the importance of considering in detail and in advance how generated funds should be made available at the unit and individual level.

13. Findings from Leslie et al. (2002) suggest that faculty entrepreneurship rarely arises from centrally mandated, collective, strategic initiatives. For these authors, such a result raises an important question: "Should incentives be targeted primarily on individuals rather than departments?" (87).

References

Alexander, F. K. 2003. Comparative study of state tax effort and the role of federal government policy in shaping revenue reliance patterns. In *Maximizing revenue in higher education. New Directions for Institutional Research*, ed. F. K. Alexander and R. G. Ehrenberg, 119: 13–26. San Francisco: Jossey-Bass.

Arnone, M. 2003. IRS ruling on naming rights for facilities may jeopardize status of some tax-exempt bonds. *Chronicle of Higher Education*, April 18, A30.

Arnone, M., S. Hebel, and P. Schmidt. 2003. Another bleak budget year: As state legislators convene, concerns over money dominate the agenda. *Chronicle of Higher Education*, January 3, A21–22.

Babbidge, H. D., and R. Rosenzweig. 1962. *The federal interest in higher education*. New York: McGraw-Hill.

Baldwin, R. G., and J. L. Chronister. 2001. *Teaching without tenure: Policies and practices for a new era*. Baltimore, Md.: Johns Hopkins Press.

Barbulies, N. C., and T. A. Callister. 2000. Universities in transition: The promise and challenge of new technologies. *Teachers College Record* 102(2): 271–93.

Biddison, G., and T. Hier. 1998. Wringing dollars out of campus space. *Facilities Manager* 14(6): 18–23.

Blumenstyk, G. 2003a. Deflated deals. *Chronicle of Higher Education*, May 9, A27–28.

———. 2003b. Donations to colleges decline for the first time since 1988. *Chronicle of Higher Education*, March 21, A29–30.

Blustain, H., P. Goldstein, and G. Lozier. 1998. Assessing the new competitive landscape. *Cause/Effect* 3:19–27.

Bok, D. 2003. *Universities in the marketplace: The commercialization of higher education*. Princeton, N.J.: Princeton University Press.

Bowen, H. H. 1980. *The costs of higher education: How much colleges and universities spend per student and how much should they spend?* San Francisco: Jossey-Bass.

Boyd, D. J. 2002. *Revenue adequacy and the Western states*. Paper presented at the annual meeting of the Western Interstate Commission for Higher Education, Broomfield, Colorado, November 11, 2002.

Breneman, D. W. 1997. The "privatization" of public universities: Mistake or model? *Chronicle of Higher Education*, June 14, B4–5.

———. 2002. For colleges, this is not just another recession. *Chronicle of Higher Education*, June 14, B7–9.

Campbell, T. I. D., and S. Slaughter. 1999. Faculty and administrators' attitudes toward potential conflicts of interest, commitment, and equity in university-industry relationships. *Journal of Higher Education* 70(3): 309–52.

Carnevale, D. 2003. Some colleges add ads to their Web sites. *Chronicle of Higher Education*, April 25, A31–32.

Caruthers, J. K., and C. L. Wentworth. 1997. Methods and techniques of revenue forecasting. In Forecasting and managing enrollment and revenue: An overview of current trends, issues, and methods. *New Directions for Institutional Research*, ed. D. T. Layzell, 93:81–93. San Francisco: Jossey-Bass.

Clark, B. R. 1998. *Creating entrepreneurial universities: Organizational pathways of transformation.* Oxford: Pergamon for the IAU Press.

———. 2002. University transformation: Primary pathways to university autonomy and achievement. In *The future of the city of intellect: The changing American university,* ed. S. J. Brint, 322–42. Palo Alto: Stanford University Press.

Collis, D. J. 2002. New business models for higher education. In *The future of the city of intellect: The changing American university,* ed. S. J. Brint, 181–202. Palo Alto, Calif.: Stanford University Press.

Davies, J. L. 2001. The emergence of entrepreneurial cultures in European universities. *Higher Education Management* 13(2): 25–43.

Day, J. H. 1997. Enrollment forecasting and revenue implications for private colleges and universities. Forecasting and managing enrollment and revenue: An overview of current trends, issues, and methods. In *New Directions for Institutional Research,* ed. D. T. Layzell, 93:51–65. San Francisco: Jossey-Bass.

Eckel, P. D. 2003. Capitalizing on the curriculum: The challenges of curricular joint ventures. *American Behavioral Scientist* 46(7): 865–82.

Ehrenberg, R. G. 2000. Financial forecasts for the next decade. *The Presidency* (Spring): 30–34.

Etkowitz, H., A. Webster, and P. Healy, eds. 1998. *Capitalizing knowledge: New intersections of industry and academia.* Albany: State University of New York Press.

Feller, I. 1997. Technology transfer from universities. In *Higher education: Handbook of theory and research,* ed. J. C. Smart, 12:1–42. New York: Agathon Press.

Geiger, R. L. 2002. The American university at the beginning of the 21st century: Signposts on the path to privatization. In *Trends in American and German higher education,* ed. R. M. Adams, 33–84. Cambridge, Mass.: American Academy of Arts and Sciences.

Grassmuck, K. 1990. Colleges fight bootleggers as sales boom for goods that bear logos and emblems. *Chronicle of Higher Education,* February 21, A32–33.

Hearn, J. C. 1996. Transforming higher education: An organizational perspective. *Innovative Higher Education* 21(2): 141–54.

———. 1999. Pay and performance in the university: An examination of faculty salaries. *Review of Higher Education* 22(4): 391–410.

———. 2003. *Diversifying campus revenue streams: Opportunities and risks.* Report for the American Council on Education series Informed Practice: Syntheses of Higher Education Research for Campus Leaders, July. Washington, D.C.: American Council on Education.

Hearn, J. C., and M. S. Anderson. 2001. Clinical faculty in schools of education: Using staff differentiation to address disparate goals. In *Faculty work in schools of education: Rethinking roles and rewards for the 21st century,* ed. W. Tierney, 125–49. Albany: State University of New York Press.

Hearn, J. C., R. Clugston, and R. Heydinger. 1993. Five years of strategic environmental assessment efforts at a research university: A case study of an organizational innovation. *Innovative Higher Education* 18(1): 7–36.

Hebel, S. 2003. If you build it, they will come. *Chronicle of Higher Education,* February 7, A16–19.

Hinchcliff, J. 2000. *The globalisation of education.* Paper presented at the Technological Education and National Development Conference, April 2000. Abu Dhabi, United Arab Emirates. ED447296.

Hirsch, W. Z. 1999. Financing universities through nontraditional revenue sources: Opportunities and threats. In *Challenges facing higher education at the millennium,* ed. W. Z. Hirsch and L. E. Weber, 75–84. American Council on Education Series on Higher Education. Phoenix, Ariz.: Oryx Press.

Hitt, J. C., and J. L. Hartman. 2002. *Distributed learning: New challenges and opportunities for institutional leadership.* Washington, D.C.: American Council on Education, Center for Policy Analysis.

Horwitz, M. D., and R. L. Rolett. 1991. Retirement communities: A financially rewarding educational approach. *Business Officer* 24 (January): 33–35.

Hovey, H. A. 1999. *State spending for higher education in the next decade: The battle to sustain current support.* Washington, D.C.: National Center for Public Policy and Higher Education.

Immerwahr, J. 2002. *Meeting the competition: College and university presidents, faculty, and state legislators view the new competitive academic arena.* A report by Public Agenda for the Futures Project: Policy for Higher Education in a Changing World. Providence, R.I.: Brown University.

Institute for Higher Education Policy and the National Education Association. 2000. *Benchmarks for success in Internet-based distance education.* Washington, D.C.: Institute for Higher Education Policy.

Johnstone, D. B. 2002. Challenges of financial austerity: Imperatives and limitations of revenue diversification in higher education. *Welsh Journal of Education* 11(1): 18–36.

Kaludis, G., and G. Stine, 2000. From managing expenditures to managing costs: Strategic management for information technology. In *Dollars, distance, and online education: The new economics of college teaching and learning,* ed. M. J. Finkelstein, C. Frances, F. I. Jewett, and B. W. Scholz, 256–68. Phoenix, Ariz.: Oryx Press and the American Council on Education.

Karlin-Resnick, J. 2004. Blueprints: A look at a campus building that is generating discussion. *Chronicle of Higher Education,* July 9, A7.

Karr, S., and R. V. Kelley. 1996. Attracting new sources of research funding. In *Strategies for promoting excellence in a time of scarce resources,* ed. D. W. Breneman, 33–43. *New Directions for Higher Education* (No. 94). San Francisco: Jossey-Bass.

Katz, R. N., and Associates. 1998. *Dancing with the devil: Information technology and the new competition in higher education.* San Francisco: Jossey-Bass.

Katz, R. N., E. M. Ferrara, and I. S. Napier, 2002. *Partnerships in distributed education.* Washington, D.C.: American Council on Education, Center for Policy Analysis.

Kerr, C. 2002. Shock wave II: An introduction to the 21st century. In *The future of the city of intellect: The changing American university,* ed. S. J. Brint, 1–19. Palo Alto, Calif.: Stanford University Press.

Kienle, J. 1997. Facilities that help pay for themselves. *Planning for Higher Education* 26(1): 14–17.

Kirp, D. L., and P. S. Roberts. 2002. Mr. Jefferson's university breaks up. *The Public Interest* (Summer): 70–84.

Knapp, L. G., J. E. Kelly, R. W. Whitmore, S. Wu, L. M. Gallego, and S. G. Broyles. 2002. *Enrollment in postsecondary institutions, fall 2000 and financial statistics, fiscal year 2000.* NCES 2002–212. Available at http://nces.ed.gov/pubs2002/pubsearch.

Koger, D. 2001. Expanding sports facilities. *American School and University* 73(11): 48–51.

Kozeracki, C. 1998. *Institutional entrepreneurship in higher education.* CELCEE Digest No. 98–5. Ewing Marion Kauffman Foundation, Kansas City, Mo. Center for Entrepreneurial Leadership.

Leder, M. 2002. Your alma mater wants to become your bank. *New York Times*, August 25, 8.

Leslie, L. L., R. L. Oaxaca, and G. Rhoades. 2002. Revenue flux and university behavior. In *Incentive-based budgeting systems in public universities*, ed. D. M. Priest, W. E. Becker, D. Hossler, and E. P. St. John, 55–91. Northampton, Mass.: Edward Elgar.

Leslie, L. L., and S. A. Slaughter. 1997. The development and current status of market mechanisms in United States postsecondary education. *Higher Education Policy* 10(3–4): 239–52.

Levine, A. 2000a. *Restructuring higher education to meet the demands of a new century*. Twenty-second annual Pullias Address, University of Southern California, Los Angeles, July 1.

Levine, A. 2000b. The soul of a new university. *New York Times*, March 20, A25.

Lewis, D. R., and J. C. Hearn, eds. 2003. *The public research university: Serving the public good in new times*. Lanham, Md.: University Press of America.

Mansfield, E. 1995. Academic research underlying industrial innovations: Sources, characteristics, and funding. *Review of Economics and Statistics* (February): 55–65.

Matkin, G. W. 1997. Organizing university economic development: Lessons from continuing education and technology transfer. In *New Directions for Higher Education* 97: 27–41. San Francisco: Jossey-Bass.

McPherson, M. S., and M. O. Schapiro. 1998. *The student aid game: Meeting need and rewarding talent in American higher education*. Princeton, N.J.: Princeton University Press.

Miles, R. H., and K. S. Cameron. 1982. *Coffin nails and corporate strategies*. Englewood Cliffs, N.J.: Prentice-Hall.

Morrell, L. R. 1997. Success in investing: Integrating spending policy with asset allocation strategy. *Business Officer* 30: 38–42.

National Association of State Universities and Land-Grant Colleges [NASULGC]. 1997. *Value added: The economic impact of public universities*. Washington, D.C.: National Association of State Universities and Land-Grant Colleges.

Newman, F. 2000. Saving higher education's soul. *Change* (Sept./Oct.): 16–23.

Newman, F., and Couturier, L. K. 2001. The new competitive arena: Market forces invade the academy. *Change* (Sept./Oct.): 11–17.

Nicklin, J. L. 1992a. Many institutions conduct research for companies for a fee, but others assail the practice. *Chronicle of Higher Education*, February 19, A29–30.

———. 1992b. Discipline-minded president credited with reviving Northwestern. *Chronicle of Higher Education*, June 3, A29.

———. 1993. Colleges seeking new sources of revenue herald creation of the cashless campus. *Chronicle of Higher Education*, February 3, A29.

———. 1996. Finding the green on the fairway. *Chronicle of Higher Education*, July 5, A37–38.

Oblinger, D. G., C. A. Barone, and B. L. Hawkins. 2001. *Distributed education and its challenges: An overview*. Washington, D.C.: American Council on Education and EDUCAUSE.

Press, E., and J. Washburn. 2002. The kept university. *Atlantic Monthly*, 39–54.

Priest, D. M., W. E. Becker, D. Hossler, and E. P. St. John, eds. 2002. *Incentive-based budgeting systems in public universities*. Northampton, Mass.: Edward Elgar.

Primary Research Group, Inc. 1997. *Forecasting college and university revenues*. New York: Primary Research Group.

Sekera, J., B. Baran, and S. Teegarden. 1999. *California community colleges and economic development: Options and opportunities.* Economic Development Coordination Network (EDNet), California Community Colleges. Sacramento: California Community Colleges, Office of the Chancellor.

Slaughter, S., and L. L. Leslie. 1997. *Academic capitalism.* Baltimore, Md.: Johns Hopkins University Press.

Spitz, W. T. 1999. Investment policies for college and university endowments. In *Roles and responsibilities of the chief financial officer,* ed. L. Lapovsky and M. P. Mc-Keown-Moak, 51–59. *New Directions for Higher Education* 107. San Francisco: Jossey-Bass.

Swanquist, B. 1999. A new trend in dining design. *College Planning and Design* 2(45): 34, 36.

Teitel, L. 1989. Managing the new frontier between colleges and companies. In *Maximizing opportunities through external relationships,* ed. D. T. Seymour, 43–64. *New Directions for Higher Education* 68. San Francisco: Jossey-Bass.

Tierney, W. G., ed. 1999. *Faculty productivity: Facts, fictions, and issues.* New York: Falmer.

Tornatzky, L. G., P. G. Waugsman, and D. O. Gray. 2002. *Innovation U.: New university roles in a knowledge economy.* A Report of the Southern Technology Council and the Southern Growth Policies Board. Research Triangle Park, N.C.: Southern Growth Policies Board.

Toutkoushian, R. K. 2001. Trends in revenues and expenditures for public and private higher education. In *The finance of higher education: Theory, research, policy, and practice,* ed. M. B. Paulsen and J. C. Smart, 11–38. New York: Agathon Press.

Wellman, J., and R. Phipps, R. 2001. *Funding the "infostructure": A guide to financing technology infrastructure in higher education.* Report for the Lumina Foundation for Education. Indianapolis, Ind.: Lumina Foundation for Education.

Wertz, R. D. 1997. Big business on campus: Examining the bottom line. *Educational Record* 78(1): 19–24.

Wetzel, J. N. 1995. *The effect of tuition differentials on student enrollment patterns and university revenues.* Final report of a FIPSE-sponsored project. Richmond, Va.: Virginia Commonwealth University. ED414833.

Winston, G. C. 1999. Subsidies, hierarchy, and peers: The awkward economics of higher education. *Journal of Economic Perspectives* 13(1): 13–36.

Yanikoski, R. A., and R. F. Wilson. 1984. Differential pricing of undergraduate education. *Journal of Higher Education* 55(6): 735–50.

Zemsky, R., S. Shaman, and D. B. Shapiro. 2001. Higher education as competitive enterprise: When markets matter. *New Directions for Institutional Research* (No. 111). San Francisco: Jossey-Bass.

Zimbalist, A. 1999. *Unpaid professionals: Commercialization and conflict in big-time college sports.* Princeton, N.J.: Princeton University Press.

CHAPTER FIVE

Students and Families as Revenue:
The Impact on Institutional Behaviors

Don Hossler

In recent years much has been written about trends in higher education finance and the upward spiral of college tuition at public colleges
and universities. Well-documented declines in state funding in the public sector, the inability of institutions to find ways to reduce the costs of
providing a college education, and the ever-increasing competition for
status and prestige have resulted in significant rises in college tuition
(Dickeson 2004; Heller 2001; Zumeta 2004). The annual study of college costs produced by the College Board indicates that during the past
ten years (ending in 2004), tuition costs at private four-year institutions
have risen by 36 percent. Among their public counterparts, tuition has
risen by 51 percent at four-year public colleges and universities and by
26 percent at two-year public colleges (College Board 2004a).

The majority of private colleges and universities have always relied
on tuition for large portions of their revenue. Most private colleges garner between 80 and 90 percent of their revenue from student tuition.
Indeed, the history of higher education finance in the United States reveals that many private colleges and universities have struggled to enroll a sufficient number of students to sustain economic viability. In
Higher Education and Its Useful Past (1982), Thelin chronicles college
presidents traveling the countryside, offering families a guaranteed seat
in return for early tuition payments, accepting gifts of farm crops in lieu
of tuition payments, and using other schemes to capture as much tuition revenue as possible. In the context of this edited book, we state the

obvious when we note that, when it comes to their financing strategies, private institutions have always been *privatized* and as such have been heavily reliant on student tuition to cover most of the operating costs. This chapter focuses on the increasing reliance of *public* institutions on student tuition dollars to cover operating costs and the institutional and public policy impacts of this trend towards increasing privatization.

The extent to which individual public colleges and universities have been increasing tuition to fund operating expenses varies by state and by sector. Factors such as the student demand for admission, whether a campus is primarily a regional commuting student population or is residential with a wider geographical draw, the degree of autonomy for setting their tuition rates, and current tuition levels all influence the degree to which higher tuition rates (privatization) are possible and desirable. Generally two-year colleges have the lowest tuition and public research universities the highest tuition, but there can still be significant differences in costs. For example, being a full-time student at a community college in California still costs less than $300 per semester but more than $800 at Ivy Tech State College in Indiana. Tuition for resident students at the University of Mississippi is about $2,000 per semester and nearly $4,000 at the University of Michigan. The primary focus of this chapter is on tuition increases and their effects as part of the privatization trends that are taking place at four-year public institutions, especially public flagship universities. It is at these institutions, where tuition levels are growing and are sufficiently large to generate larger revenue streams from the tuition of both resident and nonresident students, that the impact of the privatization of higher education has been most evident.

Privatization and Tuition Revenue

The increased reliance on tuition is a relatively new trend among public sector institutions. Toutkoushian (2001) reports that between 1979–1980 and 1994–1995 the number of students enrolling in public institutions increased. At the same time, state and local funding per enrolled student declined. Not only did the amount of state appropriation per enrolled student decline, but the actual percentage of dollars coming from state and local governments to fund public institutions also declined. St. John (2003) found that state funding declined from 76.5 percent of all revenues in 1970–1971 to 67.5 percent in 1996–1997 (table A.3, p. 316). Thus, at a time when enrollments were increasing at public institutions, appropriations from state and local governments have been declining. Like many other public sector entities, public colleges and universities have been asked to do more with less.

This has placed public institutions in a difficult situation. They have, in some sense, been forced to increase tuition to find sufficient revenue to provide classes and services for the students who are enrolling. Between 1993–1994 and 2003–2004, the average tuition in constant dollars at four-year public institutions went from $3,188 to $4,694. As previously noted, this represents an increase of nearly 51 percent. Average tuition costs at two-year colleges (in constant dollars) rose from $1,566 to $1,905—a 22 percent increase (College Board 2004a, 11). These developments demonstrate that tuition policies at public institutions have started to move along the continuum toward higher costs and toward privatization.

In recent decades changes in public policy and societal norms have made the increasing reliance on tuition and larger tuition increases more politically and socially acceptable. Both the economic and higher education literature are replete with discussions of the public and private benefits of higher education. Throughout the first seventy-five to eighty years of the twentieth century, tuition policies at public institutions suggest that public policy makers believed that since society is the primary beneficiary, society through federal and state subsidies should bear most of the costs of postsecondary education. During the last part of the twentieth century, as tuition levels rose and federal need-based aid shifted from grants to loans, scholars and higher education observers have suggested that public policy makers had shifted their views to the belief that *individuals* were the primary beneficiaries of postsecondary education and thus should pay most of the costs. It is hard to discern whether the ideological perspective on this debate actually shifted first and then public policies followed, or whether public policy makers adopted ideological rationales for the decisions they had to make in an era of federal and state budget deficits. In any case, during the last decades of twentieth century higher education moved from primarily being seen as a public good to being seen as a private good. This shift is consistent with less public support and higher tuition rates, and with a shift to the privatization of higher education.

It is from this perspective that the remainder of this chapter considers five focal points. The next section of the chapter provides a brief historical examination of the roles of competition and tuition pricing in shaping the move of public sector institutions toward privatization and the emergence of the market-oriented behaviors among colleges and universities. This is followed by an analysis of the potential financial benefits that accrue to universities that are able to increase their tuition costs. The third section considers the impact on access and equity for students in an environment of higher tuition costs at public institutions. The fourth section shifts from a focus on broad institutional and public policy issues to a consideration of the operational costs of privatization that public colleges and universities need to consider as they compete for undergraduate students in an environment where low tuition costs are no longer one of the largest competitive advantages for public institutions. This analysis of the impact of privatization on institutional behavior closes with a set of conclusions and recommendations.

Privatization, the Public Sector, and the Higher Education Marketplace

To some extent, colleges and universities have always competed for students. During the nineteenth century and the westward expansion, having a college in a community was a common aspiration for many large and small towns and cities. As a result, colleges were created at a rapid rate. To emphasize this point, in the early 1870s England had four universities for a population of 23,000,000; the state of Ohio, on the other hand, had thirty-seven colleges for a population of 3,000,000 (Rudolph 1962, 48). There were simply not enough potential college students to support the large number and variety of colleges that had been established in the United States. As a result, many institutions of higher education had to be creative in devising new ways to attract students.

Competition for new students continued into the twentieth century. During the Great Depression and World War II, there was a shortage of students who could pursue a college degree. Even after World War II, when GIs were entering colleges and universities in unprecedented numbers, and later during the baby boom years, the increase in the number of community colleges and in the expansion of regional public four-year institutions resulted in a competitive environment for many regional private colleges (Thelin 1982).

When the decline in the number of high school graduates hit colleges and universities during the 1980s, many institutions adopted marketing techniques and strategies that had been developed for business and industry. These business-oriented marketing strategies were soon followed by the evolution of the concept of enrollment management

(Hossler and Hoezee 2001). If there had been any doubt that competition for students had created a higher education market and that a college degree had become a commodity to be *sold* to prospective students and their families, that doubt has been erased during the last fifteen years. Marketing and the commodification of colleges and universities has become widespread. Now all sectors of higher education in the United States compete with each other on the following dimensions:

1. Range of academic degree programs
2. Perceived quality and reputation
3. Tuition and financial aid packages
4. Locations in which they offer courses and degree programs
5. When courses are offered (day, evening, weekends, on-line)
6. Quality of student life and out-of-class facilities and activities
7. Early application and early admissions practices in some instances.

As a result of public policy trends, both private and public institutions have become more reliant than ever before on tuition revenue for their support. Many public universities have started to describe themselves as "state-assisted" rather than "state-supported." St. Mary's College of Maryland, a public college, successfully lobbied state legislators to give them almost complete freedom to set tuition in return for no increases in state funding. Miami University of Ohio recently announced that it would charge both resident students and nonresident students the same tuition but provide scholarships to all resident students that would reduce their net costs of attendance to the equivalent of the in-state tuition. The state of Colorado is permitting public institutions to raise their tuitions and is providing vouchers, basically student financial aid, that is portable among public and private institutions. All of these are indicators of a growing movement toward the privatization of public higher education. These trends, when viewed from a broader perspective, also reflect the growing marketization and commodification of higher education. They reflect the desire of campuses to enroll more students and/or increase tuition charges in order to garner more tuition revenue.

In their seminal analysis of the increasingly entrepreneurial behavior of universities, Slaughter and Leslie (1997), use the phrase "academic capitalism" to describe the behaviors of many colleges and universities, especially those located in industrialized countries. They indicate that colleges and universities in the United States as well as those in many industrialized countries have increasingly turned to new sources for funding—including student enrollments. Slaughter and Leslie acknowledge the emergence of the higher education marketplace where institutions compete for students, grants, contracts, revenue, and prestige. In addition, in their examination of the global changes taking place in postsecondary education, Henry, Lingard, Rizvi, and Taylor (2001) observe that in the United States and throughout many developed countries, colleges and universities are being asked to find more self-funded sources for teaching, research, and service.

Swail and Heller (2004) document the recent effects of privatization on the costs of higher education in five Western industrialized countries (Australia, Canada, England, Ireland, and the United States). In the last decade these trends have expanded to include even former and current communist countries such as Russia and the People's Republic of China (International Comparative Higher Education Finance and Accessibility Project 2004). Returning to a focus on trends in the United States, Newman and Couturier (2001) suggest that the American higher education system has always been rooted in the competitive forces that both motivate and enable public and private institutions to look for competitive advantages. They conclude that competitive strategies—ranging from merit-based awards for students to developing Web-based education degrees—are the result of this growing trend toward marketization and the quest for institutional revenue.

Hossler, Schmit, and Vesper (1999) introduce one more construct related to this discussion of privatization and marketization. They have noted that, in an ever more competitive environment where colleges and universities vie to enroll students, the decision to attend a specific college is increasingly being viewed as just one more consumptive decision. Colleges and universities are competing for students, and often for the support of their parents, like other commodities, in order to enroll the desired number of students with the desired academic and sociodemographic characteristics. Although much has already been written about this move toward increased reliance on tuition and the attendant shifts toward privatization of higher education in the United States, there have been few holistic examinations of the implications of these trends. Key developments that merit examination include the emergence of a market model for student enrollments and how this phenomenon is being influenced by privatization; the influence of these trends on the public good, particularly the impact on service to the states in which universities are located; and the impact on equity and access issues in public higher education. In their examination of privatization, Zemsky and Wegner (1997) have observed the tensions:

"This questioning of postsecondary education's commitment to public purposes, accompanied as it has been by reduced public funding, now erodes postsecondary education's credibility as an agent of public improvement. It makes the market, rather than public policy, the dominant shaper of the nation's postsecondary institutions" (77).

Incentives for Students and Their Tuition Dollars

In an era of declining support for public institutions, the quest for additional revenue through higher tuition and/or the enrollment of more students are predictable responses. The benefits to public colleges and universities can appear to be transparent. For example, tuition for resident students at Penn State University in 2004–2005 was $10,856, and approximately 34,000 undergraduate students were enrolled. A 5 percent increase in tuition would produce nearly $18,500,000 additional revenue. Recently, many public institutions have enacted tuition increases of 10 percent or more. A 10 percent increase would generate approximately $37,000,000 additional revenue for Penn State. An increase of 500 additional undergraduates would produce $5,428,000 in additional campus revenue for the Penn State campus. If the increase of 500 students was composed of nonresident students (whose tuition rates were $20,784 in 2004–2005), an additional $10,392,000 would result. In a period of declining state support, additional revenue can be a powerful push toward greater reliance on student fees and can push institutions further down the path toward privatization.

National trends over the past decade reflect the quest for more tuition revenue to offset declines in state funding. *Trends in College Pricing* (College Board 2004a) reports that in constant dollars, tuition rates during most of the 1990s increased at rates of 1 percent to 2 percent. In 2003–2004 and 2004–2005, however, tuition increases in constant dollars at public institutions was 9 percent. In 2004–2005, in current dollars, 35 percent of all public institutions increased their tuition by 9 percent or more. This is not the first time college tuition at public universities has risen precipitously. Indeed, in the early 1990s public college tuition increases hovered around 10 percent per year, and this paralleled another period of 10–15 percent declines in state and local support for public institutions. What appears to be different about this current period is a public policy environment more receptive toward the privatization of public higher education.

As has already been noted, presidents from many public institutions are increasingly advocating for higher tuition for state citizens. In nearly every state, college and university presidents have advocated for the freedom to charge higher levels of tuition in order to generate more revenue to cover instructional and administrative costs. Presidents from states ranging from Colorado to Florida to Texas have been outspoken in their support for higher tuition for resident students (Curtin 2003; McGee 2003; Tate 2003). The governor of South Carolina has proposed privatizing all public higher education in the state (Smith 2003). The voucher system that has been put into place in Colorado also demonstrates broader support for privatization (Henley 2004).

In addition to the general move toward higher tuition rates, many public universities have also started to look more closely at their tuition rates for nonresident students. Campus administrators have reviewed their tuition rates and have often decided to increase tuition for out-of-state students. Indeed, an analysis of published tuition rates for resident and nonresident students at a selected set of public institutions indicates that the tuition rates for nonresident students attending public institutions increased at twice the rate of tuition increases for resident students. This trend has likely occurred for the following reasons:

1. Most states do not provide state subsidies for nonresident students, so the campus costs to educate a nonresident are higher;
2. State coordinating boards and trustees typically do not try to restrain tuition costs for nonresident students;
3. The parents of nonresident students do not vote for state legislators; and
4. Most institutions that attract large numbers of nonresidents are more selective and are more highly regarded; as a result, the students who enroll tend to be more affluent, with parents who can afford to pay higher tuition rates.

Because of the attractive incentives associated with enrolling nonresident students, at the same time that many public institutions are increasing tuition rates for nonresident students, they are also enhancing their efforts to attract an increasing percentage out-of-state students. Both domestic and international nonresident students create a more diverse student body, and they also pay higher tuition. For example, tuition and fees for nonresident students at Indiana University was $325 for residents in 1970–1971 and $745 for nonresidents. In 2004–2005, tuition and fees for residents had grown to $6,776 and $18,589 for nonresidents. Thus, nonresident tuition grew by nearly 250 percent during this time, while resident tuition increased by 200 percent. Similar increases are evident at many public universities. In 1975 nonresident tuition at Iowa State University was $3,700 and resident tuition was $2,000. By 2004–2005, nonresident tuition had nearly quadrupled to $14,500, while resident tuition had increased by a factor of 2.5 to $5,000. Tuition at Colorado State has risen from $1,152 in 1984–1985 to $13,520 in 2004–2005.

These tuition differentials have created incentives for public institutions to recruit nonresident students aggressively in order to increase tuition revenue. At a public university that charges $5,000 in tuition and fees for residents and $15,000 for nonresidents, recruiting 100 additional resident students would generate $500,000 in revenue. Adding an additional 100 nonresident students would produce $1,500,000—a threefold increase in revenue. It should not be surprising that a job description for a senior enrollment management position at a large multicampus public university included the request for a candidate who could help the individual campuses that comprised this system to develop successful strategies to attract out-of-state students.

It is important to acknowledge that increasing enrollments just to attract more revenue is not always a wise method to generate more campus revenue. To the uninformed observer of higher education it seems quite logical—more students produce more income. However, this movement can often be counterproductive because additional students may result in increases in instructional costs that exceed the tuition revenue these students pay. Thus, institutional capacity is a key variable in whether simple enrollment growth is a sensible strategy to garner more dollars for operating expenses. However, if the physical plant has additional capacity, and academic and financial administrators have determined that they have excess capacity in some majors, then the marginal costs of additional students does not exceed the tuition they pay. The structure and composition of the instructional faculty is also an important consideration. If an institution has to hire more full-time faculty to meet the instructional needs of additional students, then adding more students may cost more than the additional revenue they generate. This is one of the reasons many institutions are hiring part-time and adjunct faculty who are paid less. This lowers the cost of instruction so that student tuition dollars may cover all instructional costs and administrative support costs. In other instances, academic and financial administrators have determined that they have excess capacity in some majors and that the marginal costs of additional students does not exceed the tuition they pay (Breneman 1994).

The benefits of increasing revenue through higher tuition and/or enrolling more students, when possible, are self-evident. Nevertheless,

117

greater reliance on student tuition raises some interesting equity and operational concerns for public colleges and universities. These equity concerns in particular include some thorny issues that campus and state policy makers need to consider.

Equity and Access

If the current shift toward privatization through higher student tuition continues, public and institutional policy makers will need to recast many of the factors they considered in the areas of financial aid and enrollment. Historically, public universities have not provided large amounts of campus-based financial aid for needy students or to reward high academic achievement. They have relied upon their low tuition costs to assure access and to attract a modicum of academically talented students. However, in the new marketplace of higher tuition, public colleges can no longer rely on their low tuition to assure equity and access or to attract their fair share of high-ability students. Indeed, several higher education researchers have concluded that rising costs at four-year public institutions, coupled with failures of both the federal and state governments to increase need-based financial aid, have resulted in increased socioeconomic segregation, as more and more low- and moderate-income students enroll in low-cost, two-year colleges (Hearn 2001; St. John 2003).

Until recently, scholarly and public policy analyses of the access problem have focused almost exclusively on the responsibility of the federal government and the states to provide need-based aid to assure access to public sector institutions. Recently, however, as public institutions raise their tuition costs, the appropriate role for public universities in providing more of campus-based financial aid for low-income students is being discussed. Comprehensive campus need-based financial aid approaches that have been announced at the University of North Carolina at Chapel Hill and at the University of Virginia (Associated Press 2003) have resulted in national attention being focused on the responsibilities of public institutions to use some of their own financial aid dollars to help solve the access problem.

Unfortunately, no national databases exist that enable researchers to identify easily the range and amount of awards going to need-based and merit-based campus-based financial aid for undergraduate students. However, it is possible to make some informed inferences. In *Trends in Student Aid 2004*, the College Board reports that between 50 percent and nearly 65 percent of all enrolled low-, middle-, and high-income students attending four-year private colleges and universities receive some form of institutional grant. The average grant ranges between $6,000 and $7,500. Middle-income students tend to receive the largest awards, followed by low-income students, and then high-income students. This distribution is the result of two factors: (1) federal and state need-based awards that provide additional need-based aid for low-income students, and (2) high-income students who can more readily afford to pay the tuition costs at more private institutions.

In contrast, only 18 to 29 percent of all students attending public institutions receive institutional grants. However, high-income students, on average, receive the largest campus-based awards; and low-income students receive the lowest average awards. In addition, the dollar value of awards for low-income students (in constant dollars) has declined in recent years, and the dollar value of awards to the highest income quartile has increased the most as the number of high-income students receiving awards has increased the most (College Board 2004b, 16). These are disturbing trends.

In total, these patterns suggest that public universities provide less institutional financial aid and, in comparison with their private college colleagues, public institutions are less committed to providing need-based aid. Indeed, Heller (2004) has pointed out that public institutions have increased their commitment to campus-based merit aid more than their allocations to need-based aid in recent years. Given the strong correlations between family income and academic ability, it is likely that the increases in campus-based aid going to high-income students at public universities is an indirect indicator that more money is being dedicated to merit aid and, in many instances, to students who could afford to pay their costs of attendance.

Along with these financial aid trends, there are other indications that access and equity issues are at greater risk at public colleges and universities. Hearn (2001) and St. John (2003) have demonstrated that low-income and minority students are increasingly being segregated at community colleges because of rising costs and too little financial aid at four-year institutions. In addition, a series of studies conducted in the 1990s (Florida Postsecondary Education Planning Commission 1994; Minnesota Private College Research Foundation 1992; Oregon State System of Higher Education 1995) consistently found that there were more low- and moderate-income students enrolled in private colleges and universities than in public four-year institutions in the states of Oregon, Minnesota, and Florida. These studies suggest that these enrollment patterns were due to private institutions providing more need-

119

based aid, thus reducing the net cost of attendance and more effectively serving low- and moderate-income students.

The cumulative impact of these policy shifts is not only on the actual distribution of need-based financial aid to admitted students. There is also a potential impact on the types of students who even apply to higher-cost public colleges and universities. Hossler, Schmit, and Vesper (1999) found that as tuition costs rise (also often described as the "list cost"), students from lower-income families are less likely to apply because they assume they cannot afford to attend. As a result, another task that publics with rising tuition costs face is not only to provide more need-based aid for low- and moderate-income students but also to let them know during their junior and senior years in high school that they provide need-based aid. Otherwise, many low-income students will not even apply for admission.

Impact

Collectively, these trends indicate that many public institutions are drifting toward a high tuition model. This approach received a good deal of attention in the early and mid-1990s as a result of an influential article by James Hearn and David Longanecker (1985) in which they laid out a rationale for a high tuition and high financial aid model for public universities. However, research conducted at that time (Gumport and Pusser 1994; Hossler et al. 1997) and current trends suggest that while the high tuition part of this proposal is gaining ground among more costly four-year public institutions, the need for state institutions to invest more in need-based aid is not being systematically addressed. Hossler et al. (1997) concluded that this was the case in the mid-1990s when they reported that neither public nor institutional policy makers had identified agreed-upon measures to determine what constituted low, moderate, or high financial aid environments. Indeed, they concluded that in the states where they conducted their research, institutions were drifting toward higher tuition and low to moderate financial aid. Gumport and Pusser (1994) reached similar conclusions in their research conducted in California. The College Board reports that in constant dollars, since 2000–2001, allocations to state financial aid programs have risen by just 17 percent (2004b, 7), while college costs at public four-year institutions have risen by 27 percent (College Board 2004a, 8).

Equally problematic from an equity perspective, during the last ten years, the percentage of state financial aid dollars being devoted to need as opposed to merit has declined from 90 percent to 75 percent (College Board 2004b). In many respects these trends are not surprising. St. John (1994) notes that the lack of coordinated federal and state policies for funding student aid and institutional subsidies has accentuated the financial pressures facing college students, their families, and postsecondary educational institutions.

However, there is a key difference in these earlier discussions about higher tuition and higher financial aid focused primarily on the role of states and their need to let public institutions' tuition increase (and reduce state subsidies to institutions) and investing those state dollars in need-based financial aid. Little or no attention was given at that time to the need for public institutions also to invest some of their increases in tuition revenue in need-based aid; the focus was on states to provide more need-based aid as public tuitions rose. Much has changed since 1985, however; and as tuitions at public institutions continue to rise and trends toward privatization and marketization push forward, senior administrators and trustees need to consider investing more of their own resources in need-based aid.

It is interesting to note that senior administrators at private institutions have longer histories of balancing issues of affordability and higher tuition prices. For many senior administrators and trustees at public colleges and universities, however, these are new issues to consider. As I have already noted, historically they have not given much attention to access issues because low tuitions, along with state and federal financial aid, were perceived to address the access and equity issues. No databases or surveys exist to establish empirically the validity of my observations; however, anecdotal conversations with many senior enrollment managers at public universities lend strong support to my assertion that public institutions are just now starting to consider the role of campus need-based aid in assuring access to low- and moderate-income students. Initiatives announced by the presidents of the University of North Carolina at Chapel Hill, the University of Virginia, and the University of Nebraska have garnered public attention because they are focusing on major new financial aid programs to provide need-based aid for undergraduate students.

This issue has two dimensions: What is the obligation of a public state-supported college or university to provide need-based aid for resident students *and* what is the obligation of a public state-supported college or university to provide need-based aid for *non*resident students? It has been my experience that it is easier to engage campus administrators about the need to provide need-based aid for resident students than for nonresident students. The access concerns of state citizens are perceived to be more compelling than those of nonresident students. However, as public institutions move increasingly toward privatization, it is difficult not to make the following comparison. Private institutions typically do not distinguish between in-state and out-of-state students when they are developing institutional policies that address need-based aid and access questions. As more and more public institutions pursue market-oriented models similar to those pursued by private sector institutions, it is only a matter of time before these questions will have to be more openly and systematically addressed.

Operational Concerns

In addition to the broader institutional and public policy issues raised by privatization, some interesting internal operational questions are also emerging for public institutions. Campus-based costs associated with greater reliance on student tuition to meet the revenue goals of public universities need to be carefully considered. Historically, offices of admissions at public institutions and offices of financial assistance were not staffed to recruit new students aggressively and proactively. At one time most public institutions relied on a combination of lower tuition costs, convenient location, and less selectivity to assure that they enrolled the requisite number of students. However, in a more competitive, market-oriented context, this is no longer sufficient.

A national survey conducted by the Noel-Levitz consulting group indicates that to recruit a new student the average public college spends about $456, compared to approximately $1,965 spent by private institutions (2002). The calculations used to derive these figures are simple and revealing. To calculate the cost to recruit a new student, the total budget of the admissions office is divided by the number of new students enrolled in any given year. The costs are so much higher at private institutions because they usually have larger staffs and they spend more money on publications, electronic recruitment, and travel than do their public counterparts. Private institutions make this investment in their offices of admissions because the number of students enrolled —as well as other characteristics of the enrolled student body, such as diversity or quality—is important. As public institutions rely increasingly on tuition, it seems likely that they too will have to increase their investments in new student recruitment.

Not only will public institutions have to increase their investment in admissions recruitment, but they will also have to increase their investment in campus-based financial aid. In 2001, the average discount rate at four-year private institutions was 38.2 percent (Davis 2003). Less is known about discounting practices at public colleges and universities.

Several years ago, working with a graduate student, I tried to study discounting practices at public flagship universities. Few public institutions were willing to discuss their discounting practices. Indeed, in one state, a senior administrator at one public flagship said, "We do it, but I can't share this information." However, a senior administrator at the other public flagship in the state reported, "We don't discount because state-level policies do not permit publics to use campus funds for scholarships." (In fact, further informal contact revealed that this campus also was engaged in tuition-discounting practices). More recently, public institutions are starting to discuss more openly the extent to which they are using campus funds for student financial aid—need- or merit-based financial assistance. A recent confidential internal report produced by public flagships that are members of the same consortium revealed that their discount rates ranged from approximately 8 percent to 17 percent. As public colleges and universities raise their tuitions and are forced to compete more aggressively with private institutions for students, they will be forced to compete on the net costs of attendance as well as on the quality of their academic programs.

In addition, just as admissions offices need more staff to compete in the marketplace for students, financial aid offices face a similar situation. There is less documentation of the comparative staffing levels and costs for offices of student financial aid in the public and private sector. Nevertheless, informal conversations with senior financial aid administrators suggest that private institutions also have larger staffing ratios per enrolled student when compared to public institutions. This is not surprising. Private universities have learned that the decision to attend a higher-cost private institution was often linked with questions about how families would be able to afford the costs and structure their tuition payments. In addition, aid administrators need time to review individual financial aid applications personally to determine whether unusual circumstances justify making some students eligible for more federal or state need-based aid. Personalized service is part of the business model that private institutions have had to provide as part of their higher-cost structures. The financial aid offices at public institutions often have smaller staffs and rely more heavily on automated processes to determine the aid eligibility of students. Except for the most assertive families, staffing patterns at public institutions typically do not permit the personalized reviews or the application of professional judgment that is found at private colleges.

Thus, as public institutions move more aggressively to privatize themselves in the areas of tuition costs, the areas of admissions and financial aid also face increased cost structures. There is a need for a greater investment in campus-based financial aid as well as in larger staffs and more personalized recruitment and financial aid offices. There is a need for more travel as well as for electronic and direct-mail recruitment activities. These developments are quite consistent with the tenets of Resource Dependency Theory (Pfeffer and Salancik 1978). Tolbert (1985), for example, found in her research that the structure of both for-profit and nonprofit organizations is associated with the resources from the external environment on which the organizations depend. Hossler and Hoezee (2001) assert that, as colleges and universities depend more on student enrollments for revenue and prestige, they will devote more organizational energy and financial resources on enrolling the desired number of students. As institutions that derive significant portions of their revenue from tuition, they are likely to devote attention and resources to revenue optimization. These become some of the additional costs associated with privatization and marketization among public sector institutions.

Conclusions and Recommendations

It is important to emphasize that the move toward greater reliance on student tuition among public colleges and universities is not an isolated phenomenon. As the costs of higher education have increased, state governments have been torn between providing for the public good by holding down costs and paying for their expansive public postsecondary educational systems in a context of competing demands for public funds. Nevertheless, the shift toward greater reliance on tuition is one of the most visible and potentially significant outcomes of this move toward privatization of public colleges and universities.

It is premature at this time to conclude that the move to privatization among public institutions will continue or that increases in tuition at public institutions will continue to hover near 10 percent for several more years. However, if these trends should continue, or if policy proposals like those being advanced in Colorado or South Carolina should become common, a number of important public and institutional policy questions need will need to be monitored and evaluated.

Although it goes beyond the scope of this chapter, the concerns articulated by Zemsky and Wegner (1997) merit careful consideration. What are the public policy implications if the marketplace, rather than public policy, becomes the dominant force in shaping higher education in the United States? Historically, state and federal governments have been a powerful force in areas including institutional mission and goals; curriculum; meeting local, state, or national labor market needs; access and equity; redressing past injustices; and stimulating public institutions to achieve other federal and/or state goals. It seems clear that if public institutions move further along the continuum toward greater privatization, public policy makers will have less influence and control over these previously public entities that have often been instruments for addressing concerns of state and sometimes federal policy. Certainly public policy makers would have to adjust how they conceptualize their legislative activities. State and federal lawmakers might have to shift from legislative initiatives designed to determine institutional policies and practices to policies that are intended to incentivize institutional policies in the context of an academic marketplace.

Clearly, issues of access and equity are already becoming more complicated as tuition levels rise at public institutions. In an era of limited state funds, should state governments attempt to shift funds from state appropriations directly to public colleges or universities, or to state financial aid programs? Should state financial aid programs emphasize merit or need in the formulas used to provide state grants to students? What are the obligations of the federal government to help insure access and equity as the costs of attendance at public institutions increase?

These questions have been at the center of public policy debates for nearly two decades; they are not new issues. However, for most senior campus policy makers, questions about the obligations of public institutions to provide need-based aid for both resident and nonresident students is new terrain, raising larger questions about the use of campus-based financial aid. It is common to read about financial aid discount rates among private sector institutions, but until recently it has not been a topic that garnered much attention among public sector policy makers. The issue of need-based aid for nonresident students is particularly interesting. Private institutions typically do not have different policies for meeting need among resident and nonresident students. They often realize that generous need-based state scholarship programs will reduce their need to provide campus-based aid for needy resident students, but private colleges and universities do not often have policies that specifically discriminate against nonresident students. Public institutions, if they invest much money in need-based aid at all, often have de facto policies that discriminate against nonresident students.

Finally, as public institutions privatize their tuition structures and increase the costs of attendance, they will find themselves competing more directly with private sector colleges and universities. They are also likely to have to invest more money in campus-based financial aid and in larger admissions and financial aid staffs. These costs should give senior administrators at public universities pause. It is possible that if the tuition levels at their institutions are not high enough, it will not be a wise investment. If a public college or university moves assertively because more expensive peers are doing so, they may discover that the costs of such initiatives outweigh the financial costs of the efforts. The additional revenue may not be sufficient to justify the costs. Similarly, attempting to increase enrollments in order to increase revenue if the campus is at capacity could well cost more in expenditures on faculty and physical plant than the increase in revenue will generate.

Privatization and the marketization of public higher education has the potential of placing many trustees and senior campus administrators in a new external environment. For those who have spent most of their careers in public institutions, this may be a context for which they are ill prepared and have much to learn. It will be interesting to revisit these themes in another five to ten years to see how public and institutional policy makers are faring in the academic marketplace. Decisions made in the next years could have a significant impact on public institutions, on the students who enroll, and on those who would be likely to enroll.

References

Associated Press. 2003. University of Virginia considering "Carolina Covenant." *The Charlotte Observer*, October 6. Available at http://www.charlotte.com/mld/observer/news/local/6945912.htm.

Breneman, D. 1994. *Liberal arts colleges: Thriving, surviving, or endangered.* Washington, D.C.: The Brookings Institution.

College Board. 2004a. *Trends in college pricing 2004.* New York: College Board.

———. 2004b. *Trends in student aid 2004.* New York: College Board.

Curtin, D. 2003. State colleges' finance in a vise, presidents warn of closures by 09. *Denver Post*, December 19.

Davis, J. S. 2003. *The unintended consequences of tuition discounting.* The New Agenda Series, Vol. 5, No. 1. Indianapolis, Ind.: Lumina Foundation. Available at http://www.luminafoundation.org/publications/Tuitiondiscounting.pdf.

Dickeson, R. C. 2004. *Collision course: Rising college costs threaten America's future and require shared solutions.* Policy Brief. Indianapolis, Ind.: Lumina Foundation.

Florida Postsecondary Education Planning Commission. 1994. *How Floridians pay for college.* Technical Report of the Florida Family Funding Study. Tallahassee, Fla.: Florida Postsecondary Education Planning Commission.

Gumport, P., and B. Pusser. 1994. *Public to private isomorphism: A case study of rising public university fees.* Paper presented at the annual meeting of the American Educational Research Association, New Orleans, April.

Hearn, J. C. 2001. Access to postsecondary education: Financing equity in an evolving context. In *The finance of higher education: Theory, research, policy and practice,* ed. M. B. Paulsen and J. C. Smart. New York: Agathon Press.

Hearn, J. C., and D. Longanecker. 1985. Enrollment effects of alternative postsecondary pricing policies. *Journal of Higher Education* 56 (September/October): 484–508.

Heller, D. E. 2001. *The states and public higher education policy: Affordability, access, and accountability.* Baltimore, Md.: Johns Hopkins University Press.

———. 2004. State merit scholarship programs. In *Readings on equal education: Vol. 19. Public policy and college access: Investigating the federal and state roles in equalizing postsecondary opportunity,* ed. E. P. St. John, 99–108. New York: AMS Press.

Henley, K. 2004. Voucher experiment expands to colleges. *Christian Science Monitor,* May 3. Available at http://www.christiansciencemonitor.com/2004/0503/p03s01-uspo.html.

Henry, M., R. Lingard, F. Rizvi, and S. Taylor. 2001. *The OECD, globalisation, and education policy.* Oxford, UK: Elsevier Science.

Hossler, D., and L. Hoezee. 2001. Conceptual and theoretical thinking about enrollment management. In *Strategic enrollment management revolution,* ed. J. Black, 57–72. Washington, D.C.: American Association of Collegiate Registrars and Admissions Officers.

Hossler, D., J. P. Lund, J. Ramin-Gyurnek, S. Westfall, and S. Irish. 1997. State funding for higher education: The Sisyphean task. *Journal of Higher Education* 68(2): 160–90.

Hossler, D., J. Schmit, and N. Vesper. 1999. *Going to college: How social, economic, and educational factors influence the decisions students make.* Baltimore, Md.: Johns Hopkins University Press.

International Comparative Higher Education Finance and Accessibility Project. 2004. http://www.gse.buffalo.edu/org/inthigheredfinance/.

Mcgee, P. 2003. UT system approves higher tuition. (Dallas/Fort Worth, Texas) *Star-Telegram,* November 19. Available online at http://www.dfw.com/mld/dfw/news/7298859.htm?1c.

Minnesota Private College Research Foundation. 1992. Ways and means: How Minnesota families pay for college. St. Paul: Minnesota Private College Research Foundation.

Newman, F., and L. K. Couturier. 2001. The new competitive arena: Market forces invade the academy. *Change Magazine* 33(5): 10–17.

Noel-Levitz, Inc. 2002. *2001–2002 national enrollment management survey: Executive summary.* Analysis prepared by S. E. Bodfish. Available at http://www.noellevitz.com/pdfs/2002_NEMS.pdf.

Oregon State System of Higher Education. 1995. *Oregon family resource study.* Eugene, Ore.: Author.

Pfeffer, J., and G. R. Salancik. 1978. *External control of organizations: A resource dependency perspective.* New York: Harper and Row.

Rudolph, F. 1962. *The American college and university: A history.* New York, NY: Vintage Books.

Slaughter, S., and L. L. Leslie. 1997. *Academic capitalism: Politics, policies, and the entrepreneurial university.* Baltimore, Md.: Johns Hopkins University Press.

Smith, B. 2003. Sanford proposes letting state colleges go private. (Columbia, S.C.) *The State,* December 5. Available at http://www.thestate.com/mld/thestate/news/local/7422811.htm.

St. John, E. P. 1994. *Prices, productivity, and investment.* ASHE/ERIC monograph, No. 3. San Francisco: Jossey-Bass.

———. 2003. *Refinancing the college dream: Access, equal opportunity, and justice for taxpayers.* Baltimore, Md.: Johns Hopkins University Press.

St. John, E. P., E. H. Asker, and S. Hu. 2001. The role of finances in student choice: A review of theory and research. In *The finance of higher education: Theory, research, policy and practice,* ed. M. B. Paulsen and J. C. Smart, 419–38. New York: Agathon Press.

Swail, W. S., and D. E. Heller. 2004. *Changes in tuition policy: Natural policy experiments in five countries.* Montreal, Quebec: Canada Millennium Scholarship Foundation.

Tate, S. G. 2003. *College bound.* Special issue. Publication of the Florida Prepaid College Board. Available at http://www.florida529plans.com/pdf/CollegeBoundSpec.pdf.

Thelin, J. 1982. *Higher education and its useful past: Applied history in research and planning.* Cambridge, Mass.: Schenkman Publishing Co.

Tolbert, P. S. 1985. Institutional environments and resource dependence: Sources of administrative structure in higher education. *Administrative Science Quarterly* 30(1): 1–13.

Toutkoushian, R. K. 2001. Trends in revenues and expenditures for public and private higher education. In *The finance of higher education: Theory, research, policy, and practice,* ed. M. B. Paulsen and J. C. Smart. New York: Agathon Press.

Zemsky, R., and G. Wegner. 1997. Shaping the future. In *Public and private financing of higher education: Shaping public policy for the future,* ed. P. M. Callan and J. E. Finney, 60–73. Phoenix: American Council on Education and Oryx Press.

Zumeta, W. 2004. State higher education financing: Demand imperatives meet structural, cyclical, and political constraints. In *Public funding of higher education: Changing contexts and new rationales,* ed. E. P. St. John and M. Parsons, 79–107. Baltimore, Md.: Johns Hopkins University Press.

CHAPTER SIX

Patents and Royalties

Joshua B. Powers

Today's convenience store, grocery, and pharmacy have many products for sale that, when purchased, directly enrich a university. In the beverage aisle, for example, likely filling an entire refrigerator case, will be Gatorade, a product invented at the University of Florida to give their football team an "edge" that today comes in seven brands and twenty-two flavors. Now owned by PepsiCo, Gatorade sales have provided the University over $80 million in revenues since they began flowing in 1973. Moving to the oral hygiene section, almost every brand of toothpaste contains fluoride, a chemical additive invented and patented at Indiana University in the 1950s. By the time the patent ran out in the mid-1970s, the University had received approximately $4 million from their licensee, Proctor and Gamble, who were the first to use the additive in their brand of toothpaste, Crest. Had the institution chosen to tie their royalty payments to product sales, the norm with patent licensing, instead of to how much fluoride was in Crest, that amount could easily have surpassed $100 million. Even a stroll through the produce aisle finds products that financially benefit a university. The University of California, for example, owns patents on fifteen varieties of strawberries that, combined, have brought in over $2.5 million in royalties annually since at least the mid-1990s.

The pharmacy, however, is where universities have enjoyed the greatest financial bonanza. Florida State University, for example, has realized more than $200 million from its patent license to Bristol-Myers Squibb for a process for manufacturing Taxol, a popular cancer-fighting drug, while Michigan State University has realized over $300 million from its line of chemotherapy drugs. Columbia University in just one year (2001) enjoyed more than $100 million in revenues from their pharmaceutical-related patents. While Columbia's windfall outpaced all other universities in that year, many others have enjoyed at least modest returns on their life-science-related patents.

In a time in which public universities have been experiencing reductions or threats of reductions to their most critical resource, state appropriations, patenting "success" stories such as those described above have fueled a patenting and licensing arms race in American higher education. Institutions are seeking to make proprietary their most valuable esource, intellectual capital, with the hope of leveraging it into tomorrow's Gatorade or Taxol. Unfortunately, very few universities have enjoyed blockbuster revenue flows from their patent portfolio, and those that have, generally experience it with a single technology. Yet just one big "hit" is often all it takes to make a patenting program financially profitable. Hence, the normally conservative universities of America appear unusually willing to lose money, sometimes lots of it, out of the belief that their own "success" story is right around the corner. Thus, "Patenting 101" sessions get scheduled for faculty with increasing frequency, attorneys get hired to do the requisite patent work, technology transfer offices get established or expanded, and business incubators and research parks get built—all in the name of economic development.

What has led America's universities, especially its public institutions, to make these uncharacteristically risky choices, and what have been the implications? The purpose of this chapter is to explore why universities in general and public universities in particular have increasingly sought to privatize their "intellectual commons" by making proprietary what was once widely accessible and usually freely given. It will also describe how these activities are typically organized and executed and will draw parallels to patenting and licensing practice in industry. Furthermore, the chapter will discuss what is known from the research regarding factors that influence success with a patenting and licensing program as well as the ethical manifestations of its practice. Recommendations on what public universities in particular might do to better manage their social responsibilities in light of their increasing privatization tendencies will conclude the chapter.

Historical Context

The application of universities to meet the practical needs of society has been an issue of interest since at least the middle of the nineteenth century. With the advent of the Morrill Land Grant Act of 1862 and later the rise of the research university, a number of public and private institutions had by the turn of the century formed applied research laboratories, agricultural extension programs, and other targeted research activities. Although universities were engaged in practically oriented research, the idea of profiting from these efforts was nevertheless anathema to most in academe. Research, it was felt, was to be freely given for the benefit of society.

A first contrarian voice to this belief was Frederick Cottrell, a noted professor of chemistry at the University of California, Berkeley. In 1907, Cottrell pursued and received a patent on his electrostatic precipitator technology, a groundbreaking pollution control technology for cleaning ash, dust, and acid from the smoke pouring out of industrial smokestacks. Believing that a proprietary technology was more likely to entice industry to license and develop the technology for use than one freely given to any interested party, Cottrell had tried but failed to get the university to patent and "own" the technology. Instead, Cottrell patented it himself but wished to use the royalty revenues from his precipitator to support the work of other researchers. Hence, in 1912, together with Charles Wolcott, secretary of the Smithsonian Institution, he set up the Research Corporation, a private nonprofit corporation that had as its mission the distribution of seed funds for researchers in the physical sciences. He and other public-minded researchers who also held patents used their resources to support many projects during a pre–World War II period when federal funds were scarce. The Research Corporation continues to operate today with the same mission, although in 1987 it spun off a separate entity called Research Corporation Technologies (RCT) that specializes in handling patenting and licensing portfolios for client universities.

With the exception of Cottrell and a few others, most universities and many faculty researchers resisted the idea of making inventions proprietary. Even Cottrell worried that if universities became too directly involved in the management of patenting and licensing operations, their thirst for funds could lead to an erosion in the critical openness necessary for research to flourish. Nevertheless, a few universities, such as the University of Wisconsin (1925), Iowa State University (1935), and the Massachusetts Institute of Technology (1940), began to get more intensively involved in patenting. However, despite the enormous influx of federal resources for research that began after World War II, most universities up until the mid-1970s still resisted the idea of adopting a proprietary view of what was produced on the laboratory bench. The reluc-

131

tance to become involved stemmed from a variety of sources, including a cumbersome process for obtaining patents based on technologies arising from federally sponsored research, a belief that it would lead to the erosion of the pursuit of critically important basic research, and/or a view that proprietary control of medical research in particular was wrong, given its public health implications. Where patenting and licensing did occur, it was usually at arms length, allowing an organization such as Cottrell's Research Corporation to manage the portfolio.

Starting in the mid-1970s, however, a sea change in attitude began that continues to this day. In 1973, two academic researchers, Stanley Cohen from Stanford University and Herbert Boyer from the University of California, San Francisco, discovered recombinant DNA, a process by which genetic material could be transformed from one organism to another. This seminal breakthrough in life science led to the creation of an entirely new industry, biotechnology, and clear evidence that substantial money could be made by exploiting it. Once Stanford and the University of California began licensing the recombinant DNA technology—ultimately via over 200 licenses that brought in over $100 million in royalty revenues—other universities began to see the enormous potential stemming from patenting academic research.

At the same time that the biotechnology industry was emerging, the nation was waking up to the reality that the world economic domination it had enjoyed since World War II was threatened, especially by the Japanese. As such, Congress was eager to provide a stimulus to national innovation, one outcome of which was the Bayh-Dole Act of 1980. Concerned that many valuable technologies languished on the university lab bench, Congress enacted the Bayh-Dole legislation to help America regain its economic dominance by creating incentives for universities to benefit financially from their intellectual output via patenting and licensing their technologies to industry. Almost overnight, the federal government legitimized university pursuit of profit under the banner of economic development and competitiveness, while also removing the considerable hurdles required to patent a technology stemming from federally supported research. An examination of patent data during this time demonstrates just how catalyzing the Bayh-Dole Act was to university involvement in patenting (see figure 6.1).

As can be seen in figure 6.1, academic patents were few and the numbers did not rise for many years prior to 1980. In the years following, academic patenting grew exponentially. In the 1970s, patent awards to all academic institutions were in the 250–350 per year range. In 1980 it was 390, while a decade later it had jumped 200 percent to 1,182. By

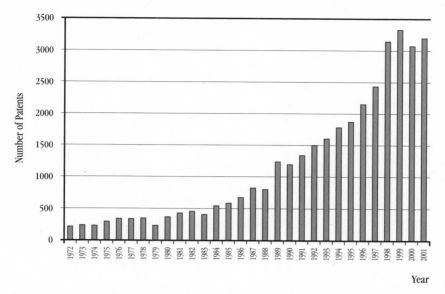

Figure 6.1. Academic patenting: 1972–2001. (*Science and Engineering Indicators* 2002 [2004] and 1993 [1995].)

2001, the most recent data available, academic patents had reached 3,203, a more than 800 percent increase since 1980. The number of universities involved in patenting technologies also more than doubled over the 20-year period between 1981 and 2001 (from 84 to 190), although the top 25 universities in terms of patenting activity have consistently accounted for approximately half of all academic patents issued throughout this period. These increases outpaced those that were also occurring in industry, affirming higher education's embrace of privatization.[1]

Much of the growth in academic patenting has been in the life science fields, stimulated by the possibilities of biotechnology. In 2001, almost one-half of academic patents came from the life sciences, most notably in the areas of chemistry, molecular biology, and microbiology, up from 15 percent of the total in 1980 (National Science Board 2004). Ironically, in the same year that the Bayh-Dole Act was legislated, the U.S. Supreme Court, in its *Diamond v. Chakrabarty* decision, made it legal to patent artificially engineered living organisms, a legal case that undoubtedly also helped to stimulate patenting in the life sciences.

A third force catalyzing university interest in patenting was a more gradual one but a phenomenon that has become especially influential in recent years. As has been presented in earlier chapters of this book, universities have experienced an increasingly competitive environment for scarce resources, whether they be students of the caliber desired, grant funds to support a large and expensive research program, or, for public institutions, state appropriations. In an effort to respond to threats to traditional resource flows, by the 1990s universities had become increasingly entrepreneurial, or more highly engaged in what Slaughter and Leslie (1997) called "academic capitalism." One manifestation of university efforts to reduce dependence on threatened or reduced core resource bases has been to exploit other opportunities for revenue generation, most notably through technology transfer, the process by which an academic innovation is made proprietary and licensed to industry. The dream was and continues to be that a patented and licensed technology will be developed by a firm into a bona fide product for sale, thereby creating a royalty revenue stream back to the institution.

The Mechanics of Patenting and Licensing in Higher Education

The process for patenting and licensing a technology is fairly straightforward. First, a faculty member discloses to the institution's technology transfer office an invention that he or she believes has the potential to be commercially exploited. Professional licensing officers then make an assessment of the technology's potential, thereby driving the decision whether or not to proceed with the expensive patenting process.[2] The decision to patent might also be driven by the ability to identify a potential licensee in advance, a benefit to a university, since the typical licensing deal involves the firm paying the patenting costs.

Once a patent is obtained, and assuming it has not already been licensed, the staff of the technology transfer office then seeks a potential licensee through their industry contacts and/or postings of their technology portfolio onto a website. Technologies are licensed in one of two ways—either exclusively to one company, or nonexclusively to multiple companies. Data collected by the Association of University Technology Managers (AUTM) indicates that approximately half of the licensing deals that are made are executed exclusively, with the rest being executed nonexclusively such that a patent can be licensed to multiple firms (AUTM 2003). With increasing frequency, universities are also licensing technologies to start-up companies established for the specific purpose of developing the technology. The theory behind this practice is that an institution can, over the long run, obtain better returns if a technology has moderate to blockbuster success than if it had licensed the technology to a large, established firm. Furthermore, many of the start-up company licensing deals involve the university accepting stock equity in the firm in lieu of the traditional up-front licensing fees. Assuming that the company is later acquired by a larger firm or grows large and strong enough itself to become a publicly traded company, the value of the stock may be considerable (Bray and Lee 2000). However, the risks of company failure are higher for smaller firms; hence, the potential for success is speculative at best. This is especially true since many of the technologies emerging from universities are of the basic variety and need considerable further development time and, in the case of pharmaceuticals and medical devices, time to proceed through the clinical trials process.

The norm for revenue distribution is to split any royalties three and sometimes more ways. One portion goes to the university (the norm being one-third), another to the faculty inventor (often another one-third), and the last portion most commonly goes to the technology transfer program, the faculty member's department, and/or the university research office. Many universities today also allow the institution, and often the faculty member, to accept stock equity. However, for a number of public institutions, this freedom has only emerged in recent years as state legislators have amended laws preventing state entities and employees from benefiting financially from outside business interests. Universities also often expect product development milestone payments as a means of realizing at least a small revenue stream relatively soon after a licensing deal is made. Relevant clauses are incorporated into licensing contracts, with a means of canceling the contract should the company not adequately develop the technology within a designated time frame. Enforcing such clauses, however, has proven somewhat problematic. It is often difficult to prove breach of contract since many firms can point to unexpected stumbling blocks to the adequate development of the technology.

Finally, as a component of the Bayh-Dole Act, universities are expected to provide annual documentation to the federal government on technology transfer activity stemming from federal research funds. The federal government is ostensibly supposed to use this data to track what products arise from federal dollars and to inform a decision to exercise its own march-in rights to a technology it funded if, in its estimation, it is not being developed appropriately. In the almost twenty-five years that the act has been in existence, however, the government has essentially never exercised this right. Furthermore, it is clear that until very recently, the decentralized and haphazard nature of data collection has made it difficult to tell just what federal investment in academic R&D has actually purchased in downstream innovations.

Research on Technology Transfer Performance

As has been described, higher education is increasingly behaving like private-sector industry, given its embrace of technology patenting and licensing. Institutions are treating their academic R&D enterprises more like producers of private goods to be leveraged into potential sources of income. Despite the rapid pace at which universities are incorporating technology patenting and licensing into their missions, however, research to inform its responsible practice has been appearing in the literature with much frequency only recently. Furthermore, most of what has been done is descriptive rather than inferential and is focused on data since 1991, the year when the primary association of professional licensing officers in higher education, the Association of University Technology Managers (AUTM), began collecting data from their member institutions. Nevertheless, what is now known is quite revealing about the practice of patenting and licensing on the university campus and how it has changed over time.

Growth Patterns in Patenting and Licensing

As mentioned earlier, the growth in academic patenting since 1980 has been enormous. However, owning a patent is only the first step — the hope of realizing an income flow requires a critical second step, licensing the technology to industry. To be reasonably effective at both of these tasks requires a professional staff infrastructure that has also grown significantly in recent years. Since 1991, this corps of specialized professionals has increased almost fourfold, from approximately 438 total FTEs to 1,686 total FTE among institutional respondents to AUTM's annual surveys (AUTM 2003). This growing core of technology transfer staff undoubtedly helped stimulate faculty interest in commercialization as evidenced by an almost 100 percent growth rate in faculty disclosures of potentially commercializable technologies (Campbell, Powers, Blumenthal, and Biles 2004), the vital commodity necessary for patenting and licensing to occur.

Growth in the area of licensing technologies to industry has been substantive as well. In fiscal year 2002, 156 universities reported that 3,739

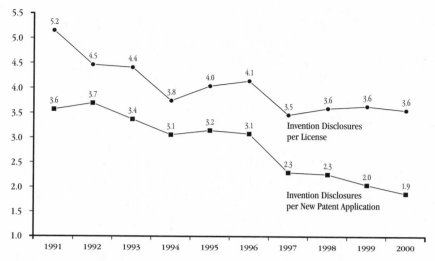

Figure 6.2. Ten-year trends in university technology transfer activity (*n*=51). (Ten-year recurrent respondents to annual AUTM licensing surveys for which complete data is available.)

licenses and options to license were executed; whereas in 1991, 98 universities reported 1,991 licenses and options executed (AUTM 2003). Thus, not only has licensing activity almost doubled in a decade, but many more universities are becoming involved in licensing activity, with each carrying on average a larger portfolio of patented and licensed technologies.

Although patenting and licensing have increased substantially since 1991, what is less well known is that universities appear to be showing a greater proclivity to patent a greater proportion of the disclosed inventions, leading some to comment that the overall quality of university patent portfolios is declining (Mowery and Ziedonis 2000). Figure 6.2 suggests this to be true in recent years, judging by the fact that since 1997 invention disclosures per license have remained flat, while invention disclosures per new patent application have declined. Universities are patenting more of their disclosures but are not licensing them at an equivalent increased rate.

Leveraging Patents into Royalty Income

On one level, the above data is clear evidence that the intent of the Bayh-Dole Act, the facilitation of university-sourced inventions to industry, is being achieved. However, assessing its ultimate success, the

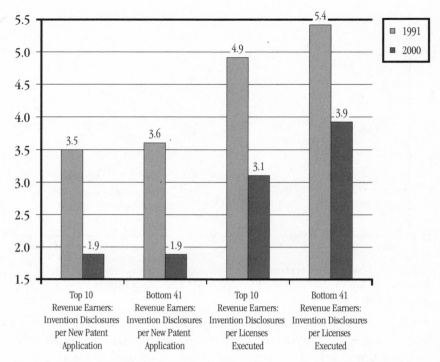

Figure 6.3. Trends in university technology transfer activity by royalty revenues performer group (*n*=51). (Ten-year recurrent respondents to annual AUTM licensing surveys for which complete data is available.)

development by industry of a university-licensed technology into a bona fide product such as Gatorade, fluoride, or Taxol, requires evidence that these licenses have resulted in product sales, a proxy of which is royalty revenues to a university. AUTM has also tracked royalty income over the past decade. In 1991 royalty income from all university respondents was approximately $130 million, while by 2002 it had reached $787 million (AUTM 2003). A close analysis of the data for the past few years, however, reveals that 60 percent of all licensing revenues came from just ten universities and that among these ten institutions, most derived from one or just a few very lucrative licenses, primarily from the life sciences field (Campbell, Powers, Blumenthal, and Biles 2004). Thus, some of the blockbusters described at the start of this chapter, as well as others like the hepatitis B vaccine from the University of California, San Francisco, make up the lion's share of the revenues. Furthermore, there are sizable differences among institutions in terms of how successful they have been at leveraging a license into a royalty stream. As shown in figure 6.3, among universities that have reported their revenues every year between 1991 and 2000, the top ten and bottom 41 royalty revenue earners showed an almost identical enthusiasm for patenting technologies disclosed to the technology transfer office.

In 1991, one patent application was made for every 3.5 disclosures. In 2000, this figure had fallen to one application for approximately every 2 disclosures. However, the ability of universities from each group to translate invention disclosures into licensed technologies was not the same. In 1991, the top ten revenue earners could leverage one license from 4.9 disclosures, a figure that declined to one in 3.1 in 2000. For the vast majority of institutions that have not enjoyed sizeable royalty streams, their leveraging rates were one in 5.4 and one in 3.9 respectively. Thus, the financially successful institutions enjoy a performance premium in licensing, a gap that increased from 0.5 invention disclosures in 1991 to 0.8 in 2000. This data suggests that the risk of engaging in technology commercialization activities is not universally the same for all institutions and that many have a more difficult time consummating an industry licensing deal, let alone seeing that technology reach the marketplace as evidenced by a royalty stream.

What accounts for differences in performance among institutions in terms of licenses executed and royalty income generated? The small amount of research on the topic suggests that the quality of the faculty, the number of professional licensing staff, the level of federal R&D support, and possibly the close availability of venture capital are important (Powers 2000, 2004; Shane and Stuart 2002) as well as the number of licenses held by an institution (Carlsson and Fridh 2002). However, there does not appear to be any empirical evidence yet that constructing business incubators and research parks provides any noticeable licensing royalty benefits (Powers 2000), even though investment in these areas in recent years has been substantial. Furthermore, despite the considerable attention paid to faculty incentives for patenting— namely, a share of the royalty income—there also appears to be no evidence that various royalty-sharing configurations have any stimulation effect on licensing and/or licensing income (Powers 2000), and they may possibly have a negative effect (Markman, Gianiodis, Phan, and Balkin 2004).

Some recent research provides insights into how public universities have performed vis-à-vis their private institution counterparts. First, after controlling for the quality of the faculty and the size and age of the technology transfer office, a statistical comparison of private and public institutions in terms of licenses executed and royalty income revealed

139

no differences between private universities, land-grant institutions, and other public universities (Powers 2003). Patenting "success" stories do not seem to be a function of institutional type. However, an analysis of trend data indicates that patenting and licensing activity has been growing the fastest at public non-land-grant institutions, suggesting that they have been the most aggressive at getting involved in technology transfer and likely playing catch-up with their private and land-grant counterparts. Non-land-grant public universities appear to be expanding their missions most noticeably among the three institutional types.

Furthermore, there is evidence that some public institutions are investing too heavily in their technology transfer programs in circumstances where the external environment already provides many of the supportive elements needed, such as resources for small business growth like incubators and abundant venture capital (Powers and McDougall 2004). Other public institutions located in weak external environments are being too selective about what to patent and not being adequately supportive of what they do patent and seek to license, given their weak external environment. Both of these approaches can be recipes for disaster (Roberts and Malone 1996), the former likely driven by trying to inappropriately emulate places like Stanford and MIT, the latter by inadequate investments and/or inexperience. Thus, not only are public universities becoming more like private industry in terms of its embrace of R&D for income generation purposes, but some public institutions appear to be investing in these activities in inappropriate ways in a likely quest to stimulate their own version of Silicon Valley or the Boston Route 128 Corridor.

Leveraging Other Forms of Income from Licenses

Although royalty revenues are a primary way that universities measure performance (i.e., as an indicator that a technology did reach the marketplace via its financial support of the university research and commercialization enterprise), other sources of revenues are becoming important to universities. For example, as mentioned earlier, universities are increasingly taking stock equity as part of a licensing agreement, particularly with the small companies that the Bayh-Dole Act seeks to favor in technology licensing. While many private institutions have been engaging in this practice for some time, public universities have generally been newcomers to this approach to licensing. State and institutional conflict of interest laws have been relaxed in recent years to allow universities and their faculty to accept stock in a company for which they may do research and/or serve as an officer (Schmidt 2002). A few universities have enjoyed big gains from the sale of equity taken in a licensee firm when it was starting out and then ultimately became successful after going public (e.g., the Medarex company by Dartmouth College, Akamai Technologies by MIT). Yet predicting which small companies will be successful is especially fraught with risk, particularly among those built around basic and untested technologies commonly emerging from universities. Unless a company makes a public offering or is purchased by a larger firm while still private, the stock owned by a university is essentially worthless.

Patent infringement suits as well as attempts to extend lucrative patents represent another source of considerable revenue or anticipated revenues for universities. A vigorous suit against Genetech by the University of California, for example, resulted in a $200 million settlement for the university in 1999, an amount that dwarfed the $67.8 million in actual royalties and fees that the entire campus system received that year. The University of Rochester waged a similar suit against Searle in the hopes of obtaining royalty payments on Celebrex, the number one–selling drug product worth potentially billions in royalties over the lifespan of the patent. As it regards efforts to extend patents, a noted example involves Columbia University and its patented technique for genetically engineering animal cells that has been used by a number of biotechnology firms to develop new drugs such as Interferon. The patent expired in August of 2000, and after a failed attempt to get Congress to extend the patent, the university filed for additional patents, one of which was approved in late 2001. Five biotechnology firms sued Columbia University, alleging that the University sought to illegally extend the life of their most lucrative patent and later to apply for new patents on the old technology. Some have suggested that Columbia University is doing exactly what so many have complained that pharmaceutical companies do in a concerted effort to maintain revenue flows (Pollack 2003). This is one more example of how universities are behaving more like private industry.

Ethical Issues

Closely associated with the issue of patenting and licensing of university-sourced technologies and arguably receiving the most press attention, have been the ethical conflicts it engenders. There is evidence that the fundamental norms of academic science are eroding. The opportunities afforded through biotechnology, combined with a policy environment favorable to commercialization, have led to a change in the core academic values of communality and disinterested inquiry (Merton 1942). The open sharing of data and study results and the pursuit of research free from personal financial gain motives appear to be increasingly replaced by an environment of solitariness and self-interestedness (Anderson and Louis 1994). Faculty and their institutions are increasingly viewing data, research findings, and innovative devices and processes as an intellectual property to be protected and nurtured for personal or institutional financial gain.

Derek Bok (1994) spoke to this changed environment and how it may compromise core academic values. According to Bok, relationships with industry can

> divert the faculty. Graduate students may be drawn into projects in ways that sacrifice their education for commercial gain. Research performed with an eye towards profit may lure investigators into conflicts of interest or cause them to practice forms of secrecy that hamper scientific progress. Ultimately, corporate ties may undermine the university's reputation for objectivity. (1994, 78–79)

This quote encapsulates many of the worst fears about the negative repercussions arising from university commercialization efforts. First, as it regards its effect on graduate education, a survey of 693 graduate students and postdoctoral fellows in the life sciences at six universities revealed that 34 percent of those with industry-supported projects felt constrained in discussing their research results with other scientists (Gluck, Blumenthal, and Stoto 1987). The study also found that graduate students and postdoctoral fellows whose projects were supported by industry had significantly fewer publications on average than those with no industry support. In their qualitative study of 37 science and engineering faculty, Slaughter, Campbell, Holleman, and Morgan (2002) found that faculty were often willing to use their graduate students as "tokens of exchange" to land a lucrative industry contract. In other words, a faculty member could often consummate a research deal with industry because of ready access to a source of cheap bench-side labor. A recent *Wall Street Journal* article suggests that this issue is not limited to graduate students. Marcus (1999) described undergraduate students at MIT who had been recruited to work for Akamai Technologies, a company in which the university had a sizable equity stake as described earlier in this chapter. The students found that they could not use their work at the firm as a basis for a computer science homework assignment because they had signed a nondisclosure agreement with the company. The students were unable to secure permission from the company founder, an MIT faculty member, who feared that the assignment amounted to company espionage since the course professor who assigned the project also happened to be the founder of a rival company.

The conflicts of interest issue that Bok (1994) articulated in the above quote have also received considerable attention. Conflicts of interest generally center on the degree to which faculty or institutional judgment is clouded when one or both holds a financial interest in or depends on revenue flows from a company for whom research is conducted by faculty. Examples of note include universities or faculty failing to ensure the safety of human subjects because they have a financial stake in the outcome of a study, universities becoming reticent to resist industry encroachment on the design and execution of lucrative clinical trials, and faculty biasing research results to please an industry sponsor—a finding in a number of studies (see Bekelman, Li, and Cross 2003). Furthermore, there is evidence that faculty may be increasingly lured away from basic research topics to more applied ones. Blumenthal, Campbell, Causino, and Louis (1996) found that faculty members with industrial support were significantly more likely than those without such support to report that their choice of research topics had been influenced somewhat or greatly by the likelihood that the results would have commercial application.

To date, private or public university attempts to manage these conflicts have been haphazard at best, with a considerable diversity of policies in place that range from the restrictive to the laissez-faire (Cho, Shohara, Schissel, and Rennie 2000). Harvard Medical School's recent debate over whether or not to raise the limits on stock ownership and consulting fees highlights the difficulty that universities face when attempting to balance conflicts of interest with the need for a favorable work environment for faculty (Mangan 2000).

Increased secrecy in academic science can take a number of forms, most notably faculty delaying publications for an extended period of time and refusing to share research results and materials when asked by other academic scientists. Blumenthal et al. (1997) found in their 1994–1995 survey of academic life scientists that faculty researchers with industry funding were significantly more likely to have delayed publication of their research longer than six months compared to faculty without industry funding ($p < .001$). Furthermore, a national survey of geneticists (Campbell et al. 2002) found that for almost half of academic geneticists who had asked other faculty for additional information, data, or materials regarding published research, at least one of their requests had been denied in the preceding three years. Because they were denied such access, more than a quarter of geneticists reported that they had been unable to confirm published research. Perhaps the most visible example of secrecy involved the alleged cold fusion "discoveries" at the University of Utah in 1989. The two researchers, Stanley Pons and Martin Fleischmann, refused to share the exact techniques used in their experiment so others could seek to replicate it. Although the underlying reasons for their reluctance to share the results are still debated, it was certainly in part due to efforts by the researchers and the university to pursue intellectual property protections and a $25 million grant from Congress to advance their project.

An emerging ethical concern centers on the issue of licensing basic technologies and whether or not they should be licensed exclusively, nonexclusively, or not at all. Basic technologies, the ones most likely to emerge from university research, are generally those for which no clear application is evident but that appear likely to have a considerable impact. For example, with the mapping of the human genome complete, particular gene sequences certainly hold the keys to curing any number of diseases. Yet is the cause of public health advanced if that sequence is patented and licensed to a single company who then has the monopoly rights on that technology's development and sale? A similar case can be made for stem cell lines. For example, the University of Wisconsin, a major center for stem cell research, has licensed some of its cell lines on an exclusive basis to the Geron Corporation.

The licensing exclusivity concern was very recently raised by the U.S. Public Health Service, which has advanced a draft document entitled *Best Practices for the Licensing of Genomic Inventions*, with the nonbinding recommendation that these kinds of technologies should be licensed on a "nonexclusive basis when possible" but that if it must be done exclusively, it should be for a very narrow field of use. Unfortunately, when it is not clear what field or fields of use might be applicable, it is difficult to define it narrowly enough. Furthermore, given the very long, expensive, and risky incubation period most likely necessary for the refinement of a basic technology for practical application, industry makes a compelling case that exclusivity protections are important. Thus, universities find themselves in the challenging place of trying simultaneously to meet their public benefit responsibilities while also having to pursue a course of limited access to their potentially lifesaving health innovations.

Recommendations for
Public Universities

As this chapter has described, America's research universities are increasingly seeking to leverage financial benefit from their most valuable asset, their intellectual capital. A confluence of forces have led to this behavior—the opportunities associated with biotechnology, a policy environment supportive of entrepreneurial endeavor, and increased competition for limited resources, especially state appropriations in the case of public institutions. Thus far, while few universities have experienced the blockbuster success story, all are confronted with daunting ethical implications stemming from the pursuit of "profit." Below are some recommendations for what public universities in particular might do to better address the opportunities and the risks of technology transfer.

Facilitating Technology Transfer

Given current state and federal policy environments, it is unlikely that policy makers are going to roll back efforts to stimulate regional and national innovation, especially given the real and perceived beneficial effects on economic development. However, at the same time, there clearly are challenges that universities, especially public universities, face when attempting to deliver on federal, state, and even institutionally self-established technology transfer goals. Hence, the following recommendations are offered to enhance the movement of university-sourced inventions into the marketplace from public institutions.

First, public universities need to recognize the need for benchmarking against appropriate peer institutions. Much has been made of the successes of the MITs and Stanfords, and as such, many seek to model their programs after the experience of these two noted institutions. The reality is, however, that both of these universities have a unique culture of faculty entrepreneurship, function in regional environments that are enormously important to the nurture and development of small companies, enjoy a caliber of faculty near or at the forefront of their fields, have been engaged in technology transfer for many decades, and are both private. This last point is especially important in terms of the kinds of policy options generally available to private institutions and the requisite flexibility to put into place needed elements supportive of patenting and licensing activities. In sum, public institutions need to benchmark against similar public institutions that are located in regions with similar external infrastructures.

Second, public universities would be wise to better educate state and federal policy makers on the downstream challenges of transforming a newly licensed infant technology into a saleable product. There is considerable evidence, for example, that while universities have enjoyed success in licensing patented technologies, the post-license steps and development times are often substantially more challenging and time consuming. This is especially true with new pharmaceutical compounds that must endure multiple rounds of intensive clinical trials before approval. Public universities might press the federal agencies to create new incentives for post-license product development through such venues as new university-industry partnership grant opportunities, increased resources for such programs as SBIR and STTR,[3] and a slight revision to the Bayh-Dole Act to require institutions also to share milestone payments with faculty inventors. Royalty streams may be a long time in coming, if they ever arrive, and faculty might be stimulated to stay more engaged with the inevitable product development issues that arise during interim periods if universities were to share those resources as well. At the state level, lobbying the legislature to address the critical infrastructure needs to support the kinds of high-technology businesses likely to be interested in licensing a university-sourced technology is also of high importance.

Finally, state policy makers should do a careful assessment of the strategic capabilities of their various state universities to ascertain where various, and limited, economic development resources should best be invested. Thus, for instance, it may not be wise to allow all or even most of the public universities in the state to launch their own business incubation programs, but rather look to where resources might be shared and/or invested for other economic growth needs such as workforce development. State policy makers might also focus on key institutional needs like keeping faculty salaries competitive so as to attract and retain the most important resource needed for a successful technology transfer program, a high-quality faculty.

Addressing Ethical Conflicts

If public universities are to maintain the public trust and fulfill their service role to the citizens of a state, attention to the inevitable ethical conflicts associated with patenting and licensing is critical. Three key steps in this regard are essential. First, careful crafting of conflict of interest policies with specifics is necessary. Many institutional conflict of interest policies are either outdated or insufficiently specific regarding

146

the finer points of what the conflicts might be or the ramifications of having been accused or found to have violated one. Thus, for example, mere statements that "conflicts of interest are taken seriously and will not be tolerated" do not go far enough. It is important that the language of these policies outlines in clear terms what conflicts will not be tolerated, offers case examples, presents the investigatory and sanctioning mechanisms, links to key federal and state policies of relevance, and maps out the processes for policy revision/expansion during this dynamic period in which universities are finding themselves.

Second, institutions should adopt good practice principles such as have been advanced by the Public Health Service and the National Institutes of Health among others. These might include a shift toward more nonexclusive licensing whenever possible; equity policies that carefully manage the circumstances under which a faculty inventor can accept equity in a licensee firm; expectations of full-disclosure of any financial interests that a faculty member may have in a firm, especially when publishing research; and statements that affirm the primary teaching, research, and service responsibilities of an academic. While some universities and faculty have resisted, or at least bristled, at the notion that their integrity could ever be compromised, the social contract under which universities function necessitates that such concerns are taken seriously and are addressed, irrespective if an ethical breach has actually occurred.

Last, new research to inform the responsible practice of technology transfer needs to be accelerated. Most of what is known still remains anecdotal or characteristic of a single institutional circumstance. For example, there have been no studies to date that investigate if exclusive licensing actually slows the pace of innovation and/or what the short- and long-term implications of such an approach might be. Cost-benefit research is also largely absent from the study of university technology transfer. We know that certain factors lead to greater technology transfer output, for instance, but we do not know whether the costs of such investment outweigh the benefits. Finally, there is some exploratory research suggesting that the level of state appropriations for public institutions may have an effect on technology transfer activity at both the public and private institutions in a state but with only speculative insights into why this might be or its implications (Powers 2004). Empirical studies to explore these issues and related others would do much to inform practitioners, policy makers, and future researchers on an important phenomenon transforming America's universities.

147

Tomorrow's Public University

This chapter began by describing everyday products that came from industry but were developed from university research. While university research has long been a source of industry innovation, what has changed is that higher education now wants a piece of the financial action whenever you or I buy sports drinks, toothpaste, fruits and vegetables, or drugs. So long as economic development remains front and center in legislators' minds and state appropriations continue to be threatened or reduced, it is likely that the distinctions between public universities and private for-profit businesses will become even more blurred in the future. The challenge, of course, is to strike the appropriate balance between the longstanding social responsibilities of collegiate institutions and the needs and requirements of the changing marketplace.

Notes

1. Although outpacing industry growth in patenting, academic patenting remains small by comparison (about 5% of all patenting from the private or nonprofit sectors).

2. Domestic patents generally cost between $15,000 and $20,000 to pursue and obtain, whereas international patents can be into the hundreds of thousands of dollars depending on the extent of the coverage.

3. SBIR stands for the Small Business Innovation Research Program and STTR for Small Business Technology Transfer Program. Both are competitive grants programs to assist small businesses with product incubation.

References

Anderson, M. S., and K. S. Louis. 1994. The graduate student experience and subscription to the norms of science. *Research in Higher Education* 35: 273–99.

Association of University Technology Managers. 2003. *AUTM licensing survey FY 2000.* Norwalk, Conn.: Association of University Technology Managers.

Bekelman, J. E., Y. Li, and G. P. Cross. 2003. Scope and impact of financial conflicts of interest in biomedical research. *JAMA* 389: 454–59.

Blumenthal, D., E. G. Campbell, M. S. Anderson, N. Causino, and K. S. Louis. 1997. Withholding research results in academic life science. *JAMA* 277: 1224–28.

Blumenthal, D., E. G. Campbell, N. Causino, and K. S. Louis. 1996. Participation of life-science faculty in research relationships with industry. *New England Journal of Medicine* 335: 1734–39.

Bok, D. 1994. The commercialized university. In *University-business partnerships: An assessment,* ed. N. E. Bowie. Lanham, Md.: Rowman and Littlefield.

Bray, M. J., and J. N. Lee. 2000. University revenues from technology transfer: Licensing fees vs. equity positions. *Journal of Business Venturing* 15: 385–92.

Campbell, E. G., B. R. Clarridge, M. Gokhale, I. Birenbaum, S. Hilgartner, N. A. Holtzman, and D. Blumenthal. 2002. Data withholding in academic genetics. *JAMA* 287: 473–80.

Campbell, E. G., J. B. Powers, D. Blumenthal, and B. Biles. 2004. Inside the triple helix: Technology transfer and commercialization in the life sciences. *Health Affairs* 23(1): 64–76.

Carlsson, B., and A. Fridh. 2002. Technology transfer in United States universities. *Journal of Evolutionary Economics* 12: 199–232.

Cho, M. K., R. Shohara, A. Schissel, and D. Rennie. 2000. Policies on faculty conflict of interest at U.S. universities. *JAMA* 284: 2203–208.

Gluck M., D. Blumenthal, and M. A. Stoto. 1987. University-relationships in the life sciences: Implications for students and postdoctoral fellows. *Research Policy* 16: 327–66.

Mangan, K. S. 2000. Harvard weighs a change in conflict-of-interest rules. *Chronicle of Higher Education*, May 1, A47–48.

Marcus, A. D. 1999. MIT students, lured to new tech firms, get caught in a bind. *Wall Street Journal*, June 24, A1, 6.

Markman, G. D., P. T. Gianiodis, P. H. Phan, and D. B. Balkin. 2004. Entrepreneurship in the ivory tower: Do incentives matter? *Journal of Technology Transfer* 29: 353–64.

Merton, R. K. 1942. A note on science and democracy. *Journal of Legal and Political Sociology* 1: 115–26.

Mowery, D. C., and A. A. Ziedonis. 2000. Numbers, quality, and entry: How has the Bayh-Dole Act affected U.S. university patenting and licensing? *NBER Innovation Policy and the Economy* 1: 187–220.

National Science Board. 2004. *Science and engineering indicators 2002*. Washington, D.C.: Author.

Pollack, A. 2003. Three more biotech firms file suit against Columbia over patent. *New York Times*, July 16, B2.

Powers, J. B. 2000. Academic entrepreneurship in higher education: Institutional effects on performance of university technology transfer. *Dissertations Abstracts International* 61(11): 4309. (UMI No. AAT 9993648).

———. 2003. *Do land-grant and private universities enjoy a performance premium in the technology commercialization game?* Paper presented at the annual conference of the Association for the Study of Higher Education, Portland, Oregon.

———. 2004. Commercializing academic research: Resource effects on performance of university technology transfer. *Journal of Higher Education* 74: 26–50.

Powers, J. B., and P. McDougall. 2004. Policy orientation effects on performance with licensing to start-ups and small companies. Unpublished manuscript.

Roberts, E. B., and Malone, D. E. 1996. Policies and structures for spinning off new companies from research and development organizations. *R&D Management* 26(1): 17–48.

Schmidt, P. 2002. States push universities to commercialize their research. *Chronicle of Higher Education*, March 29, A26.

Shane, S., and T. Stuart. 2002. Organizational endowments and the performance of university start-ups. *Management Science* 48: 154–70.

Slaughter, S., T. Campbell, M. Holleman, and E. Morgan. 2002. The "traffic" in graduate students: Graduate students as tokens of exchange between academe and industry. *Science, Technology, and Human Values* 27: 282–312.

Slaughter, S., and L. L. Leslie. 1997. *Academic capitalism—Politics, policies, and the entrepreneurial university.* Baltimore, Md.: Johns Hopkins University Press.

CHAPTER SEVEN

Philanthropy

Aaron Conley and Eugene R. Tempel

Just a few decades ago the functional areas of alumni relations, development, and public relations on most public college campuses were arguably considered secondary, or in some cases, insignificant functions when viewed from the overall perspective of any given institution's operational priorities. Staff sizes and budgets were minimal, and most personnel likely had limited training in their field. Organizationally, these offices were commonly not integrated in mission or scope, leaving their roles ambiguous and undefined. By contrast, America's private colleges and universities recognized long ago the importance of developing and integrating this trio of functions as a means to greater private financial support and reputational enhancement.

Commonly recognized today as "institutional advancement," this organizational unit that was once on the functional fringe of most public campuses has now become a critical central component, especially at the largest public universities. A combination of forces over the past thirty years combined to push advancement to the top of the list of nearly every administration wishing to become a premiere public institution or to retain its position there. But the economic pressures of just the past few years have sharply accelerated this trend of public institutions adopting the successful model of advancement that has been so effectively followed by their private counterparts. This chapter examines these forces, considers their impact on the public higher education landscape, and proposes that the future success of America's public colleges and universities will rely even more heavily on institutional advancement's becoming an indispensable function on these campuses.

The catalyst that began moving the independent advancement functions together can be traced to a 1957 joint conference between the American Alumni Council and the American College Public Relations Association at the Greenbrier Resort in West Virginia. The report that emerged from this gathering, "The Advancement of Understanding and Support of Higher Education," was the first to articulate the principle of consistent and integrated organization of efforts in institutional advancement (Brittingham and Pezzullo 1990). Commonly referred to as "the Greenbrier report," this effort led to the eventual joining of these two organizations to become the Council for the Advancement and Support of Education (CASE), which today represents the primary professional association for administrative staff engaged in alumni relations, marketing and communications, and fund raising. Membership in CASE includes more than 23,500 individuals at 3,000 colleges, universities, and independent elementary and secondary schools in the United States, Canada, Mexico, and forty-two other countries (CASE 2004).

Evolution of Advancement on the American Campus

Like so many features of American higher education today, the origin of institutional advancement is well documented at this nation's first college institution, Harvard. Just three short years after its founding in 1636, the fledgling seminary hired three emissaries to return to England in search of financial support for the school (Cutlip 1965), armed with "New England's First Fruits," the earliest version of a campaign brochure. The outcome of the effort was mixed, but the precedent was set, and America's new institutions of higher learning would soon follow with more efforts at raising private support.

For the first three centuries of American higher education, however, the practice of fund raising and "friend raising" was almost entirely the domain of private, non-state-related institutions. Through most of the 1700s the reason was simply because there were no public institutions. The University of Georgia was incorporated in 1785 and began classes in 1801, and the University of North Carolina was chartered in 1789, starting classes there in 1795, making them this country's first public universities. By this time, many private institutions already had decades of experience pursuing their graduates and friends for voluntary support.

Throughout the rest of the 1800s many of the earliest private institutions also had a fundamental edge over public institutions in instilling a sense of philanthropy simply because of the nature of their existence. Nearly all private institutions established prior to 1900 were church-affiliated seminaries created primarily to train clergy. As the nation expanded westward through the early 1800s, hundreds of institutions arose throughout the Midwest, and competing denominational interests ensured that each faith was represented in each new state as they staked their own claims much like land speculators moving into the new territories. Ohio provides the best evidence of this trend, claiming thirty-seven institutions of higher education in the decades that followed the Civil War. Ohio had a total population at that time of just 3 million. By contrast, England possessed just four institutions to serve a population of 23 million (Barnard 1880, cited in Rudolph 1990, 48). Denominationalism is also credited as the primary reason for the founding of eleven colleges in Kentucky before 1865, twenty-one in Illinois by 1868, and thirteen in Iowa before 1869 (Sears 1922, in Rudolph 1990, 15).

Nearly all the new institutions founded during this period faced routine financial hardship in their early years, and many did not survive. For those that did, it was commonly through a sense of Christian charity among wealthy old men or nearby God-fearing residents and farmers who gave what they could, including gifts of land, food, or labor to keep their colleges open (Rudolph 1990). As a result of this routine experience, the students were acculturated into an environment that showed them the importance of philanthropy, not only as part of their virtuous training but also in a way that showed them that their very education rested on the support of others who were keeping their institution afloat financially.

The latter half of the nineteenth century witnessed two important movements in higher education that had a monumental impact on how our institutions appear in form and function today, setting the stage for the explosive growth about to be realized in many new state colleges and universities. These factors can also be credited as the cause for the disparity between public and private schools and their approach to institutional advancement.

The first movement was the shift from seminary and liberal arts training toward more rigorous academic teaching and research methods. This adoption of the "German model" would lead to new emphases on basic research, graduate education, and the Ph.D. as the standard credential for the American professorate. In 1852 the president of the University of Michigan, Henry Philip Tappan, attempted wide-scale changes to usher in this new model and to bridge the gap between advocates for pure vocationalism and those for scholarly intellectualism. While his efforts set the trend in motion, his vision for change was too much for either side, and he was dismissed as president in 1863 (Rudolph 1990). Only after the conferral of the first Ph.D., which occurred in 1861 at Yale, and the establishment of Johns Hopkins University in 1867 did the new model for the American research university clearly begin to emerge.

The Morrill Act of 1862 represented the second key development that would dampen the emergence of institutional advancement at public institutions, but it did lead to the creation of many of the largest and most prominent state research universities operating today. This congressional act set aside federal land in each state for the purpose of establishing institutions of higher learning to focus primarily on the advancement of the agricultural and mechanical arts. This single act would transform the role of higher education in America and set the stage for growth for another century to come: "The Morrill Act of 1862 put federal largess at the disposal of every state government, and thereby helped to develop a whole new network of institutions with a popular and practical orientation, the land-grant colleges, which by 1955 would be enrolling more than 20 percent of all American college students" (Rudolph 1990, 244).

With its focus on a new, practical approach to learning, the Morrill Act sought to tie colleges and universities to the citizens of their states in order to meet the needs of a rapidly growing and developing nation. The state of Michigan led the movement as the first to utilize the land-grant resources, allocating its share to the previously chartered Michigan State College of Agriculture in East Lansing, which today is Michigan State University. The state of Indiana paired a private gift of $100,000 from John Purdue to establish Purdue University in West Lafayette, as did the state of New York through a $500,000 gift from Ezra Cornell to fund the institution in Ithaca that bears his name. While many of the institutions created under the Land Grant Act are among today's largest and most prominent public research universities, others, like Cornell, demonstrate these public funds being designated to private institutions. Others following this model include Dartmouth in New Hampshire, Brown in Rhode Island, and Transylvania College in Kentucky.

The resources provided to new state institutions through the Morrill Act in 1862, and a second act in 1890 that provided annual appropriations to the land-grant colleges, greatly diminished the need for these institutions to actively seek private support through gifts from alumni or other individuals. Generations of graduates from this period did not face the experience of attending an institution routinely on the edge of insolvency, thus setting the stage for much of the next century where philanthropic gestures toward public higher education were rarely seen or needed. For private institutions, the shift from training clergy toward a more rigorous curriculum in the sciences and liberal arts did little to damage the tradition of giving already entrenched as a central custom within the institutional culture.

Fund Raising Emerges

While the Gilded Age of philanthropy benefited many private institutions in the early 1900s, the century ended under entirely different circumstances, as public institutions increasingly resembled their private counterparts in all forms of institutional advancement. Among the largest and most prominent public institutions, advancement staff sizes and budgets grew, campaigns emerged, and endowments expanded to rival some of the most seasoned fund-raising operations at elite private schools. It appeared that public institutions could benefit from the same model of fund raising that private institutions had been using for more than three centuries. But prior to the 1980s, advancement efforts at public schools still were mostly inconsistent and poorly coordinated.

Early campaign efforts are a primary example of this random approach to fund raising. While many colleges had conducted campaigns for buildings or other special projects prior to 1900, none resembled the coordinated or systematic nature of campaigns commonly conducted today. The first campaign credited with using many of the features of a modern campaign was conducted in 1914 at the University of Pittsburgh, a private institution at that time, during a $3-million campaign effort (Worth 2002). This campaign used the "Ward method," so named for Charles Sumner Ward, a YMCA executive from Chicago who brought his expertise to a floundering YMCA campaign in Washington, D.C., in 1905 and realized success by utilizing now-common techniques such as using volunteers to screen lists of prospective donors and creating a visual "campaign clock" to keep the pressure on in order to reach the goal by a specified deadline. These original features have evolved into today's standard campaign tools, including volunteer committees, a fixed campaign time frame including a "silent phase" and a fixed end date, and campaign publications and events.

Some public schools, like Indiana University, adopted this new approach to begin coordinated efforts to solicit prospective donors (Indiana University Foundation 2004). A three-year "Memorial Fund Campaign" began there in 1921, but unlike private institutions, most public schools did not face the same urgency to undertake new efforts quickly. Indiana did not carry out another comprehensive campaign effort until 1965, when it set out to raise $25 million for the institution's "150th Birthday Fund." The campaign ended successfully in 1972 with over $51 million in contributions.

Prior to 1950 some state-supported institutions created new organizational units for the formal collection of gifts from alumni and others interested in supporting the institution, but these instances were limited and represented no widespread movement. One of the earliest examples, the Kansas University Endowment Association, was established in 1891 to receive gifts from grateful alumni of the University of Kansas (Worth 1985). Other institutions creating free-standing foundations for the same purpose included the University of Oregon in 1922, the University of Illinois in 1935, the University of Nebraska and Indiana University in 1936, the University of Oklahoma in 1944, and the University of Wisconsin in 1945. Other public institutions started alumni offices during this period, but it was not until the 1980s that it became common to find a formal development office, foundation, or central institutional advancement operation at every public institution.

Public institutions cannot be faulted for their failure to implement organized advancement efforts during this period since an implied understanding existed between public and private institutions and between many public institutions and their state legislatures that fund raising was not a necessity for their survival. Organized annual fund drives and major gift fund raising was the traditional domain of private institutions, and the same effort would have been viewed as unfair for public institutions since they were so generously funded with state resources through annual appropriations, while private institutions relied on tuition revenue and gift income to meet operational expenses.

Catching Up with the Privates

In 1990 Brittingham and Pezzullo (1990) highlighted the emergence of four major trends in educational philanthropy from its seventeenth-century beginnings through the 1980s. The fourth of these trends, recognized over a decade ago, served as an accurate predictor of philanthropy's increasing importance into the twenty-first century:

Table 7.1. Percentage of Revenue by Source (Public Institutions)

	1980–1981	1999–2000
Tuition and fees	12.9	18.5
Federal government	12.8	10.8
State government	45.6	35.8
Local government	3.8	3.8
Private gifts, grants, and contracts	2.5	4.8
Endowment income	0.5	0.7
Sales and services	19.6	21.6
Other sources	2.4	3.9

1. A wide shift away from church-affiliated and individual and personal solicitation to direct institutional appeals of an organizational and professional nature;
2. A dramatic shift away from the notion of charity and toward philanthropy;
3. The imposing role fund raising plays in all aspects, daily or yearly, of institutional life rather than being limited to crises or major changes in direction;
4. The widespread acceptance of fund raising among state-assisted colleges and universities in the last forty years.

There is little question today that if public institutions are to compete squarely with well-endowed private institutions, they must engage their alumni and other potential donors for greater private support. Higher education scholars and presidents alike acknowledged that the close of the twentieth century was bringing a fundamental shift in the way public institutions would operate in the new century, considering the continued inability of state appropriations to keep up with campus demands; the limits on their ability to raise tuition and fees; and the expanded influence of accepted corporate sector practices like marketing, incentive-based budgeting, and quality management tools that all contribute to making an institution more competitive in the higher education marketplace (see Kennedy 1995; Yudof 2002).

Of all these factors, the failure of state appropriations to keep pace with the escalating cost of running a public university is the most common justification for strengthening efforts to seek other sources of private support. In 1994 tuition income overtook state appropriations as the largest revenue source for higher education for the first time since the mass expansion of public colleges and universities a half-century earlier (Breneman and Finney 1997). In the two decades between 1980 and 2000, visible changes in percentages of revenue sources for public institutions, illustrated in table 7.1, have fueled the movement to re-place budget shortfalls through tuition increases, sales and services, and fund raising (National Center for Education Statistics 2002).

In the face of declining state support, leaders of the nation's top pub-lic institutions have no choice but to seek alternative revenue sources to continue growing and to retain their prominent standing. Speaking in 1991 on the subject of competitiveness and the push to become "elite," the late Clark Kerr, president of the University of California system from 1958 to 1967 and chairman of the Carnegie Commission on Higher Education, suggested fund raising had emerged as the primary vehicle to move institutions ahead of their peers, saying, "Private fund raising by both public and private institutions has, in recent times, in-creasingly become a mechanism for competitive advantage" (Kerr 1991, 15). Kerr understood well the evolution of flagship public research in-stitutions, having served as chancellor of the Berkeley campus from 1952 to 1958 before assuming the top system-wide position and imple-menting a master plan that built the University of California system into a complex powerhouse of academic institutions.

When the nationwide downturn in state appropriations hit Califor-nia, Kerr recognized that private support would be necessary to retain the elite status of the campuses at Berkeley, Los Angeles, Irvine, Davis, San Diego, and Santa Barbara. These campuses responded by landing some of the largest private gifts ever to higher education. The UCLA campus, in particular, received a $200 million commitment in 2002 by entertainment mogul David Geffen, which resulted in the naming of UCLA's medical school in his honor. The UC–San Diego campus re-ceived a $110 million commitment in 2003 for its engineering school from Irwin Jacobs, founder of telecom giant, Qualcomm. And in 1999 the co-founder of Broadcom, Henry Samueli, split a $50 million com-mitment, with $30 million going to the engineering school at UCLA and $20 million to UC–Irvine. Both engineering schools are now named in honor of Samueli. Kerr may not have envisioned gifts of this great magnitude to these leading University of California campuses, but there is little doubt of the impact they will have on retaining their standing as top research universities.

Another public multicampus system president, Graham Spanier of Penn State University, acknowledged in a recent report to his university faculty senate that fund raising was a critical component of the institution's areas of "special investment" for the next three years (Spanier 2004, 25). Fund raising appeared second on this list of eight areas:

1. Research commercialization
2. An enhanced investment in fund raising
3. Increased K–12 educational partnerships
4. A World Campus/resident instruction course development initiative
5. A humanities, fine arts, and social sciences initiative
6. Improvement of faculty/student ratios in selected programs
7. Conversion of fixed term to tenure track, and graduate assistants to fixed-term positions in selected programs
8. An enhanced investment in student services and recreation

While this emphasis from a president at a major public institution should not come as a surprise anymore, it is worth noting that Penn State had just completed a campaign that raised $1.37 billion between 1996 and 2003. This overt emphasis on continued fund raising, in the face of a remarkably successful campaign, aptly demonstrates the repositioning of institutional advancement from the fringes to the center of the public campus administrative hierarchy. Even though Penn State successfully completed a billion-dollar campaign, the institution only got serious about advancement two decades ago, according to R. P. Kirsch, Vice President of Development and Alumni Relations at Penn State University in a telephone interview in June 2004. While there was a development operation in place before this, the institution did not confer the title of vice president to the person leading this effort until 1982. The first comprehensive campaign began shortly thereafter, with a goal of raising $200 million between 1984 and 1990. After a successful start, the goal was raised to $300 million, and the effort finished with a final total of $352 million.

The increased investment by the institution over these past two decades further illustrates the commitment made by Penn State to obtain greater support through private sources. In 1983 the total number of salaried staff working within the institution's advancement operations totaled just 10. A decade later the staff grew to 80, and by 2003 there were 203. The total university budget allocation during these years illustrates similar growth, as the allocation in 1983 of $500,000 pales in comparison to the $3.9 million allocation in 1993 and the $11.4 million budget in 2003.

In the case of Penn State, the dramatically increased commitment of resources from the institution over just two decades has paid rewarding dividends. In addition to the two successful campaigns undertaken dur-

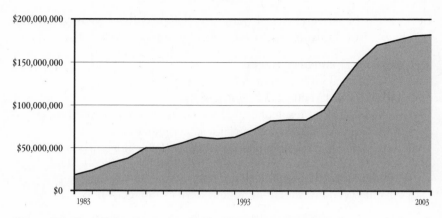

Figure 7.1. Penn State University, fund-raising totals (1983–2003).

ing this period, the growth in overall fund raising for each of the past twenty years, illustrated in figure 7.1, suggests that Penn State's investment has generated the kind of returns every public institution would like to experience. In 1983 the university's fund-raising total (cash and gifts-in-kind) reached $17.7 million. Ten years later it was nearly $71 million, and 2003 brought in more than $181.3 million.

Much of the increase in giving to public institutions over the past few decades, like that experienced at Penn State University, is attributable to gifts from individuals in general, and alumni in particular. Alumni have historically accounted for the largest source of total private support to higher education. According to the annual report published by the Council for Aid to Education, alumni giving has consistently accounted for more than one-fourth of the income from private sources, although in 2002 giving from foundations surpassed alumni giving for the first time in twenty-five years. In 2003, alumni and foundation sources both accounted for 28 percent (Council for Aid to Education 2004).

Tapping alumni from public institutions for greater support, however, is challenging and far more difficult than senior campus executives or their board members may understand. Consider table 7.2, which illustrates the top 20 public and private national universities, as appearing in the 2004 ranking by U.S. News and World Report. For the national rankings, one of the seven criteria used in the ranking methodology is the percentage of alumni who made a gift to the institution in the previous year, known as the alumni giving rate. U.S. News includes this particular criterion since alumni giving can be considered a measure of student satisfaction. Alumni who give, it is assumed, had a positive edu-

Table 7.2. Alumni Giving Rates for Top 20 National Universities
(Privates vs. Publics)

School (Private)	Overall Rank	Alumni Giving	School (Public)	Overall Rank	Alumni Giving
Top 10			*Top 10*		
Harvard U	1	49%	U of Cal–Berkeley	21	15%
Princeton U	1 (Tie)	61%	U of Virginia	21 (Tie)	27%
Yale U	3	44%	U of Michigan–Ann Arbor	25	15%
MIT	4	38%	U of Cal–Los Angeles	26	13%
Cal Tech	5	37%	U of North Carolina–Chapel Hill	29	25%
Duke U	5 (Tie)	46%	C of William & Mary	31	26%
Stanford U	5 (Tie)	38%	U of Cal–San Diego	32	8%
U of Pennsylvania	5 (Tie)	40%	U of Wisconsin–Madison	32 (Tie)	14%
Dartmouth C	9	47%	Georgia Tech	37	32%
Washington U–St. Louis	9 (Tie)	39%	U of Illinois–Urbana/Chmp.	40	12%
Top 20			*Top 20*		
Columbia U	11	32%	U of Cal–Davis	43	9%
Northwestern U	11 (Tie)	29%	U of Cal–Irvine	45	9%
U of Chicago	13	28%	U of Cal–Santa Barbara	45 (Tie)	16%
Cornell U	14	34%	U of Washington	45 (Tie)	14%
Johns Hopkins U	14 (Tie)	27%	Penn State U–Univ. Park	48	21%
Rice U	16	35%	U of Florida	48 (Tie)	18%
Brown U	17	36%	U of Maryland–College Park	53	17%
Emory U	18	28%	U of Texas–Austin	53 (Tie)	12%
U of Notre Dame	19	48%	U of Iowa	57	15%
Vanderbilt U	19 (Tie)	26%	Purdue U–West Lafayette	58	17%

Table 7.3. Twenty-five Largest Gifts Since 1990 (Public Schools in Bold)

Institution	Amount	Year
Cal Tech	$600 million	2001
Stanford U	$400 million	2001
Rensselaer Polytech. Institute	$360 million	2001
MIT	$350 million	2000
U of Arkansas–Fayetteville	**$300 million**	**2002**
Vanderbilt U	$300 million	1998
Emory U	$295 million	1996
New York U	$250 million	1994
U of Colorado System	**$250 million**	**2001**
U of Texas at Austin	**$232 million**	**2002**
Ave Maria U	$200 million	2002
F. W. Olin C of Engineering	$200 million	1997
U of Cal–Los Angeles	**$200 million**	**2002**
Johns Hopkins U	$150 million	2001
New York U	$150 million	2002
Polytechnic U	$144.2 million	1998
DePauw U	$128 million	1997
U of Nebraska	**$125 million**	**1998**
U of Utah	**$125 million**	**2000**
LaGrange C and Mercer U	$123 million	2000
U of Pennsylvania	$120 million	1993
U of Southern California	$120 million	1993
U of Southern California	$112.5 million	1998
U of Cal–San Diego	**$110 million**	**2003**
U of Southern California	$110 million	1999

cational experience, and their gift is viewed as an endorsement of the quality of education they received.

This comparison presents a compelling dilemma for leaders of public institutions. Among the top 10 institutions, no private school has less than 37 percent alumni giving. Only one of the top 10 public schools is above 30 percent, and six are at 15 percent or less. Among the next 10 ranked schools, the lowest ratio among the privates is 26 percent, while only one of the publics managed to break 20 percent. Most of the public schools in this ranking are large state universities that have built alumni populations of 200,000 or more. When these institutions' lead-

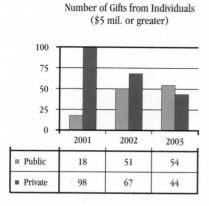

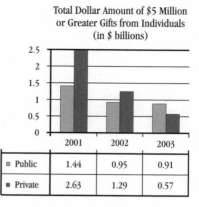

Number of Gifts from Individuals ($5 mil. or greater)	2001	2002	2003
▣ Public	18	51	54
■ Private	98	67	44

Total Dollar Amount of $5 Million or Greater Gifts from Individuals (in $ billions)	2001	2002	2003
▣ Public	1.44	0.95	0.91
■ Private	2.63	1.29	0.57

Figure 7.2. Public institutions gaining on privates in the race for mega-gifts.

ers look for sources of additional revenue, it is easy to see how a president of an institution with a lowly alumni giving rate of 10 to 15 percent could envision millions of new dollars if they could get an additional 5 percent of their alumni base to start giving back to alma mater.

While publics may be lagging their private peers in gaining widespread support and instilling a philanthropic identity with their graduates, they are making considerable advances in raising "mega-gifts." This tradition, which began a century ago with gifts from great industrialists like Rockefeller and Stanford, was once commonplace only among the private institutions. As table 7.3 illustrates, however, seven of the largest gifts to higher education since 1990 have been made to public institutions, and all these were made after 1998 (Chronicle of Higher Education 2004b).

While they may not be among the largest gifts, many public institutions are also beginning to develop a strong track record of raising multiple gifts of $5 to $10 million or more. Arizona State University (ASU) received a $50 million commitment in 2003 resulting in the naming of their business school the W. P. Carey School of Business. The donor, a successful commercial real estate developer in New York, was not an alumnus but the grandson of the institution's founder, and had earned a business degree from the University of Pennsylvania. ASU followed this with another $50 million gift announced in 2004 for their engineering programs, resulting in the naming of the Ira A. Fulton School of Engineering. The donor had attended ASU on a football scholarship but did not graduate. He went on to become a leading residential builder in the southwest U.S. through his company, Fulton Homes.

The recent success of Arizona State University does not appear to be an isolated case of mega-gifts from individuals going to public institutions. According to gifts tracked by the Center on Philanthropy at Indiana University and illustrated in figure 7.2, the three-year period between 2001 and 2003 has seen public institutions overtake privates in both the number of $5 million or greater gifts made by individuals and the total dollar value of these gifts (Center on Philanthropy 2004).

The growth in the overall number and the cumulative dollar amount of mega-gifts to public institutions is likely the source of both optimism and concern among senior advancement staff on public college campuses. As these gifts are announced by presidents and chancellors with great fanfare, there is ever-growing pressure on the advancement staff to develop a steady stream of more and even bigger gifts to meet the institution's needs. But donors at this level are increasingly becoming more demanding on how these gifts are used and whether they are having the anticipated impact promised by the institution.

The most visible example of this can be seen in the $300-million commitment made to the University of Arkansas by the Walton Family Charitable Support Foundation. This gift in 2002, the largest ever made to a public institution, took two years of negotiations to complete and came with a number of strings attached, including a required challenge campaign to match the gift with an additional $300 million from other donors by June 30, 2005, and an annual progress report that tracks campus measures including average test scores of entering freshmen, student retention rates, and progress in filling new chairs and professorships (Strout 2004). Since the gift was portrayed by the university as a way for the institution to help improve the quality of life for the entire state, other measures are required, including increases in new business starts, per-capita income, and percentages of the state population with various college degrees.

With the noted increase in multimillion dollar gifts over the past decade going to public institutions, these schools are realizing that they can pursue larger and more ambitious campaigns than they may have ever considered before. The Walton family gift to Arkansas, for example, is part of a $900 million campaign scheduled to end in 2005. Many of the largest state schools are now following the cyclical pattern emulated by so many private schools, where these campaigns seem to begin not long after the last one ended, and the goals for the new campaigns are reaching billion-dollar levels that were once only within reach of great Ivy League institutions.

The first public institution to attempt a $1 billion campaign was the University of Michigan. Since then, others have followed and succeeded, setting the bar for public institutions aspiring to build their reputation, along with their financial support, to reach this goal. The following institutions are currently in this exclusive club, and eleven more public institutions are seeking this goal and will complete their campaigns by 2007 (Chronicle of Higher Education 2004a):

- University of Michigan, $1.4 billion, 1992–1998 (Goal was $1 billion)
- Ohio State University, $1.23 billion, 1995–2000 (Goal was $1 billion)
- University of Virginia, $1.43 billion, 1995–2000 (Goal was $1 billion)
- University of Minnesota, $1.625 billion, 1996–2003 (Goal was $1.3 billion)
- Penn State University System, $1.37 billion, 1996–2003 (Goal was $1.3 billion)
- University of Colorado System, $1.026 billion, 1996–2003 (Goal was $1 billion)

With more and more large campaigns being undertaken and completed, presidents and trustees at many public institutions that have not attempted such ambitious efforts are anxiously pressing their advancement operations to get in on the action. The inherent danger here is for an institution to attempt too much too soon. When the economy soured after the dot-com crash, many institutions found themselves pushing back their campaign end dates and offering donors who had made major commitments to take longer to complete their pledges (Pulley 2003).

During this period, however, there were several surprising results at public institutions taking on their first-ever multi-year campaigns or attempting such an ambitious goal without having a substantial tradition of comprehensive institutional campaigns. Some examples follow.

Florida Atlantic University

This multicampus institution, founded in 1961, serves the coastal population of southeast Florida and has grown to a student population of 25,000. In 1995, FAU took on its first-ever capital campaign. Ignoring expert advice to set a goal of $33 million, FAU chose instead to aspire to raise $100 million by 2001. The campaign concluded with a total of more than $220.2 million, with nearly $90 million of the total designated to endowed student, faculty, and program purposes (Florida Atlantic University Foundation 2001).

Georgia Institute of Technology

One of today's premier public research universities, Georgia Tech did not have an extensive history of comprehensive campaigns or major gift fund raising when it undertook an ambitious five-and-a-half year campaign in 1995 to raise $300 million. The effort was so successful the goal was raised three times to a final target of $600 million, which it surpassed with a total of $712 million on December 31, 2000. While Georgia Tech had only had 22 endowed chairs since its founding in 1885, the campaign established 54 new endowed chairs. The campaign also funded 11 new buildings and 233 new endowed undergraduate scholarships and graduate fellowships (Georgia Institute of Technology 2001).

University of Colorado System

As an example of the dramatically increased expectations for fundraising success at state institutions, the University of Colorado stepped up from a successful $200-million campaign effort from 1986 to 1993 that raised $271.7 million, to a $1-billion campaign effort from 1996 to 2003. The campaign was a success, raising $1.026 billion, and gave Colorado the distinction of being among the first public institutions to successfully undertake a $1 billion campaign (University of Colorado System 2003).

Other notable examples of campaign success are being found in large urban institutions that not only have little experience in major campaigns but whose alumni population is primarily composed of former students who were nontraditional commuters and did not go through the same experience as four-year traditional college students. Even these institutions are finding success in their first attempts at major campaigns. A few that are pursuing campaigns include the University of California San Diego ($1 billion goal), Indiana University–Purdue University Indianapolis ($700 million goal), and the University of North Carolina at Charlotte ($100 million goal).

One of the greatest benefits for any institution of completing a major campaign is the opportunity to strengthen the endowment. The growth in endowments at public institutions, buoyed by campaigns and the run-up of the late 1990s bull market, propelled a number of public schools into exclusive territory. These successes set the tone for more public schools to build endowment reserves as a way to offset continued reductions in appropriations or unexpected mid-year budget cuts, which were all too common in the market crash that followed the dot-com

Table 7.4. Endowments of $1 Billion or More (Public Schools in Bold)

Rank	Market value as of June 30, 2003	
1	Harvard U	$18,849,491
2	Yale U	$11,034,600
3	Princeton U	$8,730,100
4	**U of Texas System**	**$8,708,818**
5	Stanford U	$8,614,000
6	Mass. Institute of Technology	$5,133,613
7	**U of California**	**$4,368,911**
8	Columbia U	$4,350,000
9	Emory U	$4,019,766
10	**Texas A&M U System and Fdns.**	**$3,802,712**
11	U of Pennsylvania	$3,547,473
12	**U of Michigan**	**$3,464,515**
13	Washington U, St. Louis	$3,454,704
14	U of Chicago	$3,221,833
15	Northwestern U	$3,051,167
16	Duke U	$3,017,261
17	Rice U	$2,937,649
18	Cornell U	$2,854,771
19	U of Notre Dame	$2,573,346
20	Dartmouth C	$2,121,183
21	U of Southern California	$2,113,666
22	Vanderbilt U	$2,019,139
23	**U of Virginia**	**$1,800,882**
24	Johns Hopkins U	$1,714,541
25	Brown U	$1,461,327
26	**U of Minnesota and Fdn.**	**$1,336,020**
27	Case Western Reserve U	$1,289,274
28	Rockefeller U	$1,278,100
29	New York U	$1,244,600
30	**Ohio State U and Fdn.**	**$1,216,574**
31	**U of Pittsburgh**	**$1,156,618**
32	California Institute of Technology	$1,145,216
33	U of Rochester	$1,127,350
34	Grinnell C	$1,111,615
35	**U of Washington**	**$1,103,197**
36	**U of North Carolina and Fdns.**	**$1,097,418**
37	Williams C	$1,082,336
38	**Purdue U**	**$1,056,767**
39	Wellesley C	$1,043,476

years. By 2003, 11 public institutions were among the 39 that held endowments valued at $1 billion or more, as illustrated in table 7.4 (National Association of College and University Business Officers 2004).

Philanthropy in the Twenty-first-century Public University

Operating within the reality of continued declines in state appropriations and limits to tuition increases allowed by their state legislatures, America's public colleges and universities are poised to place more widespread emphasis on seeking private support in the new century, following the lead set by the few dozen institutions that experienced success during the last quarter of the twentieth century. The increasingly competitive nature of higher education also seems to ensure the continued proliferation of the academic race to be the best. In defense of this trend, former Harvard University president Derek Bok makes no distinction between public and private institutions because any institution seeking success must continually acquire the resources necessary to meet its demands:

> Universities share one characteristic with compulsive gamblers and exiled royalty: there is never enough money to satisfy their desires. Faculty and students are forever developing new interests and ambitions, most of which cost money. The prices of books and journals rise relentlessly. Better and more costly technology and scientific apparatus constantly appear and must be acquired to stay at the cutting edge. Presidents and deans are anxious to satisfy as many of these needs as they can, for their reputation depends on pleasing the faculty, preserving the standing of the institution, and building a legacy through the development of new programs. (Bok 2003, 9)

As the leaders of America's public campuses continue to wrestle with this recurring dilemma, there is little doubt that institutional advancement will continue to grow in its importance as a central campus function. Advances in technology, although costly, are yielding more sophisticated ways to track and cultivate an institution's population of alumni and major gift prospects. Advancement practitioners are also entering the field with greater professional skills and knowledge, thanks to the emergence of academic degree programs in nonprofit management and philanthropic studies. More than 240 colleges and universities now offer credit programs in nonprofit management or fund raising; 97 offer graduate-level programs, and 66 offer noncredit programs (Levy 2004).

Leaders of public institutions also have reason to be optimistic for continued fund-raising success as the advancement of the profession coincides with a demographic event that holds the potential to transform many more public institutions than the few that have been highlighted here. The aging of the baby boomer population is expected to bring with it the largest intergenerational transfer of wealth ever experienced in this country, approximately $41 trillion by 2040, with at least $6 trillion going to charity (Havens and Schervish 2003).

But simply adding more staff and better technological tools to go out and ask more alumni for contributions endangers the long-term prospects for a public institution to develop a philanthropic culture among its graduates, which private institutions were able to do over their first century. As suggested earlier, this culture was developed and instilled during the student years, before graduates left the confines of their institution.

To adequately strengthen the prospects for greater financial support, especially from alumni, public institution leaders should invest in greater efforts to engage their current students into the life of the institution, giving them the understanding that their alma mater is more than just a place where they spent four years attending classes, living in dorms, or spending Saturday afternoons at the stadium cheering on the football team. As evident in the low alumni giving rates for public schools ranked in the nation's top 20, too many graduates leave public campuses without developing an "identification" with the institution, which Paul Schervish (1993, 1997) suggests must occur for an individual to become a committed donor to any cause. Only through "communities of participation" do individuals identify strongly enough with an organization to make a sustained commitment for their philanthropic support.

This theoretical construct of early engagement was applied to the alumni population of one of the nation's oldest and largest student organizations, the Indiana University Student Foundation (IUSF) (Conley and Tempel 2000). This student group was established in 1949 under the visionary leadership of Chancellor Herman B Wells and grew to become one of the largest and most active student organizations on the university campus. The purpose of the IUSF, as Wells noted in his autobiography (1980), was to acculturate a core group of students into the mission of the IU Foundation in hopes of long-term gains in greater alumni support: "From the beginning the purpose of the Foundation

169

was impressed upon them, as were the needs of the university and their role in interpreting those needs to other students. It was hoped and believed that they would carry this knowledge with them into their adult lives, when many of them might have the means and influence to have a major role in the Foundation's fund raising" (169–70).

After a half-century of activity, the 2000 study found a striking difference in giving between IU graduates from 1950 through 1989 who had been members of this organization as compared with other IU graduates. This included an analysis of donors versus nondonors, which found a far higher participation rate in giving among IUSF members, and an analysis of giving magnitude, which found that members of the organization gave as much as four to six times more than other graduates.

The lesson to be learned from this study and the data illustrated in this chapter is that greater sources of private support for public colleges and universities are out there too, but institutions run the risk of permanently turning off potential supporters. The development of a successful institutional advancement operation takes time, and those constituents who can be moved into a position of providing significant philanthropic resources will not respond to a million-dollar proposal simply because it comes from their alma mater. By following the private schools' model of offering a coordinated program that includes events for establishing and maintaining alumni engagement, publications that are informative and inspiring, and regular contact with development personnel to build relationships first before major gift solicitations, the years ahead will continue to reduce the distinction between institutional advancement programs on public and private college campuses.

References

Barnard, F. A. P. 1880. Two papers on academic degrees. As cited in F. Rudolph (1990), *The American college and university: A history*. Athens: University of Georgia Press.

Bok, D. 2003. *Universities in the marketplace: The commercialization of higher education*. Princeton, N.J.: Princeton University Press.

Breneman, D. W., and J. E. Finney. 1997. The changing landscape: Higher education finance in the 1990s. In *Public and private financing of higher education*, ed. P. M. Callahan and J. E. Finney, 30–59. Westport, Conn.: American Council on Education and Oryx Press.

Brittingham, B. E., and T. R. Pezzullo. 1990. *The campus green: Fund raising in higher education*. ASHE-ERIC Higher Education Report, No. 1. Washington D.C.: School of Education and Human Development, George Washington University.

Center on Philanthropy at Indiana University. 2004. *Million dollar list*. Available at http://www.philanthropy.iupui.edu/announce.html#million.

Chronicle of Higher Education. 2004a. Capital campaigns website: http://chronicle.
com/money/campaigns.php3.
———. 2004b. *Largest private gifts to higher education since 1967*. Available at http://
chronicle.com/stats/big_gifts.htm.
Conley, A., and G. Tempel. 2000. The student foundation as a community of participation: A study of its impact on alumni giving. *CASE International Journal of Educational Advancement* 1 (October): 120–34.
Council for Advancement and Support of Education. 2004. Website: http://www.case.
org/about.
Council for Aid to Education. 2004. *Charitable giving to higher education stabilizes in
2003: Gifts from alumni rebound after a sharp one-year decline*. Press release, March
11. Available at http://www.cae.org/content/pdf/VSE-PressRelease2004.pdf.
Cutlip, S. M. 1965. *Fund raising in the United States: Its role in American philanthropy*.
New Brunswick, N.J.: Rutgers University Press.
Florida Atlantic University Foundation. 2001. *Annual report*. Boca Raton, Fla.: Author.
Georgia Institute of Technology. 2001. *Georgia Tech celebrates $712 million campaign*.
Institute Communications and Public Affairs. Press release, April 17. Available at
www.gatech.edu/news-room/archive/news_releases/end-of-campaign.html.
Havens, J. J., and P. G. Schervish. 2003. Why the $41 trillion wealth transfer estimate
is still valid: A review of challenges and comments. *Journal of Gift Planning* 7:
11–15, 47–50.
Indiana University Foundation. 2004. Website: www.iufoundation.org.
Kennedy, D. 1995. Another century's end, another revolution for higher education.
Change, May/June, 8–15.
Kerr, C. 1991. The new race to b Harvard or Berkeley or Stanford. *Change* 23(3): 8–
15.
Levy, J. J. 2004. The growth of fundraising: Framing the impact of research and literature on education and training. In *Fundraising as a profession: Advancements and
challenges in the field*, ed. L. Wagner and J. P. Ryan, 21–30. New Directions in Phil-
anthropic Fundraising, No. 43. San Francisco: Jossey-Bass.
National Association of College and University Business Officers. 2004. Higher education endowments still struggled in FY03. Press release, February 5. Available at
http://www.nacubo.org/x2398.xml.
National Center for Education Statistics. 2002. *Digest of education statistics 2001*.
NCES 2002–130. Washington D.C.: National Center for Education Statistics.
Pulley, J. L. 2003. Struggling against the tide: Ambitious fund-raising campaigns press
on despite the economic downturn and world events. *Chronicle of Higher Education*, February 28, A29.
Rudolph, F. 1990. *The American college and university: A history*. Athens: University of
Georgia Press.
Schervish, P. G. 1993. Philanthropy as a moral identity of *caritas*. In *Taking giving seriously*, ed. P. G. Schervish, O. Benz, P. Dulaney, T. B. Murphy, and S. Salett,
85–103. Indianapolis: The Center on Philanthropy at Indiana University.
———. 1997. Inclination, obligation, and association: What we know and what we
need to learn about donor motivation. In *Critical issues in fund raising*, ed. D. F.
Burlingame, 110–38. New York: John Wiley and Sons.
Sears, J. B. 1922. Philanthropy in the history of American higher education. Washington, D.C.: Government Printing Office. Cited in F. Rudolph (1990), *The American
college and university: A history*. Athens: University of Georgia Press.

171

Spanier, G. B. 2004. *The privatization of American public higher education.* Remarks by Graham B. Spanier to the University Faculty Senate. Available at http://president.psu.edu/presentations/privatization_031604.pdf.

Strout, E. 2004. It's $300-million, but don't call it a gift. *Chronicle of Higher Education,* May 28, A24.

University of Colorado System. 2003. *Beyond boundaries campaign fact sheet,* September 12. Available at http://www.cu.edu/downloads/BeyondBoundaries_facts.pdf.

U.S. News and World Report. 2004. *America's best colleges.* Washington, D.C.: U.S. News and World Report.

Wells, H. B. 1980. *Being lucky.* Bloomington: Indiana University Press.

Worth, M. J. 1985. *Public college and university development.* Washington, D.C.: Council for Advancement and Support of Education.

———. 2002. The historical overview. In *New strategies for educational fund raising,* ed. M. J. Worth, 24–35. Westport, Conn.: American Council on Education and Praeger.

Yudof, M. G. 2002. Is the public research university dead? *Chronicle of Higher Education,* January 11, B24.

III

MODERNIZING
PUBLIC UNIVERSITIES

CHAPTER EIGHT

Incentive-Based Budgeting Systems in the Emerging Environment

Douglas M. Priest and Rachel Dykstra Boon

Allocation of institutional resources is a significant factor in university life. In theory, an institution's allocation of its resources reflects its aspirations. Chapter 4 of this volume suggests that universities will raise all the money they can and spend all the money that they raise (Bowen, 1980) in light of expanding bases of economic support for universities. Bowen was correct, and although many university administrators may not have liked to admit the accuracy of the statement then, they do even less now as budgetary times have become quite tight through economic recessions at the local, state, and national level.

Public institutions exist in a more complex environment now than in previous times. State appropriations are not keeping pace with volume increases, inflation, and institutional aspirations; and the effect is a downturn in the ratio of state funds to total university budget. The competition for students is fierce on almost every level as the advent of such publications as *U.S. News and World Report*'s annual college and university rankings have armed students and parents with information they can use in making choices about where to get a college education. However, the rankings have also shown university administrators very clearly who their competitors are and the measures on which they may choose to focus if they wish to be considered more like the institutions *USNWR* readers consider better than their own. The drive to improve in the rankings has an effect of forcing costs up. Almost no institution is without another that it emulates either in academic quality, in fund-raising prowess, or in state-of-the-art facilities. In this regard, competition between universities is not limited to battles between athletic teams but also involves admissions offices, development offices, and faculty recruiting.

In that competitive sense, all but a select few institutions are lacking in resources, and the resources that are available are highly sought after by nearly every department on most campuses. The pressure for increased revenue production has lead many to the conclusion that tuition is the most promising source for funding new ventures. Adding more tuition-paying students to the campus is the clearest way to reach that objective, though the capacity for new students is generally limited by facilities and faculty. Various pricing strategies can be employed that raise tuition, that vary charged tuition amounts in consideration of aid availability, or that adjust the mix of in-state and out-of-state students. Calls for reduction in overhead and instructional-related activities costs not directly related to the objectives of USNWR ratings are also demanded as a way to shore up resources. Decisions on how to distribute those resources gained or saved most effectively are often contentious, and that situation is not likely to change no matter what budget system or decision-making mechanism is in place.

In this environment it is natural for public universities and colleges to examine budget mechanisms that are touted as modes of reining in spending and encouraging revenue maximization. Higher education has a history of watching other sectors for guidance on best management principles for budget methodologies. Zero-based budgeting; planning, programming, and budgeting systems (PPBS); and performance-based budgeting are all examples of mechanisms that have at one time or another been appropriated by colleges or universities as much-sought-after budgeting tools.

In the last couple of decades, Responsibility Center Management (RCM), known by a variety of acronyms at the diverse institutions where it is employed, has become another way of managing budgets within an institution to encourage entrepreneurship, efficiency, and educationally sound choices. RCM has been defined as involving "decentralization of responsibility coupled with the authority to make decisions" (Whalen 2002, 11), particularly in regard to revenues and expenditures at each responsibility center. Considering an incentive-based mechanism such as RCM is not unusual for an institution, given this budget mode's claims for creating opportunities for maximizing revenue while providing incentives that inform cost reduction activities and investment of dollars. This chapter will explore private sector budgeting and its relationship to RCM, tracing the history of RCM at private and public institutions, and showing how it affects operations at public institutions of higher education in practice. An understanding of other budget mechanisms will help to illustrate what makes RCM and its incentive-producing practices an alternative route to values and standards commonly found in the private sector.

Background in the Private Sector

For-profit businesses have historically run on economic theories of profit and competition in an effort to be successful. The theory of the firm dates back to Adam Smith's idea, published in 1776, that specialization via division of labor increases productivity. Coordinating the specialization is crucial, and according to the theory of the firm, entails finding ways to "ensure the interests of the agents (specialists) are aligned with the interest of the principal (owner)" and "is achieved mainly through the use of monitoring and incentives" (Phelan and Lewin 2000, 308–309).

In the for-profit business setting, individual divisions of a larger firm are often motivated to improve performance with the tantalizing carrot of bonuses to management of the division with great innovations or profit margins in a given fiscal year. An example of such a company is the General Electric Corporation (GE). The corporation has a single "brand-name" identifier but is internally broken into three dozen units. The specialization at the unit level is to maximize the benefits of having experts doing tasks and managing each area as well as the result of company-wide efforts to increase the number and range of revenue streams. Maintaining budgets and financial targets at the unit level allows the central management a clear vision of profitability for each division as it contributes to the profits of the entire corporation. Allowing each unit to maintain excess profits for reinvestment into capital, research and development, or employee bonuses as they comply with corporate regulations gives the decentralized managers a valuable incentive to have the most efficient unit possible. This system has worked very well for GE and other companies that have done the same thing as revenues have remained strong or continued to climb.[1]

These business principles have proved easily transferable to universities, though with some important distinctions. Specialization of curriculum in universities came along, not as an internal imperative that was profit-driven, but as the outside world and the students demanded it (Rudolph 1977). In a truly capitalistic economic sense, they adapted to what consumers were demanding in order to maintain enrollments and thus ensure their survival as entities. Increased specialization through departments and separate colleges of business, education, arts and sciences, and so forth, under the umbrella of a single university demanded more monitoring; thus vice presidents, deans, assistant deans, and other positions have proliferated, culminating in the much-maligned present-day increased "administrative ratchet" (Massy and Zemsky 1990). The part of the puzzle that has been missing, however, according to the theory of the firm, is the use of incentives to encourage efficiency and motivation among these many and varied monitors of the specialized divisions of universities.

Private institutions were the first to recognize that, given the limitations of funding sources and high dependence on tuition, budgeting cues could be taken from the business world and applied to the university setting. While the ultimate goal of the firm is to earn a profit, universities tend to focus their missions on the three key faculty activities of teaching, research, and service (Middaugh 2001). The pursuit of prestige is an element within the mission that is important, even if rarely mentioned. Part of the stimulus for institutions to use business-world methods is based on the essential competitiveness that all institutions feel with each other and those they emulate. For private institutions whose funding sources are primarily tuition and private fund raising, matching goals of superior teaching, research, and service with business principles of budgeting is attractive because it would help the institutions avoid some of the limitations and politics of state-provided funding. In this vein, program reviews and financial assessments of departments have long been staples of institutions looking for a balance between educational best practice and economic efficiency.

Harvard was the first to decide that a substantial change in financial operations might improve operations on many other levels. In the 1970s Harvard's administration instituted RCM with the concept of "every tub on its own bottom" as the rule of thumb (Whalen 1991). The rest of the community of higher education budget officers undoubtedly watched with great interest and skepticism to see how this would work out for Harvard, but without much delay other private institutions began to appropriate RCM into their own operations. At the University of Pennsylvania the push for RCM began in the early 1970s with the president championing it as a way to make faculty more aware of financial issues when making demands regarding academic issues. At Penn, RCM worked to improve the communication between faculty and administration while bringing marketplace incentives to bear on the system. The University of Southern California joined the ranks in the early 1980s when an administrator moved there from Penn and with the support of other top-level officials instituted Revenue Center Management. By this time the ball was rolling with greater momentum, and other institutions across the nation were taking notice of aspects of the budgeting style that brought elements of the market to these private institutions of higher education (Strauss and Curry 2002).

Public Institutions of Higher Education

Public institutions began in the late 1980s to recognize that there might be compelling reasons to begin looking into the practices of private institutions as guideposts. During periods of economic downturn at the national and state level, budget cuts quickly trickle down to cuts in higher education appropriations, leading institutions to become much more dependent on tuition to cover expenses, a trend likely to continue in the near future. Toutkoushian (2003) notes that "theoretical and empirical studies of state funding for higher education suggest that in the current economic environment, state funding for higher education is more likely to decline than it is to increase" (33). He further notes that studies have shown that an increase in enrollments does correlate with an increase in appropriations, but the rates of increase are unequal. With many states projecting enrollment increases through 2010, the financial need of institutions will continue to outpace resources appropriated by the state. This, of course, has pushed tuition at public institutions up over the years to what today are considered "crisis levels," as many states and the federal government discuss creating tuition caps for colleges and universities (though few have been instituted).

Indiana University was among the first of the public institutions to establish a budget mechanism for the campus that followed the more firm-like principles of a private institution. RCM was established at Indiana in 1990 after a new president with successful experiences using RCM as provost at Penn arrived. He spent a few years convincing the rest of the administration and campus that it was not only feasible but was a fiscal and managerial improvement for a public institution to use this method of budgeting. The large enrollment and multi-college/school arrangement meant that the central administrators were making financial decisions regarding programs about which they knew very little. Decentralizing was logical to many because of the constraints of adequately communicating all useful information to central decision makers. This is not to say that there were no hurdles on the path to a new budgeting system. However, once faculty and the deans were adequately convinced that the ability to make their own decisions would be enhanced and academic integrity would not be jeopardized, the university was able to go ahead with launching RCM (Whalen 1991).

The size of Indiana University today (38,000 students, $1 billion operating budget) continues to merit these considerations of the power of decentralization. Regularly scheduled campus-wide reviews of RCM have allowed many adjustments and improvements to be made as elements of RCM that did not work well were adjusted to a format that made sense given the unique needs of the institution and individual units. In fact, faculty reviews have shown that involving the faculty in all stages of the process has been a key factor in its success (Ruesink and Thompson 1996; Theobald and Thompson 2000). Adjustments were made at the conclusion of both reviews, however, to better apply RCM to Indiana University. Beyond minor changes in several areas, the biggest change in 1996 was the addition of a Chancellor's Discretionary Fund to enable central campus administration to help finance on a year-to-year basis projects that supported the mission of the university, were sound investments, or improved quality. After the 2000 review, adjustments to the complex algorithms for allocations were made not only to simplify them but also to bring about changes that reflected an environment that had changed over the course of a decade (Gros Louis and Thompson 2002).

The experiences of other public institutions exhibit how different campus environments can have a strong impact on the outcomes of implementing RCM. At the University of Michigan in 1997 a version of this budgeting system called Value Centered Management (VCM) was implemented. With a strong tendency toward decentralization already present in many operations at Michigan, it seemed natural to progress to a decentralized form of budgeting. Michigan created an activity-based system that would "hold all units harmless" in the first year as they changed from the more incremental system of the past (Courant and Knepp 2002). However, several changes in leadership during the implementation time and a cool faculty reception to what was perceived as a business model being imposed on an academic system meant that adjustments were being made to VCM almost immediately. Ultimately, Michigan discovered that a system that would work for them would be a derivation of VCM. An increased amount of central control over the budget was added to the new University Budget system

(UB) to allow more control and support for campus-wide activities than one would typically be found in a RCM system (Courant and Knepp 2002). At Michigan, university history and culture were just as important in making decisions on budgeting as any financial or economic theory presented.

The University of Toronto has a much longer history of RCM-style budgeting, dating back to the late 1980s. Though it is a semipublic institution (45% of UT's revenues are from the federal government, but no level of government has formal control of the institution), the University of Toronto has maintained a high level of autonomy in day-to-day operations and planning. Shortfalls in allocations from the federal government and soaring research costs not covered through grants were two factors that pushed the institution to consider creating cost centers in the mid-1980s. Central to the model they chose was an assessment of the sources of income and the categories of expense to which the sources could be applied (Lang 2002). Also critically important was the ability to use this budget model for strategic planning purposes. It was hoped that folding the budget into this process would lead to decision making that aligned goals and resources. The budget model at the University of Toronto was affected by a mixture of market forces, educational objectives, and research goals, creating a system with varied levels of decentralization depending on the needs of each unit or situation.

Other Modes of Budgeting

Prior to RCM, other forms of budgeting have made appearances in the public sector, though they almost always have fallen by the wayside as time passed. One mode of budgeting that was prominent in the late 1970s was zero-based budgeting. This method requires explaining all expenditures each new period, as opposed to the more incremental method of only explaining and ranking the functions of a unit to request funds that might be necessary, and it has benefits in the self-examination and justification it regularly requires. For businesses, this means the impact of quarterly earnings and effective use of resources in increasing those earnings is crucial. In universities, the promise of zero-based budgeting is enticing, but many institutions have found that academic units have a very difficult time with the ranking process for funding requests (Wainwright 1992). Each program or major within a unit can seem to have equally valid reasons for its request, and the dean or vice president who decides that one gets priority over another can lose

181

credibility from any number of people after making such a determination.

Similarly, the planning, programming, and budgeting systems (PPBS) method of management has been examined for its potential for organizing budget operations. The U.S. Department of Defense has been the most chronicled user of PPBS. It is based on the concept that budgeting should flow from good plans, so developing these plans at the program level and integrating budget forecasting emphasizes this flow. Difficulties cropping up for universities can include the inability to create accurate budget forecasts when so much depends on fluctuating enrollment figures. A shortfall of a hundred students from the projected enrollment can be a serious setback for small institutions or units in particular.

Another trend has been toward performance-based budgeting, which many businesses have seen as a useful tool for decades, but to which state governments started to rally only in the mid-1980s, led by Tennessee's charge in 1978 (Burke 2002). Allocating resources based on the past performance of a unit instead of on projected needs or well-pleaded requests is the core of performance-based budgeting. Designating the appropriate indicators for measuring performance is a contentious issue, but many states and universities have made adaptations to deal with that. In states such as Florida, Missouri, Ohio, South Carolina, and Tennessee, many of the prescribed details may differ from the purest form of performance-based budgeting, but the underlying conception remains the guide (Burke 2002).

None of the incentive-based systems of budgeting, including RCM, is used in its pristine form, generally speaking. Typically, selling the values of a given system but then tailoring them to individual situations means appending a new system to what was likely some form of incremental budgeting previously in use at the institution. The attraction of incremental budgeting is its predictability, a quality that managers, deans, or vice presidents are loath to lose in the switch to any other system. Individualizing incentive-based systems to contain an element of incremental budgeting can result in having the benefit of the incentives in the new system with the stability and guarantees of the old system.

Each form of budgeting discussed above (other than strict incremental budgeting) has in common with the others the use of incentives, and that may be the real story in how the various systems play out and become effective, even in their watered-down, incrementalized forms. Understanding the theory of how any given budgeting system works in a pure form and enacting a piecemeal adaptation for one's own circumstances requires a degree of sophistication that is perhaps underappreciated at universities. Indiana, Penn, and Michigan all experienced this with RCM in varying degrees, just as the SUNY system in New York and the state system in Pennsylvania experienced it with performance-based budgeting (Burke 2002).

The Implications for RCM

The future of RCM at public universities, thus, does not necessarily look exactly like anything that can be precisely described in the application of the concepts. The myriad components need to be managed in a way that works, but a good place to start is with the three categories of incentives that need stimulation or management.

First, *assessments of the units that provide nonacademic services* on campus must be utilized as an incentive to hold down overhead costs. Assessments support activities of non-degree-granting units (e.g., student affairs services, libraries, central administration) in order to advance the mission of the university. Positive results of assessments can include energy-saving policies within units, more efficient use of space to reduce rent (which in turn frees up space for others without new construction being necessary), and a more thoughtful integration of many other university-provided, assessment-funded services. Careful management of library acquisitions, computing services, and student services also provides more accountability to academic constituencies in the use of scarce resources. RCM should be able to provide incentives to fund those support services in ways that are most conducive to achieving institutional missions, most of which are academic in nature. Providing support in ways that get at objectives while using the fewest dollars possible is the goal because institutions want as much as possible to put their resources into academic areas. This is not a concept that excludes providing more funding to support units, however. For example, activities of nonacademic units might very well help improve the retention rate at an institution by enhancing the overall quality of students' experiences. Generally speaking, a by-product of increased retention is additional tuition dollars to the institution without having to spend on recruitment to replace non-returners; so support units might require more funding to help reach this goal. Decisions regarding assessments require an enlightened focus on long-term benefits over short-term concerns.

The second category of incentives is the *management of academic planning through goal-directed expenditures*. With efficiency as a principle consideration, incentives can drive units through their academic planning process to produce sound fiscal plans simultaneously. Planning within units in most incremental systems tends to be a game of drafting a "wish list" to determine the greatest possible amount of money that can be obtained from the central administration in the next year. A unit can maintain its wish list in a system of RCM as well, but with the budgetary control largely in its own hands, the likelihood of making realistic adjustments to existing resources to create the desired opportunities is much greater.

Finally, *developing incremental resources to increase what is available for use in leaner times* is a great incentive for individual units and the wider university. It is a correlative of dependency theory that generating a reserve is a good way to provide for a year of budget shortfalls within a unit or a university as a whole.

Resource dependency theory may provide a useful way of considering the economics of universities. In this theory the economic development of an entity is explained by the external influences on it, influences that are political, economic, and cultural and that vary for each entity. Equally important for universities is how they react to these external influences, often reinforcing the pattern of dependency. For public institutions of higher education, budgetary dependence on the state (or municipality in some cases) and tuition from students affects the economic development and change that the institutions are able to undertake. A year of paltry tuition income could devastate a tuition-dependent institution that does not carefully control and manage itself. An examination of resource dependence by Pfeffer and Salancik (1978) notes that "the ease of developing the capacity to accept other inputs or for creating other outputs depends on the current state of knowledge and the flexibility of the organization's technology" (109). Without a budget mechanism like RCM that allows for carefully managed, unit-level ways of dealing with surpluses and shortfalls, a university's resource dependence could be the source of its downfall.

Studies of university financing based on resource dependence to determine if sources of income were indicating direction in the use of the funds have found that the source matters in terms of where money is spent at the university level (Hasbrouck 1997). Money talks in most institutions of higher education, and resource dependence is a culprit in the persistence of that activity. Another study (Leslie, Oaxaca, and Rhoades 2002) notes similar relationships at the department and individual faculty member levels, though the strength of the relationship is decreased.

184

Conclusion

There has been a great deal of conversation about private sector principles as they apply to public universities. It is clear that incentive-based budgeting can play an appropriate role in that application. Massy (2004) points out, however, "today's markets lack the self-correcting mechanisms needed to address current problems." Specifically, he refers to "the market's ability to constrain prices and the universities' ability to assert their own internal values through cross subsidies" (32). Incentives are an effective market tool, but matching incentives with objectives consistent with institution building is the key for universities, and that is difficult with pure economic modeling. Rather, it takes insightful administrative governance to pull the levers of various incentives in appropriate degrees and to counterbalance that with cross-subsidies to match academic aspirations. Given the complexity of participatory governance structures, this is particularly difficult. Identified incentives are complemented by this full institutional vision of resources available to support and promote goals. However, effective leadership recognizes that the value attached to various incentives will change with the ebb and flow of the environment and institutional requirements. In years past, a higher proportion of state funds for public universities likely made the idea of market-based incentives fairly unattractive. Changes in the market meant that the state was making adjustments to its spending, but institutions of higher education seemed assured of receiving a substantial portion of their budget regardless of the broader economic situation. Recent trends and predictions change that outlook, however, because increased enrollments have not resulted in increased state appropriations, and the resulting desire for new levers of control over budgets has led to incentive-based plans.

In keeping with the primary institutional missions of teaching, research, and service, one can envision how a specific mode of budgeting can affect these endeavors. Market-driven strategies of RCM can affect enrollment behavior and other revenue-generating behavior that may have implications for student access in certain programs. Service can be reduced or go unrewarded because it is not funded unless it produces revenue or reduces overhead. Finally, as is increasingly the case, research can be required to be self-sustaining or even profit-generating in ways more consistent with the private sector.

The vagaries of the marketplace are also an important consideration for institutional officers dealing with financial issues. Planning for the future to support the mission of the university can be supplemented with relationships to market forces, but only in moderation. A tool important to a top-level university administrator is a discretionary funds account. In an incentive-based system that depends on certain market forces, discretionary spending informed by university mission or values can mitigate the negativities of the market's treatment of important entities. The market is not always kind to departments of philosophy or religion, but a university with a strong emphasis on liberal arts education will support those departments with discretionary spending, thus, although removing the purity of an incentive-based system, maintaining the mission of the institution. The option of discretionary spending should not be assumed from year to year by any unit, however, since this would remove the usefulness of incentives and since devoting too much of the budget to discretionary spending will obliterate much of the effectiveness of incentives campus wide.

Competition with peers and aspirants seems to be a strong driving force for universities today. In light of flagging state appropriations and greater public accountability, it should not surprise anyone that the benefits of privatization have begun to appear attractive to university administrators. As the private sector and private universities have shown us, the use of incentives and Revenue Center Management can provide a public institution with some useful tools. These tools will not be enough, however, if the institution does not have the culture and leadership to tailor whatever budget style it chooses to the local situation. If there is an atmosphere of distrust, stability in yearly revenue disbursement can help. If deans or departments want to be self-supported and managed, the administration can provide the financial and management tools for them to make necessary decisions regarding the stream of revenues and expenditures. In either case, the values and mission of the institution need to be asserted by understanding each unit's role and supporting it in any way that is fiscally and administratively possible. The wave of the future in university budgeting and management may just be customized systems of base and incentive budgeting and funding that uniquely support the mission and strategic plan of each institution.

Notes

1. GE's 2003 revenues were $134.2 billion, an increase of 1.9 percent over 2002, which saw an increase of 5 percent over 2001's revenues of $125.9 billion. See http://www.ge.com/en/company/companyinfo/at_a_glance/fact_sheet.htm, and http://www.ge.com/files/usa/en/company/investor/downloads/4Q02_earnings_press_release2.pdf.

References

Bowen, H. H. 1980. *The costs of higher education: How much colleges and universities spend per student and how much should they spend?* San Francisco: Jossey-Bass.

Burke, J. C. 2002. *Funding public colleges and universities for performance: Popularity, problems, and prospects.* Albany: State University of New York Press.

Courant, P. N., and M. Knepp. 2002. Activity-based budgeting at the University of Michigan. In *Incentive-based budgeting systems in public universities*, ed. D. Priest, W. E. Becker, D. Hossler, and E. P. St. John, 137–60. Northampton, Mass.: Edward Elgar.

Gros Louis, K. R. R., and M. Thompson. 2002. Responsibility center budgeting and management at Indiana University. In *Incentive-based budgeting systems in public universities*, ed. D. Priest, W. E. Becker, D. Hossler, and E. P. St. John, 93–108. Northampton, Mass.: Edward Elgar.

Hasbrouck, N. S. 1997. Implications of the changing funding base of public universities. Unpublished doctoral dissertation. Tucson: University of Arizona.

Lang, D. W. 2002. Responsibility center budgeting at the university of Toronto. In *Incentive-based budgeting systems in public universities*, ed. D. Priest, W. E. Becker, D. Hossler, and E. P. St. John, 109–36. Northampton, Mass.: Edward Elgar.

Leslie, L. L., R. L. Oaxaca, and G. Rhoades. 2002. Revenue flux and university behavior. In *Incentive-based budgeting systems in public universities*, ed. D. Priest, W. E. Becker, D. Hossler, and E. P. St. John, 55–92. Northampton, Mass.: Edward Elgar.

Massy, W. F. 2004. Collegium economicum. *Change* 36(4): 27–35.

Massy, W. F., and R. Zemsky. 1990. *The dynamics of academic productivity: A seminar.* Seminar conducted at the meeting of the State Higher Education Executive Officers Association, March 2, Denver, Colorado.

Middaugh, M. F. 2001. Academic problems and faculty issues. In *Institutional research: Decision support in higher education*, ed. R. D. Howard. Tallahassee, Fla.: Association for Institutional Research.

Pfeffer, J., and G. R. Salancik. 1978. *The external control of organizations: A resource dependence perspective.* New York: Harper and Row.

Phelan, S. E., and P. Lewin. 2000. Arriving at a strategic theory of the firm. *International Journal of Management Reviews* 2(4): 305–23.

Rudolph, F. 1977. *Curriculum: A history of the American undergraduate course of study since 1636.* San Francisco: Jossey-Bass.

Ruesink, A., and M. Thompson. 1996. *Responsibility-centered management at Indiana University Bloomington: 1990–1995.* Final report of the 1995–96 Responsibility-Centered Management Review Committee submitted to the Chancellor, Indiana University Bloomington.

Strauss, J. C., and J. R. Curry. 2002. *Responsibility center management: Lessons from 25 years of decentralized management.* Washington, D.C.: National Association of College and University Business Officers.

Theobald, N., and M. Thompson. 2000. *Responsibility-centered management at Indiana University Bloomington: 1990–2000.* Final report of the 1999–2000 Responsibility-Centered Management Review Committee submitted to the Chancellor, Indiana University Bloomington.

Toutkoushian, R. T. 2003. Weathering the storm: Generating revenues for higher education during a recession. In *Maximizing revenue in higher education*, ed. F. K. Alexander and R. G. Ehrenberg, 27–40. San Francisco: Jossey-Bass.

Wainwright, A. 1992. Overview of financial accounting and reporting. In *College and university business administration: Fiscal functions*, Vol. 2, ed. D. M. Greene. National Association of College and University Business Officers.

Whalen, E. L. 1991. *Responsibility center budgeting: An approach to decentralized management for institutions of higher education.* Bloomington: Indiana University Press.

———. 2002. The case, if any, for responsibility center budgeting. In *Incentive-based budgeting systems in public universities*, ed. D. Priest, W. E. Becker, D. Hossler, and E. P. St. John, 9–24. Northampton, Mass.: Edward Elgar.

CHAPTER NINE

Privatization of Business
and Auxiliary Functions

Douglas M. Priest, Bruce A. Jacobs,
and Rachel Dykstra Boon

Business and auxiliary units have come to play increasingly significant roles in the modern American university during recent decades. Although auxiliaries are often characterized as self-supporting, this is not
universally true. As they have grown in number and scope, auxiliaries
have become targets for privatization because they have come to represent a larger proportion of college and university budgets as well as consuming the time of administrators. In some cases, auxiliaries require subsidies from the campus, some of which do not appear on balance sheets.
However, in other cases, they are providing resources to the campus at
large, an alluring prospect from many administrators' point of view.

The migration toward larger, and in some cases increasingly complex, auxiliary functions has coincided with a call for accountability and
business standards by boards, administrators, and the private sector. For
the most part, well-intentioned efforts at privatization are undertaken,
but unintended consequences can result. This chapter will examine the
history of privatizing auxiliaries at universities; discuss current issues in
auxiliary management through institutional examples; and review implications regarding institutional financial performance, culture, and
administration. The authors will discuss the nature of auxiliaries and
their functions as well as their scope and roles in the academic setting.
This is important particularly because they serve consumers and generate resources in an environment that, for public institutions of higher

education, is increasingly dependent on earned income and continually demands new ways to deliver administrative and support services efficiently and effectively.

First, it is important to identify and define key terms. For the purposes of this chapter we refer to "business functions" as those general-fund-supported activities that might include fiscal functions such as budgeting, costing and pricing, taxation, and debt management, to name but a few (Ford 1992, 17). Generally, these functions are attended to by a chief financial or business officer who must consider the benefit of the entire institution with each decision. An "auxiliary unit" represents "an activity that charges individuals for its services" (Powell et al. 1992, 1193). Examples found on many campuses include student housing, food services, bookstores, vending, health services, and laundry services. Depending on the size of the institution and the rates of on-campus residency, these services can have many thousands of constituents and customers, encompassing significant segments of the life of the institution. Finally, the terms "outsourcing" and "privatizing" are often used interchangeably, and that is largely the case in this chapter as we discuss public institutions of higher education. However, one should note that private universities are by definition already privatized in many ways; thus it is common for them to outsource their auxiliary services to other private entities.

A limited survey of public institutions showed that the proportion of university expenditures attributable to auxiliary and service units is from 10 to 20 percent at most public institutions today. This suggests operations of great significance to the campus at large in terms of service offerings but also considerable business functions taking place to manage these operations.

Background

Early in the history of higher education in colonial America, colleges became concerned with providing residence halls for their students, if for no other reason than to exert control over the particulars of students' lives. Some administrators, however, felt that they might be a "needless extravagance and an impediment to the very purpose for which they were intended" (Lucas 1994, 127). Age-old complaints about food service quality are documented from early in the nineteenth century (Rudolph 1965). Largely, though, starting around the turn of the twentieth century the increased size of enrollments and the demand for services provided the impetus for new functions, roles, and divisions to be added to universities. At the time many accusations of an overwhelming business ethos taking over were aimed at administrators by members of the faculty. Not to be excluded from the ire was one of the most attention-garnering auxiliaries at many institutions today: the athletics department. The first organized collegiate football game was in 1869 when Rutgers played Princeton (Lucas 1994), and since then these auxiliary units alone have risen to multimillion dollar expenditure levels annually at NCAA Division I institutions.

The location of many colleges and universities undoubtedly played a role in the evolution of auxiliary services as well. In the United States during the eighteenth, nineteenth, and much of the twentieth centuries, the founding and growth of institutions of higher education took place in small communities that lacked the resources, and perhaps the will, to provide services for numbers of young people that chose to avail themselves of the local institutions' curriculum. This implied that if students were to be housed, "appropriately" entertained, fed, and protected, colleges had to provide facilities such as dormitories and union buildings as well as fire and police protection (Lucas 1994). These were deemed essential to student health and academic pursuits. As time passed and perceptions of student needs and demands evolved, institutions responded with the addition of communication networks, food courts, recreational fitness facilities, and bookstores that devote much of their shelf space to anything but books. Clark Kerr notes that "yet more attention is now paid by some students to the consumer aspects of college attendance—to enjoyment of the college experience as a 'slice of life,' and to preparation for the cultural components of post-college life" (1994, 72).

Moreover, colleges and universities came increasingly to be located in metropolitan and urban settings (Rudolph 1977). In these locales, for-profit businesses not only were of a size that could provide services to the college community but also saw a large enough market to make associated profits attractive. For local businesses, this shift has also meant that institutions of higher education and their auxiliary services are viewed as competition for the local market share. Associated with this phenomenon is the fact that transportation (delivery) systems have advanced beyond anything that could have been imagined even fifty years ago. Higher education today is in an environment where partnerships with for-profit organizations appear to be mutually lucrative. The experience of these partnerships and the push toward them is worth exploring.

191

In the United States today, higher education is viewed with increasing suspicion with regard to the efficiency and effectiveness with which it performs what are thought of as essentially business or economic functions (Kerr 1994). State legislators are critical of requests for additional funds, and taxpayers are critical of rising tuition levels for their children at in-state institutions. Even within institutions, various departments view each other or business and administrative functions as being inefficient or wasteful with the limited funds available. As a result, institutions have looked for ways to increase efficiency and save funds wherever possible.

As Heller points out in chapter 1 of this volume, state funding for public universities is an ever-diminishing amount of the total budget, from just under 50 percent in 1980 to 35 percent in 2000. Tuition has become a very important way to increase revenue, but many states are weighing in by setting—or threatening to set—limits to tuition increases. Institutions are searching for revenue opportunities, for reduced if not eliminated subsidies for auxiliary and service units, and for continually greater efficiency in operation of business functions and academic support areas. The goal is to have the highest possible proportion of institutional funds devoted to the academic units' pursuit of the traditional missions of teaching, research, and service. Not only does this fit with the objectives of most institutions, but it appeals to the public's perception of the use of seemingly huge amounts of tax and tuition dollars. Contributions from auxiliary services to these academic goals can be overlooked at times, thus privatization has the possibility of actually undermining pursuit of these goals if not handled properly.

Jefferies (1996) reports that colleges and universities have been looking more and more to outsourcing as a way to reduce costs, increase service efficiencies, and boost income. A review of the data from that period supports his statement. As Agron (2001) reported in the annual survey conducted by *American School and University*, outsourcing was on the rise in the early 1990s. While this trend continued through the 1990s, a slight decrease has been seen in some areas in recent years. Agron also reported that a smaller percentage of colleges and universities plan on using outsourcing in the future. The five most outsourced services by percentages are food service, vending, bookstore operations, custodial work, and laundries. Between 1995 and 1996 each of these services saw increases in the percentage being outsourced. Custodial services for academic buildings saw the biggest increase, going from 22.8 percent of colleges using a private contractor to 30.7 percent over the one-year period. Food service followed with an overall increase of

6.6 percent, moving from 67.7 to 74.3 percent. Vending increased from 63.8 to 65.3 percent, laundries from 17.3 to 18.8 percent; bookstore operations increased the least, from 33.1 to 33.7 percent.

American School and University conducted the seventh annual Privatization/Contract Services Survey and published the results in 2001 (Agron 2001). The survey indicated that the trend, first noticed in the sixth survey in 1999, continued with a decline in the number of schools that were using outsourcing. A comparison of the five areas named above does not tell the entire story. In these areas outsourcing of bookstore operations increased from 33.7 to 45.7 percent (most likely due to incentive programs that private contractors were offering), laundry service went up slightly from 18.8 to 20.6 percent, and food service stayed virtually the same, going from 74.3 to 74.6 percent. Outsourcing of custodial services declined from 30.7 to 26.3 percent, and vending dropped off from 65.3 to 63.2 percent. A closer examination of the data shows that fewer colleges were outsourcing in 2001 than in 1999. In 1999, 5.3 percent of schools did not outsource at all, and the number grew to 6 percent in 2001. In 1999 44 percent of schools outsourced five or more services, while in 2001 only 34 percent were outsourcing five or more services. When asked in 2001, approximately 36 percent of higher education institutions projected that they would be increasing the use of outsourcing. That number is compared to 37 percent in 1999 and 54 percent in 1997. Clearly, outsourcing has a place in the management of today's colleges and universities but a lesser place than was predicted by Jefferies almost a decade ago.

Institutional Experiences
Addressing Privatization

Outsourcing can take a different shape in each institutional situation and for each different service area. A review of different decisions on outsourcing versus self-operation will show the types of considerations, implications, and consequences encountered in the process of outsourcing services. In the mid-1990s a housing operation on a large Midwestern campus was facing a number of issues related to its overall operation. It had an aging physical plant, a dining system that was not well-received by the residents, and a resulting declining occupancy rate. A decision was made to re-engineer the entire housing operation. A thorough review of the organization's finances was followed by a review of each of the discrete operations within the organization. The two reviews produced a list of operations that might be outsourced, reorganized, or eliminated. An examination of three of these outcomes will provide insight into how the process evolved and what issues informed the decision making process.

Food Service

The food service on the campus was a $22-million program that served 20 meals per week at 11 dining halls in the residence halls. Each student was paying $2,600 per year and eating only 55 percent of her meals each week. Food was cited in exit surveys as the number one reason not to renew a housing contract and instead to move off campus. A satisfaction survey conducted by a marketing specialist from the school of business reported that students rated the system C-. The food service staff was highly skilled and respected in their profession and on campus. In addition, the operation was in a strong financial position. However, the physical plant for food service was old and in need of renovation. A study committee determined that the operation should remain self-operated. The strength of the staff, including its good relationship with the students, and its strong financial position were the main reasons for the determination.

A student-staff committee chaired by a student was created to serve as a review and policy board for the food service operation. The first decision the food service committee made was to move from an all-you-can-eat meal system to a point system in which one point equaled one dollar. For example, whereas students previously paid a set price for an array of options, they now were paying per item they selected. They then decided to diversify the food offerings. Parts of the operation would be outsourced, but the university would become the franchisee. This approach allowed the food service operation flexibility to bring in new franchises as tastes and interests changed. The current food service is operated at seven renovated sites in the residence halls and four kiosk sites around campus in academic buildings and performing arts venues, and students can use their meal points in any of these locations. Currently the cost of the entry-level meal plan is $2,670 and the points are being used at a rate of 98 percent. For the last four years the cost of the entry-level meal plan has not changed. In addition, a follow-up satisfaction survey rated the food service at B+ to A-.

Laundry Service

The campus laundry service consisted of over 350 washers and dryers. The machines had not been replaced on a regular basis, and the last major purchase had taken place more than seven years ago. One staff member was assigned to maintenance and another part-time worker to coin collection. Thus, both operations were always behind schedule and less efficient than good business practices would allow. The cost of a wash was 25 cents, and the dryer was 10 cents. The operation, seen as a service, was underwritten by the institution. It was determined that the machines had to be replaced and the laundry rooms renovated. The cost of this was estimated to be $280,000 for the machines and approximately $70,000 for the laundry rooms. This would mean raising the washer and dryer cost to $2.00 and $1.00 respectively to cover the cost of replacing the cash that would be used for the project.

A request for a proposal (an RFP or bid) was issued to determine if a private vendor would assume the operation of the laundry rooms. The key in this case was to write the RFP to state clearly the specific type of service the school desired. Once a vendor was chosen, the development of a contract that specified each party's obligations was of the utmost importance. The final agreement called for all new machines, on-site vendor staff for repair and coin collection, and renovation of all the laundry rooms. This was all accomplished by raising students' laundry costs to $1.00 for a wash and $.50 for an extended dryer cycle for the life of the contract, which was three years with a three-year renewal clause. This operation, which had been a loss leader for the department, became one that contributed cash to the bottom line.

Kiosks

The four kiosks that have been established on campus in the academic buildings and performing arts venue provide additional insight into the outsourcing story. These sites had been operated by private vendors for over five years. Each site was run by a different vendor under a contract that was set for a specific building. Despite well-written contracts and good oversight by the campus, these operations generally did not serve the campus well. A review determined that each of the sites was too small to generate enough business for the vendor to make a profit and pay the guarantee to the campus. As a result, the vendors had to take steps to cut costs, which had the impact of reducing service. The campus found itself in a position of having to talk to the vendors to enforce the contract. It was decided that it would be best to take a new approach to operating these sites. Each vendor was informed that a new approach was being developed and that the contract would be extended but not renewed. This enabled the campus to have all the contracts end on the same day. The new RFP called for the vendors to bid on all the sites as a package. The economy of scale, it was believed, would enable the vendor to operate within the bounds of the contract.

The two keys to this bidding process were meeting with the vendors before the bid deadline and the interaction between the vendors and the person managing the process. The pre-deadline meeting allowed the vendors to determine better what the campus was seeking to achieve with this outsource. A tour of the sites was particularly important, and the person managing this process ensured that all interested vendors received the same information.

In a final key ingredient in the process, after identifying a top choice of vendor, the bid administrator called a meeting with all the site administrators and the top choice to address each concern that site administrators had raised during the bidding process. For example, all the sites did not request the same hours of operation. During this meeting each site's specific operating times were agreed upon and written into the contract. However, the most important aspect of this meeting was the opportunity to start to develop working relationships between the vendor and the site administrator. One of the reasons that outsourcing often fails is inadequate, or sometimes the complete lack of, communication (Bartem and Manning 2001; Wood 2000).

Planning and Environmental Considerations

The reasons to privatize center around the straightforward notion of economic advantage and high levels of service along with the desire to know what sort of arrangement will provide the institution the best service at the best price to constituents or customers over the long run. Application of this notion, however, is not so straightforward, for understanding the short- and long-term implications of these decisions requires a more complex framework. But the necessity of gaining this understanding of the environment is unavoidable if one wishes to realize the economic efficiencies and advantages desired.

First, each environment is unique, so options and solutions must vary. This is true within this country, within each state and community, and within systems of higher education institutions. The economy of a geographic area can play a large role, as can the makeup of the student body, the financial situation of the institution, and the nature of those in leadership and decision-making positions. The choice to leave any of these elements out of the decision-making equation when considering outsourcing options is at the peril of making a short-sighted, wrong decision. Each application of privatization within an institution requires careful analysis and should stand on its own merits in regard to each of these important factors. In other words, it will be rare that one answer will address all institutional concerns evenly. As is evident in the case studies in this chapter, frequently a blend of privatization and self-operation will most effectively meet the needs of a unit.

Determining what balance of private and self-operation is optimal for an institution is not a formulaic determination. Toong (2004) suggests that colleges and universities must establish well-developed strategic plans that consider the environment in which they operate. He suggests that a thorough review of the external and internal environment be conducted to determine the strengths and weaknesses of the operation and the associated opportunities and threats. Bartem and Manning (2001) report that too often colleges and universities have failed to develop innovative and effective long-range plans. Thus, schools have often found themselves managing their operations with old techniques that were tried and true but that did not allow them to capture new market trends and innovations. As a result, they have lost market share or found that their costs were exceeding their income. Take the case of the bookstore that maintained its full inventory of new books until late each semester. This practice developed years ago to respond to the fact that students often made book purchases just before final exams, and it had served them well for years. It had the downside of tying up cash in inventory that in turn reduced their flexibility to move into new markets without borrowing and incurring the resultant debt.

While changes can be good for the business operations of a bookstore, anticipation of broader implications is typically necessary too. The interplay of units on campus means that bookstore decisions may have a big effect on areas such as faculty decisions for texts in the classroom, human resources issues if vendor/employer labor practices clash with standard university procedures, or athletic department revenue from apparel sales. Assessing the full realm of possible consequences and the effect on the strategic plan for the institution has helped many institutions make the most advantageous decisions regarding opportunities to privatize.

One of the key components of developing a strategic plan and including an outsourcing option is a thorough and complete understanding of institutional culture. If a decision is made to outsource, it is important that the vendor have an understanding of the culture being

197

joined. Culture is defined as "the collective mutually shaping patterns of norms, values, practices, beliefs, and assumption that guide the behavior of individuals and groups in an institute of higher education and provide a frame of reference within which to interpret the meaning of events and actions on and off campus" (Kuh and Whitt 1988). Using this definition as a guide, the organization can develop a strategic plan that can be explained to internal and external audiences. It is important to be able to explain the organization both externally and internally. According to Gilley and Rasheed (2000), "outsourcing represents the fundamental decision to reject the internalizations of an activity" (764). Having an understanding of institutional culture can contribute greatly to knowing the implications of supporting or rejecting outsourcing activities. Thus, the members of the organization must determine if an activity is congruent with its culture and mission before deciding whether or not to outsource (Toong 2004).

This assessment of culture and mission was the approach adapted by the housing department discussed above. They decided to keep the food service internal because it was core to their mission: to connect the residence halls to the academic mission of the campus. This was accomplished through meals and programs in the dining halls that related to specific programs the department wished to promote. Thus, the food service was seen as providing more than food; it was integral to the culture and an important dimension of the overall operation. As such, it was felt that the staff and decision-making processes had to remain internal. On the other hand, the same conclusion was not reached for the laundry service. It was determined that the laundry, while important, was not core to the organization's mission. While the selected vendor had an excellent understanding of the academic environment, it was not felt that the staff and decision processes had to remain internal to maintain mission integrity.

Theoretically, in most instances, an institution of any size or administrative sophistication should not have to privatize. After all, introducing an additional entity that requires profit into an economic relationship would seem to initiate an inflationary effect on prices. For the institution to benefit, this third party must have access to something that the institution does not, on its own, have access to, thus allowing the third party to provide services at an acceptable level, to treat the institution well financially, and to generate a profit for that organization. Though difficult, this is possible—where there is access to volume, removal of competitive constraints, cheaper labor, allowed reduction of services, management strength or niche expertise, and access to capital.

Access to volume is an important and oft-cited reason for involving a third party in university activities. In some situations it is possible that external vendors will have access to high-volume purchasing arrangements that would not otherwise be available to institutions. However, many institutions of higher education are large enough for access to similar discounts, and small institutions can form cooperative purchasing arrangements with other institutions to acquire volume discounts.

Another advantage the private sector has is removal of competitive constraints. Within some states and communities, activities of not-for-profits are regulated in ways that limit options in services and lines of merchandise they can provide. These restrictions make it difficult if not impossible to operate on a basic break-even basis. In this case, external vendors will usually allow institutions to avoid such restrictions.

As institutions of higher education work to reduce their costs, one approach has been to outsource nonacademic operations so that all costs for these services are contained within a predetermined contract bond agreement. Consequently, as institutions bring in private vendors, these bodies may reduce labor costs to a level with which the institution is uncomfortable in the context of its own history and practices. Of course, this has different implications in terms of labor relations as well.

In some instances an institution may desire investment in auxiliaries but lack the finances. It may be that an external vendor can provide this sort of investment in exchange for reduced future revenue provisions to the institution. Such an arrangement may be of great interest to both parties and be mutually advantageous in times of financial stringency.

Finally, a variety of areas in which auxiliaries operate are customer-oriented. These areas often deal with frequent changes in customer interests that require adjustments in operation. Usually institutional personnel practices and policies preclude routine replacement of personnel to match the market. A most cost-effective and institutionally viable way to handle these frequently changing areas is to find an external vendor with whom a reasonable amount of flexibility to changing customer demands can be demonstrated. Management companies with expertise and training capacity for employees are best equipped to handle these areas.

Considerations in
Privatization of Auxiliaries

Given all of these characteristics that have created positive institution-vendor arrangements in many instances, many institutions of higher education have found it important also to consider the following issues:

- Being prepared to dissolve or change the contractual agreement if it is not working the way it was hoped it would;
- Knowing the levels of flexibility that are given up;
- Understanding the legal liability and tax implications;
- Understanding insurance issues and responsibilities;
- Understanding implications for the community (perhaps including the diversion of customers from other local businesses);
- Understanding what peer institutions are doing and why;
- Knowing long-term financial and service implications vs. short-run profit implications;
- Conveying institutional priorities in the contract.

Each of these considerations can be crucial to the decision-making process regarding a contract with an outside vendor. Loss of flexibility can cripple an institution in some instances and be particularly troubling if customers are dissatisfied with the vendor's service. A bookstore might not work with a specific publisher that a certain faculty member has used for years, or perhaps maintenance of certain parts of campus will not be cycled to complete in time for major fundraising or recruiting events for which the institution needs to look its best. Being able to dissolve or change a contract in such situations is an important option to maintain.

Legal, tax, and insurance issues are not minor considerations either. Ultimately, problems in these areas can far outpace cost savings of using an external vendor when some difficulty comes up. Making such issues clear from the outset and codifying the appropriate mechanisms in a contract is a vitally important step to protecting the position, liability, and values of the institution. And depending on the community relationship or responsibility that the institution holds, an assessment of the implications to local businesses, facility users, or the general taxpayer must be completed before signing the on dotted line.

Many of these issues can be identified and planned for by observing peer institutions and their experiences with outsourcing auxiliary services. Gathering information on what they are doing can help in understanding the array of options, but more important yet is to understand *why* they chose or did not choose to use vendors, what options vendors provided them with in services or products, and why they have or have not been happy with the outcome of their decisions. This information can start to generate an understanding of the long-term and short-term impacts of auxiliary decisions from financial and services perspectives. However, the more important issue is how institutional priorities can be honored and maintained through the external vendor. Some institutions have found it important, and even necessary, to include these in the contract as points to guide the vendor and ensure that the institution is empowered to maintain its own priorities through the decisions that have been made.

Conclusion

The experiences of privatizing and outsourcing various auxiliary services are instructive of the complexities of the decision-making process and reveal advantages and disadvantages. Institutions of higher education—unlike many for-profit entities that focus on the bottom line and short run—are in for the long haul. A major disservice to a college or university would be a short-run decision that changed the nature of the institution. Every decision should be made with the long term in mind because the components of the institution work synergistically, so that doing something new and different with a single component may not advance the institution's long-term mission.

As these experiences have shown, the complex fabric of the institutional culture and mission depends on sound planning and decision making, and the anticipation of the ripple effects of outsourcing is crucial. The wise application of cultural, organizational, and technical knowledge has helped institutions align privatization and outsourcing with the best interests of the entire institution.

References

Agron, J. 2001. Keeping it close to home: Schools and colleges are reducing their use of outsourced noneducational services. Privatization/contract services survey. *American School and University* (September): 24–28.

Bartem, R., and S. Manning. 2001. Outsourcing in higher education: A business officer and partner discuss a controversial management strategy. *Change* 33(1): 142–46.

Ford, F. R. 1992. Overview of financial accounting and reporting. In *College and university business administration*: Vol. 1. *Fiscal functions*, 5th ed., ed. D. M. Greene. National Association of College and University Business Officers.

Gilley, K. M., and A. Rasheed. 2000. Making more by doing less: An analysis of outsourcing and its effect on firm performance. *Journal of Management* 26(4): 763–90.

Jefferies, C. L. 1996. The privatization debate: Examining the decision to outsource a service. *Business Officer* 29(7): 26–30.

Kaganoff, T. (1998). *Collaboration, technology and outsourcing initiatives in higher education: A literature review.* MR-973–EDU. Santa Monica, Calif.: The Foundation for Independent Higher Education, RAND.

Kerr, C. (1994). *Higher education cannot escape history: Issues for the 21st century.* Albany: State University of New York Press.

Kuh, G. D., and E. J. Whitt. 1988. *The invisible tapestry: Culture in American colleges and universities.* ASHE-ERIC Higher Education Reports. Education Report No. 1. Washington, D.C.

Lee, J. 2004. Higher education and privatization. *NEA Higher Education Research Center Update* 10 (March).

Lucas, C. J. 1994. *American higher education: A history.* New York: St. Martin's Griffin.

Powell, D. B., et al. 1992. Overview of financial accounting and reporting. In *College and university business administration:* Vol. 3. *Fiscal functions,* 5th ed., ed. D. M. Greene. National Association of College and University Business Officers.

Rudolph, F. 1965. *The American college and university: A history.* New York: Vintage Books.

———. 1977. *Curriculum: A history of the American undergraduate course of study since 1636.* San Francisco: Jossey-Bass.

Toong, K. 2004. Does outsourcing work for everyone? A practical look at the effects of outsourcing auxiliary services. *College Services* 4(3): 14–18.

Wood, P. A. (2000). *Outsourcing in higher education.* Eric Digest. ED446726. Washington, D.C.: Eric Clearinghouse on Higher Education.

CHAPTER TEN

Enterprise Systems

Don Hossler and William P. Gorr

Information Systems in
Higher Education

One of the most profound changes in the management of colleges
and universities in the last fifty years is the growing use of electronic information systems to store and retrieve information and provide support
for administrative decision making. John Monro, a former dean of financial aid at Harvard University has reported that in 1965 he was able
to store all of the financial aid files for students enrolled at Harvard in
the file drawers of a large desk in his office (1984). Today financial aid
administrators would simply be unable to do their jobs without the aid
of large and sophisticated electronic information systems. In the area of
student information systems, for example, Hossler (2000) has observed
that these systems have become the foundation for successful enrollment management strategies. Attracting and retaining the desired number of students, enrolling a sufficient number of high ability students or
underrepresented students, retaining students, and generating tuition
revenue have become dependent on the functionality of student information systems.

In recent years, however, the implementation of new administrative
information systems has garnered much attention in *The Chronicle of
Higher Education* and other higher education trade publications. Much

of the press has been negative, focusing on the high costs of implementing new electronic information systems as well as on some of the problems colleges and universities have encountered during the implementation process. For most faculty members, administrators, and trustees, the problems and costs of new information systems are often a surprise. Information systems for areas like human resources (HR) and payroll, student systems (such as admissions, financial aid, and registration and records), and financial management are typically back room operations. At their best, when they are functioning well, they are both ubiquitous and invisible. They support a variety of important administrative functions such as enabling universities to bill students, making it possible for colleges to pay their employees, or keeping track of the courses students have taken so administrators know when they have taken the right mix of courses to be able to graduate. Few senior administrators or faculty have established their reputations for understanding administrative information systems and their contributions to the efficient operation of a university campus. It is a rare faculty member or senior academic administrator who has a sense of the costs and difficulties associated with developing and maintaining these information systems. Yet these systems have become the administrative backbone of colleges and universities.

Historically, each institution would invest the time and resources to develop its own applications that would run on the institution's computers. In the early days of the development of computer-based student information systems, commercial software systems were few, so many colleges and universities, especially larger universities with bigger information technology (IT) staffs, built their own systems. Over time, however, commercial vendors emerged. At first they sold stand-alone systems for financial aid, registration and records, or student financials. By the 1990s, however, integrated systems—enterprise resource planning (ERP) systems—emerged. These new systems provide an integrated platform for many administrative services, including financials, human resources, and student services.

In this chapter we examine the issues associated with vended ERP solutions and their potential as vehicles for outsourcing and privatizing administrative information systems. We define relevant terms used in student information systems and include a brief overview of these systems. This is followed by a critique of both ERP systems and what is commonly referred to as the "build-your-own" alternative. The chapter also includes an examination of the unique characteristics of colleges and universities that make this debate and the decisions more complicated than in other organizational settings and considers the costs associated with these two alternatives. The chapter closes with a summary and a set of recommendations for senior campus administrators tasked with leading new information system implementations.

Definitions

Student Information System

A computer system or application that provides the business logic and functionality to support primary student services provided on most campuses is called a student information system. Although both ERP and build-your-own systems vary in the range of services they provide, generally these include systems for the functions of academic advising, admissions, financial aid, records and registration, housing, and student financials (bursar functions).

Legacy System

The *Free Online Dictionary of Computing* defines a legacy system as

A computer system or application program that was developed or purchased several years ago, often ten or more years ago, but which continues to be used because of the cost of replacing or redesigning it. Often legacy systems are dated and lack the power and functionality of modern equivalents. Legacy systems are often large, monolithic and difficult to modify. If legacy software only runs on antiquated hardware, the cost of maintaining this may eventually outweigh the cost of replacing both the software and hardware unless some form of emulation or backward compatibility allows the software to run on new hardware. (Howe 2004)

Enterprise Resource Planning (ERP) System

"ERP systems are predominantly intra-enterprise focused, and provide, at least in theory, seamless integration of processes across functional areas with improved workflow, standardization of various business practices, improved order management, accurate accounting of inventory, and up-to-date operational data" (Bendoly, Soni, and Venkataramanan 2004, 80). ERP systems on campuses also track and integrate a multitude of processes and functions, as well as maintain accurate accounting of students, faculty, and staff. In the context of this chapter, "ERP student system" refers to services provided for the func-

tions of academic advising, admissions, financial aid, records and registration, and student financials (bursar functions).

Build-Your-Own System

The effort to build a new system incorporates three distinct phases.
The initial phase incorporates systems analyses functions, whereby a
team of personnel identify the functional requirements of the system,
typically working with operational personnel. The effort focuses on capturing business rules, processes, and standardizing data elements. The
next stage includes system design, when the project manager and his/
her team determine the system's technical specifications and performance parameters, including the system's architecture and associated
project milestones. After the system is designed, the programming team
then begins to develop applications within the established technical
framework. The team of programmers writes and tests the code until
system implementation. Frequently the developers elect to use already-
developed software components, modules, or subsystems — often in the
open-source domain — and can thereby reduce development and testing time.

Open-Source Software

Howe (2004) defines open-source software as "a method and philosophy for software licensing and distribution designed to encourage use
and improvement of software written by volunteers by ensuring that anyone can copy the source code and modify it freely."

A Brief Overview of
Student Information Systems

In the early stages of the emergence of computer-based student information systems, before commercial off-the-shelf (COTS) products
became available, the development of build-your-own systems was the
only choice available for institutions of higher education. As these
legacy systems matured over the years, they included various nuances
of business rules and procedures employed by the functional unit supported by the software. The staff had the ability to make desired
changes on site with little need for coordination between functional offices since most applications ran in a stand-alone environment. The nu-

merous systems on campus would contain redundant data elements, though the data between systems may not have been identical due to the difficulty in transferring and updating data on multiple systems. Interoperability, the ability of a system to work with other systems without special effort on the part of the user, was typically cumbersome, and often nonexistent.

In the late 1990s, the use of vended systems became more common on university campuses. Most of these systems included common core functionality required by institutions of higher education. Often the functionality was extracted from ERP systems designed to help businesses reduce data redundancy and improve efficiency. Though some schools chose to develop their own ERP systems, many institutions opted to outsource the development and implementation of systems on their campuses. The desired result is an integrated system, operating from the same database, providing users with a real-time view of institutional operations.

Purchasing a suite of new information systems (including HR, financial management, and student systems) from a vendor or building one's own system can be a multimillion-dollar commitment. Depending on the size of the campus and the scope of the implementation effort, the cost can range from as little as $1 to $2 million at a single small private college to nearly $500,000,000 in the case of a large, complex, multi-campus implementation like the one taking place at the twenty-three campuses of the California State University system.

Upon reflection, it is perhaps not surprising that the implementation of these new systems has garnered so much attention. To acquire and implement the desired advances in technology, many institutions of higher education are grappling with the task of re-engineering their business rules in order to provide students, faculty, and staff secure access to needed information. The desired goal is to provide better service to all institutional constituents, and to enhance efficiency of operations. Unfortunately, most institutions of higher education have little experience with technical projects of this magnitude and complexity. University administrators certainly have many years of experience with the use of information systems to retain records and make decisions. However, as Haigh (2004) notes, prior to the widespread use of computers these systems relied on the use of paper and manual retrieval systems. The history of computer-based information systems in higher education has yet to be written, but conversations with many college administrators who have worked with information systems for many years suggest that most colleges and universities first began to develop their own electronic information systems in the mid-1970s through the mid-1980s. These first efforts were for specific tasks such as billing students or enabling students to register for classes without standing in multiple long lines inside the college gymnasium. Most information systems used at universities until the 1970s fell under the umbrella of finance and accounting systems and were usually referred to as data processing systems. In subsequent years, vendors started to develop stand-alone systems to support the many different administrative functions required on college campuses. Initially, these systems were unable to provide an informational enterprise view of the campus, necessitating different reports from multiple campus systems to provide the consolidated information required by senior administrators.

Although no data are available, anecdotal evidence suggests that many universities and colleges continued to use their own home-grown systems or they failed to continue to upgrade their vended systems after installing them. Much like the deferred maintenance on brick-and-mortar buildings, universities chose to invest their resources in other visible priorities while continuing to use aging technology without investing sufficient resources to keep them current and functioning effectively. This strategy appeared to pay off for colleges for several years. However, the costs and benefits of this approach changed dramatically when the Y2K problem emerged in the late 1990s. Indeed, much of the impetus for the massive upgrading of information systems on many campuses can be traced to that problem. Campus administrators became aware that their invisible, ubiquitous, but vital information systems were at risk because they might not function when we entered the twenty-first century. As a result, large numbers of colleges and universities, for the first time, undertook a comprehensive look at their mix of home-grown or vended systems and asked fundamental questions about their viability: Could they upgrade their current systems, or should they develop entirely new systems or purchase new ERP systems that held the promise of placing all of their administrative information systems on one technology platform?

In asking these questions, most institutions of higher education were raising questions that had not been systematically raised before. University administrators were faced with significant decisions that would influence how they would manage their institutions—decisions that would precipitate other organizational changes. Information systems were now an integral part of the university infrastructures, and though they were designed to improve effectiveness, institutions had woefully limited resources to evolve these systems in order to provide the support expected by students, faculty, and staff. In many instances, they were in a position to consider major changes in these systems for the first time since they had been developed. This lack of experience explains many of the problems that have been encountered as institutions of higher education have worked through the complex issues associated with enhancing or replacing their information systems.

There are no simple solutions to sustaining the increasingly complex and sophisticated electronic information systems that have been created. Throughout this chapter we will refer to the "hydraulic effect": the attempt to suppress costs unrealistically in one area, which often leads to increased costs in other areas. For example, some vendors will advocate a "vanilla implementation," which means that the vended software is installed as designed with no customizations. To do this, university administrators are told to change their business practices to mimic the embedded logic of the software. Light (2001), however, notes that this is seldom a realistic approach. For example, a unique and complex curriculum can be a key part of the distinctiveness of a college of business (and it is often a competitive advantage for some business schools). Faculty of a prestigious business school are unlikely to endorse a vanilla implementation enthusiastically if it means altering their curriculum to a standard, normalized approach that lacks any unique courses, requirements, or other educational experiences. Any university administrator involved in the implementation of student systems should be skeptical of claims of saving costs by advocating a completely vanilla implementation.

On the other hand, because information systems are typically invisible and ubiquitous, in the past, senior administrators and faculty groups may have insisted on institutional policies in areas like personnel or financial aid without asking the question: Is this policy worth the ongoing costs to customize our legacy or new ERP system and to maintain it long term? The greater the integration of system applications, the greater the difficulty of changing functionality in one area without affecting other areas.

For example, many integrated ERP student systems require high degrees of accuracy and completeness for every student record from the first time the student's name is entered into the student information system. This need for data integrity is in direct conflict with the messy world of admissions offices at what is called the prospect stage. Prospects are students who call in and leave their addresses, who partially fill out a prospect card, or who send an incomplete e-mail. Admissions officers are rightfully loath to lose a single prospect, but prospect information often lacks the full name, address, and social security number that new integrated ERP systems require to function effectively. And unfortunately, from the perspective of ERP systems, student prospects represent the largest group of new students campuses deal with during an annual new student recruitment cycle. Adding the myriad of campus support systems under the one ERP umbrella necessitates strict data management, and this comes with added costs. In other words, campus administrators and faculty governance groups are looking more carefully not only at what new or existing systems will do for them, but at what the total costs of implementation and maintenance are and how to contain these costs. In recent years the costs of system implementation and the costs of modifications and customizations have become a major focal point of information system implementations.

One concrete example of these interdependencies—the complexities and the hydraulic effect that we previously mentioned—can be found in the implementation of a new system at Indiana University. To do a standard implementation of one part of the student financials system from an ERP vendor would have resulted either in the university spending millions of dollars more on graduate student fellowships or in the bursar offices on each campus spending more than $200,000 annually on additional staff to award graduate fellowships and monitor them manually. The cost to customize the software was less than $100,000. Successful efforts to implement new ERP systems or to build (or enhance) your own systems require a careful balancing of these hydraulic effects. A savings in the software implementation process may result in considerably higher personnel costs in other campus offices. On the other hand, making too many customizations to the software can lead to significant ongoing programming costs every time there is an upgrade to an existing vended software product.

Outsourcing or Building Your Own: Myths and Realities

There is no dearth of assertions that have been offered by either the proponents of build-your-own systems or the supporters of buying an established ERP system. The proponents of build-your-own systems contend that these solutions enable institutions to develop systems that meet the unique business processes and curricular and competitive needs of individual campuses. Some institutions choose to incorporate the code of existing legacy systems on new platforms, although the extent of required modification reduces, and may negate, the associated cost benefits. Another approach chosen by institutions that decide to build their own involves using open-source software—potentially bypassing the use of commercial products. The growing number of institutions attempting and succeeding in developing their own systems, using and sharing developed open-source software, enables institutions to save the expenses associated with the escalating licensing costs for commercial products.

Migrating to an infrastructure based on open-source software often increases the implementation risks undertaken by the institution. Whereas a commercial software partner shares in the risks of a contracted implementation, the onus for success for open-source ventures lies solely with the university. Institutions that embark on this venture must invest a significant amount of resources during the development cycle to establish and foster cooperation with other developers; to discuss bugs, fixes, and needed refinements; and to share and exchange software. The staff that successfully develop and then maintain the institution's software will likely have a greater depth of knowledge about the software than staff involved in the implementation of a vended product. Consequently, they will likely be more adept in customizing the software to meet evolving requirements.

Build-your-own enthusiasts may advocate using open-source software because it is free. It is true that open-source software does not have any licensing costs. However, this is not to claim that the implementation of open-source software has no costs. The institution must devote the resources for customization and implementation and the additional time to train the development staff.

Institutions electing to embrace fully the option of open-source software may forego licensing costs and can own, operate, and modify their software without any vendor encumbrance. They are then fully responsible for making all software changes—including changes to the operating system and all applications and executable software. The IT staff will likely spend more time coordinating with users at other institutions —comparing notes on problems, sharing software components, and discussing software components available in the open-source arena—than staff who employ vended solutions.

Build-your-own solutions, including the use of open-source software, offer more institutional control over system enhancements and upgrades and thus enable institutions to exert more control over the costs of ownership—which leads, theoretically, to savings. In addition, supporters of build-your-own approaches note that vended solutions often require the purchase of additional third-party vended products or customizations, thereby diminishing many of the benefits of ERP solutions.

Advocates of contracted ERP solutions assert that vended products offer cutting-edge technological solutions, enable colleges and universities to have all systems on a single technology platform, and reduce the costs of ownership because the software vendor maintains the integrity of the underlying code and provides regular software upgrades, including updates in areas like changes in federal tax codes and federal financial aid regulations. Supporters of vended solutions suggest that student systems have become so complicated that few institutions have the technical staff to build their own systems successfully and that the costs of doing so are high. In addition, they note that colleges and universities that build their own systems then have to retain a large technical support staff to maintain their systems over time. Another significant benefit associated with vended products is the ability to acquire complex, state-of-the art enhancements that have been partially funded, tested, and implemented at other institutions. As the vendor responds to change requests from user institutions, all institutions that have purchased the software may be able to reap the benefits of system enhancements when system upgrades are procured. In the following sections we take a critical look at the propositions offered by advocates of each approach.

Build-Your-Own/Legacy Systems

As institutions of higher education began to use computers to help various functional areas manage their resources better in the 1960s and 1970s, separate systems emerged, and each system managed different data sets. Typically, the first applications in these first-generation systems were focused on managing financial data (numerical data)—tracking expenditures and revenues, and generating reports enabling managers to make decisions and monitor resource allocations better. These early systems often were developed and maintained by functional users, that is, users who knew the existing business rules and practices and could apply that knowledge to the unstructured design and development effort. These users also had the ability to make and test changes to the software quickly, enhancing the feeling of control over system development. The software tools, procedural programming languages, and hardware used were independently selected by these same functional communities/developers with little oversight from higher administration. Indeed, in most instances functional areas developed their own systems, often on different technological platforms, using different programming logic and different business rules. These early systems were not designed to interact with each other in order to share data readily.

Those who developed, modified, and maintained these systems soon became highly skilled and gained expert power as they amassed greater knowledge relative to other members of their respective groups (Hughes, Ginnett, and Curphy 2002). Though the systems supported each functional community, the system experts were often forced to compete with each other for resources to make enhancements or upgrades, and they often worked on similar projects using separate technological solutions, thereby negating any economy of scale benefits that could have been derived. Consequently, though these first-generation legacy systems did assist users in the organization to perform their tasks effectively, they did not necessarily enhance performance with fewer personnel.

The early history of legacy systems reveals one of the greatest strengths of legacy systems: they enable colleges and universities to organize, systematize, and consolidate the institution's ever-evolving business logic. As a result, these systems quickly become integral components of administrative operations. Personnel soon find it difficult to perform even the most basic business functions without having access to these legacy systems.

Indeed, one of the reasons some universities consider building their own systems is that they have a history of developing and maintaining their own systems, and they have the personnel on staff with the required capabilities. Migration efforts—to move the embedded business logic from older platforms to newer platforms—are sometimes the aim of build-your-own enthusiasts. However, the additional work associated with normalizing databases and converting procedural languages of one environment to work in another often requires time and skill sets that are not readily available. Even when institutions opt to develop their own systems, they often are forced to seek outside support to provide assistance in their development effort. The use of information technology consultants is widespread in higher education and affords institutions access to expertise to develop complex functionality (i.e., security and electronic commerce) that may be too time-consuming to undertake with existing staff. Often institutions attempt to limit the expenses by tying consultant's costs to certain deliverables, ensuring that the institution acquires specified functionality at a predetermined cost.

Harrison and Walton (2002) note that in legacy systems most maintenance is done for changes in program functionality rather than in fault correction. As system maintainers have sought to be responsive to users, over time the complexity of various legacy systems has increased (as new capabilities are added and existing deficiencies are corrected). Software maintenance has typically been performed to adapt to changes in the environment (to accommodate new data reporting requirements or to prepare for a new release to the operating system), or in response to failures in processing. These observations point out one of the most powerful reasons that many campuses are attracted to build-your-own solutions: legacy systems enable functional users to develop local solutions to new policies and procedures adopted by the institution. For example, a unique curriculum or customized approach to student billing can be supported through the customization of locally developed software more readily than with vended software. Some external observers of higher education and some campus administrators fail to recognize that customizations like these can be part of the strategic advantage of home-grown, customized systems. Unique curricula can be one of the reasons that a small college or a professional school is highly ranked and prestigious. Complex student payment plans for expensive private institutions can be an integral part the recruitment process because they help families afford to send their children to this institution.

The primary benefit to devoting resources to develop and mature systems in-house pertains in large measure to control. Vended products have many different customers, and over time all of them are likely to advocate for changes and enhancements to be made in the software. Unlike build-your-own systems that enable campuses to make their own changes as needed, vended software may require patience on the part of campus administrators, who often have to wait to see if vendors will make the desired changes. If few other customers are advocating for similar changes, they may never be implemented. Also, the cost for the vended system includes functionality that is sometimes not used. Essentially, the institution is forced to allocate resources for system features that are not required and to forego other features that are desired. Through developing one's own system, the school has the ability to build a cadre of personnel with the skills and knowledge to maintain the system indefinitely—though the recurring costs of keeping a full complement of trained IT developers and maintainers may be cost prohibitive for many institutions.

Another hidden benefit for build-your-own systems can be that they provide more discretion to senior campus administrators as to when

214

they will choose to invest institutional resources in information systems. This, of course, can be a two-edged sword; as with buildings, choosing to defer maintenance and upgrades on software eventually leads to having to spend significant amounts of money to re-engineer legacy systems completely or to purchase vended systems. Nevertheless, most campus administrators defer investments in buildings or software because they believe they have more pressing institutional concerns. We address this issue again in the section on vended systems. At this point we simply note that the timelines for spending money on commercial information systems are not discretionary. Vendors support versions of their systems only for specific periods of time, often four to six years. After that, new tax laws, human resource regulations, or financial aid regulations no longer work as required in the older versions. As a result, institutions are forced to invest in upgrades.

Despite their many strengths, institutionally owned and developed systems often have inherent weaknesses. First, these systems are usually noted for their lack of documentation and for the difficulty system-support personnel encounter when they attempt to migrate the applications to newer, more reliable hardware platforms (Rahgozar and Oroumchian 2003). Also the various systems supporting administrative operations in the institution usually require separate support staffs (or at least teams), so the system maintainers can continue to be responsive to users' needs. This necessitates a larger and more skilled IT staff. The more integral the information systems are to the performance of the institution's core mission, and the more often the system is used, the greater the amount of continuous maintenance and support is required (Harrison and Walton 2002).

Maintaining a sufficient number of appropriate staff is an ongoing problem with institutionally owned and developed systems. Within a few years after a system is implemented, the original system's designers and developers are likely to take on new responsibilities and often new employment positions. Newly hired maintainers are then faced with the daunting challenge of adding functionality without compromising the existing capabilities of the system. Resources are rarely allocated to develop training plans and documentation for new programmers. Software maintenance consequently becomes increasingly difficult as the complexity of the system increases and as ready access to resident system experts wanes. Like other university infrastructure issues, the problems of supporting legacy software become increasingly difficult and expensive over time. As a result, as in the analogy made above to deferred maintenance of buildings, information systems can languish, become fragile and dated, and no longer effectively serve the needs of a campus. In some instances they can become so fragile that they fail when the institution is issuing payroll checks, awarding financial aid, or registering students.

Another risk associated with the build-your-own option is that information systems have become very complex and require highly skilled software engineers and programmers. Hence these systems are costly to develop and typically take several years to build. As a result, senior campus executives have to be willing to set aside large sums of money over several years. Most university presidents or provosts do not find information systems a compelling institutional priority. They are analogous to the plumbing or electrical systems of a building—out of plain sight and expected simply to work. In this context, there is a risk that funds set aside for the new system will be reduced over time, making it impossible to develop the system envisioned in the original plan or to allocate the required funds if the original cost estimate was inaccurate. A slow erosion of funding can place the entire project at risk.

Vended Information Systems

In many instances, the greatest strength of vended systems is the greatest weakness of build-your-own systems.

STRENGTHS

Vended ERP systems have many desirable attributes. With respect to the technology backbone of new ERP systems, they offer a major cost-of-ownership advantage by placing all administrative systems in the same technological environment; they can use the same standards and tools, and they afford enhanced interoperability and facilitate system maintenance. In older legacy environments it is common to find, for example, that the records and registration system was written in COBOL, accessing a hierarchical database; the financial aid system was developed in FORTRAN, accessing flat files; and the admissions system was developed using a fourth-generation language (e.g., Pac-base, SQL), accessing a relational database. In addition, there may be several additional smaller support systems developed in FoxPro, PowerBuilder, or Java—each with different software standards and programming conventions. This requires institutions to attempt to make these different applications and data repositories interoperable and to retain staff with expertise in all of these different programs, though some may no longer be fully supported in the industry. ERP systems, on the other hand, all rest on the same technological platform. This is a significant advantage that facilitates training and retaining personnel with the requisite skills for system development and maintenance.

Another standard weakness of legacy systems, especially older home-grown systems, is that they often lack documentation for programmers and users. This means that as new staff are hired or as new programming is required, it can be difficult to train new users or to change programming features. Several years ago, a major university became almost unable to deliver student financial aid because it had only one remaining programmer who knew enough about the university's legacy system to make all the system changes required when the federal government enacted several major changes in the federal financial aid policy. That programmer simply did not have enough time to get all of the programming changes made in a timely fashion, and no one else knew enough about the 20-year-old system to assist in the effort.

Administrative systems have become very complicated, and IT managers are constantly faced with the challenge of retaining enough trained staff to keep them operating effectively. Vended systems alleviate many of these problems. The IT staff does not need to have the same technical skill sets; true design and development activities are only undertaken by the vendor. Consequently, the institution does not have as great a need for staff to sustain the system. Vended ERP systems also typically provide better documentation, and when campus users run into technical or functional problems, the vendor's call center has the required staff available to answer most questions or ready access to technical experts to help resolve seemingly insurmountable problems. At the system level, at the very least, enterprise systems help organizations eliminate redundant data in information systems, standardize user interfaces, and approach data standardization. Enterprise systems also reduce the requirements for support staff to maintain and develop system enhancements, though support staff will still be involved with developing data products (e.g., reports).

Another advantage of ERP systems is that the companies that create and market them have established higher education user groups to find optimal business solutions, workarounds, and customizations. User groups are composed of technical and functional staff from the colleges and universities who have purchased the student, HR, or financial system from a specific vendor. Higher education, unlike the for-profit sector, has a history of sharing and collaboration between institutions. Thus, if one campus's user group is running into a problem with its vended financial system, they can ask user groups on other campuses about their experience with, and possible solutions for, the problem.

Another benefit of vended ERP systems is that they assure that colleges and universities stay current with their technology. Because the companies that produce ERP systems regularly release upgrades in both the technological platform and the functionality of their systems, institutions of higher education are less likely to have the kinds of problems they have had in the past when their home-grown legacy systems simply are no longer adequate to do the important work of the campus.

A key advantage of adopting an ERP strategy is that it gets the new functionality in the hands of users faster. Typically, institutions elect to implement a skeleton version of the software, running in parallel with the legacy systems, and add functionality once users become familiar with the system. This enables the institution to get user buy-in to the new system and allows users to adapt to the new environment. Similarly, as new system features become technologically feasible, the vendor has the ability to marshal resources to provide system-wide enhancements that computer support staffs at other institutions do not have the training or expertise to implement.

A final advantage of vended ERP systems is that once you buy a system it creates an imperative to "get it in." By this we mean that once senior administration has purchased a product, it creates a strong perceived need to install the new system and start accruing the benefits of the investment. Often the implementation of a new system turns out to be more difficult and expensive than senior campus administrators imagined, but nevertheless the system does get implemented. One of the problems with a build-your-own solution to administrative systems is that because new systems are costly and take several years to implement, their budgets can become an easy target for reductions and reallocation, since there is not an external contractual commitment. This slowly and imperceptibly erodes the probabilities of a successful implementation of a new home-grown system. More than one college or university, after several years of work on a build-your-own solution, has cancelled the project and lost the investment in this approach only to turn around and purchase a vended solution and start the implementation process all over again.

WEAKNESSES

Many of the weaknesses of vended systems have been described in the section on build-your-own solutions. One weakness is that they never meet all needs for unique business practices, leading to customizations or additional third-party products, which increase the long-term cost of ERP systems. In addition, some of the unique strengths of build-your-own systems provide institutions competitive advantages in areas like new student recruitment and help them achieve their enrollment or revenue goals. In contrast, vended systems can actually cause colleges to become less competitive in their market niche by leveling the playing field. When everyone, initially, has the same system, it is difficult to stand out from the crowd.

Another key weakness lies in the area of cost control and enhancements. Universities with home-grown legacy systems have complete control over whether and when to develop enhancements for reaching their goals more efficiently or effectively. In ERP systems, campuses are tied to the enhancement and upgrade plans of the vendors. Local customizations at the campus level can be so expensive as to be prohibitive. On the other hand, ERP solutions can actually increase the number of functional staff because labor-saving solutions require customizations that are too costly. ERP systems also remove some of the discretion campus administrators have over administrative information systems expenditures.

In a certain sense, ERP systems remove the budgetary discretion that comes with deferred maintenance. Universities often have no choice about ERP system upgrades, patches, and fixes. If they do not implement them, they do not have long-term access to changes in income tax codes that are part of HR systems or the changes in federal financial aid policies that are part of financial aid modules. In effect, this means that the concept of deferred maintenance in administrative information systems is no longer relevant. This may be one of the most important factors for institutions to consider under the broad conceptual umbrella of privatization. In this instance at least, privatization can reduce institutional control over key administrative systems and also over tight control of discretionary expenditures. This is because there are costs that go with implementing system upgrades that campus administrators will have to build into their budgets. Once an ERP system is purchased, these kinds of costs are no longer discretionary. One of the risks that we address later in the closing sections of this chapter is that if senior administrators try to keep the costs of their systems close to the costs of their legacy systems, they will, because of the built-in costs of upgrades, inevitably try to reduce costs on the functional side of their information systems. In doing so, coming back to the concept of the hydraulic effect, they may lose competitive advantages that could increase revenue or reduce expenditures in other key areas of the university.

Another risk associated with vended products pertains to whether the vendor is able to maintain the quality of support that users expect. If firms are merged or are the target of a hostile takeover, the new company may not have the same commitment to support the developed products if their return on investment is not in accordance with the new company's strategic plan.

Complexities of New Information Systems in Higher Education

Colleges and universities have some unique characteristics that can affect decisions about the development and implementation of administrative information systems.

Governance and Decision Making

Most of the literature on information systems indicates that there have to be clear lines of authority for decisions regarding the purchase, implementation, and operation of ERP systems (Brown and Vessey 2003). Seasoned university administrators and faculty governance leaders will realize the problems institutions of higher education are likely to face if this is true. Brown and Vessey indicate that successful implementations require a strong and involved senior administrative group to make key policy decisions. However, when it comes to student information systems, who owns the purchase and implementation process? The senior enrollment officer who is worried about attracting and retaining the requisite number of students? The chief information officer whose goal is to get all systems on one standard platform to contain technology support costs? The chief financial officer who has to find the money to pay for a new system and support it long term? Or is it the faculty, who influence academic policies that are contained in the offices of the registrar and admissions?

Streamlined decision making is not typically one of the strengths of colleges and universities. As Ehrmann (1999) notes, clear lines of separation and specialization are often seen as the inherent structure that provides strength to the "knowledge factory." Though businesses and governmental bureaucracies are noted for hierarchical decision making, higher education has a strong tradition of shared governance—giving faculty managerial power (Lazerson 1997). Lazerson observes that faculty tenure—providing permanence of work and academic freedom, fostering freedom of expression—is seldom seen in the corporate world and adds layers of complexity in adopting changes to the organization. Given that most changes in the informational systems' infrastructure influence a broad spectrum of university constituents, there are ample opportunities for conflict. How university leadership proposes and eventually implements the changes—and gets "buy-in" from faculty—will determine in large measure the success of the new system's implementation. However, it is possible to identify some characteristics of higher education institutions that provide some guidance to senior campus administrators trying to anticipate what the development and maintenance of new information systems will be like.

The independence of faculty governance and the degree of faculty authority typically vary across institutional sectors. Traditionally, institutional prestige and emphasis on research are associated with stronger faculty governance. Thus, large well-established research universities and highly selective private liberal arts colleges are more likely to have stronger faculty governance models. At the other end of the continuum, community colleges tend to be more administratively dominated (Cohen and Brawer 2003), so that faculty have less influence in management and governance decisions. For this reason any changes wrought by information systems that touch faculty policies are more likely to be contentious and difficult to implement at research universities and elite private colleges. Changing academic policies or student expectations because "the software will not support these practices" may not be accepted as a reason for change. University administrators are wise to take these factors into consideration when developing plans for new information systems.

Tierney (1988) claims that "an organization's culture is reflected in what is done, how it is done, and who is involved in doing it. It concerns decisions, actions, and communications both on an instrumental and a symbolic level" (3). The independence evident in creating separate, stand-alone systems is one reflection of organizational planning and decision making. A shift in decision making, even for what functions are supported by information systems, becomes increasingly important as plans are formulated to replace existing legacy-system functionality.

Enterprise systems, specifically, force institutions to grapple with the requirements of prioritization and the notion of compromise. Studies of successful enterprise systems ("up-and-running system[s] with agreed-upon requirements delivered within schedule and budget") identify several factors associated with successful implementation projects (Brown and Vessey 2003, 66). Brown and Vessey identify a satisficing mindset, whereby limiting the need for customization and accepting 80 percent solutions helps eliminate cost overruns. However, this does require organizational changes in some business practices. In a legacy-system environment, users only had to compete with others in the same functional area for system configuration changes (i.e., system enhancements, or modifications).

Institutional size and mission also have an impact on both the implementation and long-term costs of ownership for vended or home-grown systems. Large campuses are certain to have more needs and unique characteristics that require modification of ERP systems or more development of home-grown solutions that inevitably increase the costs and complexity of administrative systems. Multicampus implementations are even more complex and thus more expensive. For example, in a multicampus system where some campuses primarily enroll full-time residential students and other campuses mostly enroll part-time commuting students, the needs and behaviors of the two student populations are different in many respects. Forcing all the campuses to use a build-your-own system or vended system designed for a full-time student body can cause problems for the campuses that serve mostly part-time commuting students. A residential campus that enrolls primarily full-time students whose enrollment patterns tend to be relatively stable may not need a financial aid system that daily tracks changes in the number of credit hours in which students are enrolled. On the other hand, part-time students are more likely to decrease or increase their number of courses from the first time they register until the semester actually begins. This can require that automated financial aid modules be able to track changes in credit hours enrolled so that financial aid packages can be adjusted almost daily as the start of classes nears. This is needed because the total dollar value of some federal and many state financial aid awards are dependent on the number of credit hours students are taking. In these situations a financial aid system that does not take this into account can either result in fewer students returning because of insufficient financial aid, or it can require increased staff to monitor the changes in students' registration manually and regularly. There are costs associated with either developing an automated system or with hiring additional staff to track shifts in student enrollment behaviors. Such factors must be taken into consideration when planning to implement or sustain administrative information systems.

In an enterprise system environment, all requested changes and enhancements must compete with each other. Additionally, the cost for customization usually exceeds the cost for equivalent changes in a legacy-system environment. Systems that were once owned, maintained, and supported by various in-house experts now also serve as the same systems that support various back-office functions of the organization (e.g., human resource management, financial management), along with the core functions of administration (e.g., admissions, registration, financial aid). The end user often will find it difficult to see what advantages are derived from the enterprise solution. Indeed, faculty at institutions with strong faculty governance are likely to favor build-your-own solutions intuitively. They are less likely to accept being told that the software cannot easily accommodate their policies or practices. This makes the implementation of ERP systems on campuses that have had a history of building their own system more contentious and difficult.

Costs

A large body of systematic research comparing the associated costs of build-your-own systems to vendor-delivered enterprise systems has not yet emerged for higher education institutions. However, the EDU-CAUSE Center for Applied Research has conducted extensive studies addressing the costs of vendor-delivered enterprise systems (Kvavik and Katz 2002), comparing the estimated costs to actual costs after implementation. Some of their findings, particularly with respect to customization, may rightfully apply to build-your-own systems as well—considering that a build-your-own system is designed as a one-of-a-kind, customized system.

Kvavik and Katz's 2002 study notes that, contrary to suspicion, the majority of vendor-delivered ERP implementations do not take longer than planned. Additionally, most of the institutions studied (two-thirds) finished their implementations on or under their original budget (43). However, the bigger the institution and the more customization that was specified, the less likely the institution would come in on time and under budget. Of the 258 ERP institutions in the study, 70 percent reported some degree of customization, with 48 percent of institutions reporting modifications of only up to 10 percent of the software. Kvavik and Katz note that customization improved customer satisfaction but increased costs. Though the findings are not surprising, they identify a critical tradeoff—and one that must be evaluated with respect to an institution's culture and environment. Institutions that succeeded in implementing without any customizations were able to avoid cost overrun. Some institutions were adamant about not making any changes to the software until the vanilla implementation was fully installed and functioning. This enabled the schools to identify and then rank re-

223

quired changes after other alternatives to alleviate customization were explored. By opting for tight controls over change proposals *after* a successful vanilla implementation, many nice-to-have but nonessential changes were avoided, reducing the corresponding cost outlays.

In budget estimations for the Kvavik and Katz study, there were numerous areas of significant cost increases after implementation, which came as a surprise to survey respondents. The cost area that showed the highest degree of underestimation—post-implementation—pertained to user training. Kvavik notes the need for more training was compounded by two simultaneous system changes: a new user interface and new business processes. Change management—preparing campus constituents for the impending change—must include a comprehensive training program, which is time-consuming and expensive. Similarly, the costs for generating reports proved to be much higher than institutional planners anticipated. Though the system may be able to maintain the same data, unless the information can be presented in a way that is compatible to user requirements, implementers will exacerbate user dissatisfaction and spend resources to develop an abundance of unique, nonstandardized reports.

Another cost typically incurred and often underestimated in the majority of ERP implementations was for consultants. Consultant services were used to provide skill sets not existing on the staff; consultants were often used with system selection, initial user training, and ongoing project support. Ninety percent of the institutions employing consultants reported the procured support was instrumental in helping the institution meet its objectives for system implementation.

When building one's own system, it is also important to evaluate the development costs—*fixed* costs—with the operating costs after the system is installed. The costs for vendor updates may or may not be greater than the costs for in-house developers to make required changes. The degree to which an institution opts to retain and train development staff or hire consultants to make required changes affects both recurring and future costs.

Following the Kvavik and Katz study, another survey, which focused at a broader sector of ERP implementations in industry and government, found that 51 percent of firms that implemented ERP systems (232 firms responded to the survey) were dissatisfied with the results (Jahnke 2002). The greatest area of dissatisfaction pertained to higher-than-anticipated costs and lower-than-expected returns on investment.

Build-your-own, uniquely customized systems, as well, are often plagued by grossly inaccurate cost estimations. However, this really should not come as a major surprise. In designing one's own system, requirements are typically less rigid and more evolving. Since software estimates are typically done at the beginning of the project—before the requirements phase is complete and the needs are fully understood—cost estimation often occurs at the wrong time. Glass (2001) notes that estimates for build-your-own systems are often made by upper management and not by the people who will build the software and their managers. It is worth noting, however, that in our conversations with university administrators around the country who are leading the implementation of ERP systems, it appears that this is also often the case for the estimated budgets for ERP systems. Evidently, pressure to achieve the estimated targets causes programmers to abbreviate or forego good software engineering practices and processes, resulting in less resilient and capable products.

Though ERP systems typically enable institutions to get a better gauge of the associated costs for a system, numerous institutions have been successful in building and implementing systems that meet established requirements. Senior administrators must evaluate a myriad of factors, especially in-house technical capacity, before embarking on a decision of whether to build or buy a vended system—including if and how they plan to customize the vended system.

Closing Thoughts

In closing, we offer several recommendations to senior campus administrators who are involved in these key outsourcing and privatization decisions about student information systems.

1. The larger and more complex the institution at which you work, the harder it will be to implement vanilla ERP systems or simple build-your-own solutions. With size and complexity come greater costs.
2. Institutions with strong traditions of faculty governance will also find it hard to implement vanilla ERP systems or simple build-your-own solutions. Strong faculty governance also results in more contentious implementations and greater costs.
3. Colleges and universities that have not had a history of large IT staffs and strong functional staffs should not consider build-your-own solutions. They are likely to be ill prepared for the costs and risks of building or of sustaining the staff required to maintain home-grown systems.
4. Campuses with a tradition of building their own systems will find it harder to implement and sustain vended solutions. Faculty, func-

tional, and technical staff are accustomed to having systems that meet their unique policies and business practices. Exploring open-source solutions may be worth the investment of resources. The constraints of vended systems will create friction and resistance during the implementation process.

5. Do a thorough, open, and critical assessment of the strengths and weaknesses of vended and home-grown solutions. There are no easy or inexpensive solutions, only solutions that are better or less adequate for the unique context of each college and university.

6. Use the high-range cost estimates for building your own systems or purchasing vended systems. Costs are almost always higher than anticipated; therefore, be skeptical of advocates of build-your-own or vended systems who promise significantly lower implementation costs than peer institutions. When administrators want to argue for more money, we do benchmarking to prove we should get the money. However, we sometimes use the same data to prove how much more efficient we are. Projecting too much efficiency with new student information systems can result in problematic implementations.

References

Bendoly, E., A. K. Soni, and M. A. Venkataramanan. 2004. Value chain resource planning: Adding value with systems beyond the enterprise. *Business Horizons* 47(2): 79–86.

Brown, C. V., and I. Vessey. 2003. Managing the next wave of enterprise systems: Leveraging lessons from ERP. *MIS Quarterly Executive* 2(1): 65–77.

Cohen, A. M., and F. B. Brawer. 2003. *The American community college*, 4th ed. San Francisco: Jossey-Bass.

Ehrmann, S. C. 1999. Technology's grand challenges. *Academe* (September–October): 42–46.

Glass, R. L. 2001. Frequently forgotten fundamental facts about software engineering. *IEEE Software* 18(3): 109–11.

Haigh, T. 2004. A veritable bucket of facts: Origins of the database management system. In *The history and heritage of scientific and technological information systems: Proceedings of the 2002 conference*, ed. W. B. Rayward and M. E. Bowden, 73–78. Medford, N.J.: Information Today, Inc.

Harrison, M. S., and G. H. Walton. 2002. Identifying high maintenance legacy software. *Journal of Software Maintenance and Evolution: Research and Practice* 14:429–46.

Hossler, D. 2000. *The Enrollment Management Review* 16 (Summer). (Newsletter). College Board.

Howe, D. 2004. *The free online dictionary of computing*. Available at http://burks.bton.ac.uk/burks/foldoc/.

Hughes, R. L., R. C. Ginnett, and G. J. Curphy. 2002. *Leadership: Enhancing the lessons of experience*, 4th ed. New York: McGraw-Hill Irwin.

Jahnke, A. 2002. *What's wrong with the IT consulting model?* Available at http://comment.cio.com/soundoff/020702.html.

Kvavik, R. B., and R. N. Katz. 2002. *The promise and performance of enterprise systems for higher education.* Boulder, Colo.: EDUCAUSE Center for Applied Research.

Lazerson, M. 1997. Who owns higher education? *Change* 29 (March–April): 10–15.

Light, B. 2001. The maintenance implications of the customization of ERP software. *Journal of Software Maintenance and Evolution: Research and Practice* 13: 415–29.

Monro, J. 1984. *A personal history of student financial assistance.* Paper presented at the College Board Annual Forum, November, New York.

Rahgozar, M., and F. Oroumchian. 2003. An effective strategy for legacy systems evolution. *Journal of Software Maintenance and Evolution: Research and Practice* 15: 325–44.

Tierney, W. (1988). Organizational culture in higher education: Defining the essentials. *Journal of Higher Education* 59: 2–21.

CHAPTER ELEVEN

E-Learning

James Farmer

When computers arrived on campus in the 1960s and 1970s, e-learning pioneers Pat Suppes at Stanford University and Don Bitzer at the University of Illinois began using computers for instruction. Displays were limited to text, and lessons were hand coded. But that early work established that students can learn from computer-aided instruction, as it was called. Suppes's work revealed diverse learning styles—length of sessions and time to complete a course—even among the homogenous student body at Stanford and the local high school. Bitzer, with support from Control Data Corporation, began to employ multimedia—first audio and then a new plasma display. The early courses focused on drill and practice—for learning language, chemistry, and mathematics.

Tilton's analysis of multimedia in the classroom at Yavapai College (Tilton 1995) demonstrated that retention and completion rates could be increased in the Biology 180 Biology Concepts, a Gateway course (see Farmer 1996, 483–84).[1] Users of Plato's algebra course cite similar success.[2] Several types of e-learning have emerged, and they are quite different. These were well summarized by Allen and Seaman as shown in table 11.1. Early implementations of learning management systems focused on Web-facilitated courses. As used in this chapter, e-learning focuses on those delivered online.

Cost was an early barrier to online learning. In the late 1960s one estimate of the cost of providing a terminal hour to a student was $48.[3] Following computing's cost-performance curve, the cost now is between 25 and 50 cents per hour as compared to $10 per hour per stu-

Table 11.1. Types of Generic E-learning Technology Use in Course Delivery

Portion of Content Delivered Online	Type of Course	Typical Description
0%	Traditional	Course with no online technology used. Content is delivered in writing or orally.
1–29%	Web-facilitated	Course which uses web-based technology to facilitate what is essentially a face-to-face course. Uses a course management system (CMS) or web pages to post the syllabus and assignments, for example.
30–69%	Blended/Hybrid	Course that blends online and face-to-face delivery. Substantial proportion of the content is delivered online. Uses online discussions. Has some face-to-face meetings.
80+%	Online	Course in which most of the content is delivered online. Has no face-to-face meetings.

Source: Allen & Seaman 2004.

dent in a classroom.[4] Yet now, when colleges and universities are straining to accommodate enrollments, when the content of courses continues to increase, and when faculty have students with sharply different levels of preparation and learning styles, e-learning is only beginning to have an impact on teaching and learning. But it is beginning and should sharply increase as enrollments are diverted from the public universities to the public community colleges (California Performance Review Commission 2004).

With each new generation of technology, educators and policy makers dream of a new world of education with greater efficiency and better quality. William Massy wrote, "Technology can be brought into the educational process in three ways: as a productivity aid for individuals, as enrichment add-ins, and as stimulants and enablers of education process engineering" (2000). However, unlike most uses, the new technologies have not been labor saving in U.S. higher education. Of the waves of technology—from television through computing and telecommunications—the converged technologies, delivered through a new generation of programs known as e-learning, may have the greatest potential of changing educational delivery in fundamental ways, reaching more people with new forms of pedagogy, but not yet at a lower cost (Farmer 2004), at least not in the United States. To date, the British

Open University and some American community colleges are the only educational organizations to realize an economic benefit from the electronic delivery of educational programs.

The reasons why it has been difficult to realize efficiencies in the American system are related to the nature of the technology and to the system of education. It took the film industry a substantial period of time and several iterative and adaptive ventures to adapt to the new technologies.[5] As with the film industry, it will take many ancillary changes in publishing and other related industries for higher education to be in a position to capitalize fully on the new technologies in the learning process. It is unlikely that great new efficiencies will be realized from technology in the short term. Rather, the integration and adaptation of technologies is likely to add to the costs of higher education for students and states in the near future, adding to the complexity of decisions about public investment in technology. This chapter examines the emergence of the dilemmas associated with funding the investment in e-learning, then suggests steps toward a rethinking of the challenge.

The Promise of Technology
and the Dilemma of Funding

In the late 1960s and 1970s computer-based training (CBT) appeared to provide new alternatives for meeting public policy goals of universal access to higher education, equal opportunity for success, and sharply lower unit costs of instruction. Research has confirmed that instructional and learning technologies, offered as distance learning or complementing classroom instruction, can be more effective than traditional classroom instruction, especially for marginally prepared students, and can increase access, retention, and completion.[6]

But these benefits have been elusive because the cost of instruction using these technologies at most colleges and universities exceeds available funding. The publishing industry has similarly failed to produce learning materials for colleges and universities that would be profitable. Yet publishers have produced training materials for industry that have achieved broad utilization and have been profitable or appear likely to be so in the near future. This is the case because employers incur the full costs of training and receive the benefits of convenient time and place and increased productivity, while colleges and universities do not receive these benefits. In the case of higher education, the student incurs both the cost of traveling to class and the inconvenience or barrier of class schedules, and benefits from the more effective methods of learning.

For e-learning to become economically viable, changes will be required in colleges and universities that transcend the boundaries of finance and instruction. Some faculty must become more specialized in authoring learning materials. Academic planners will have to segment the market based on student characteristics, make the most of appropriate methods of teaching and learning, and make facilities available to each segment. Business officers will have to explore market segment pricing. Federal, state, and local governments and those firms that finance employee education may recognize the benefits of improved learning technology and increase their contribution to higher education for these benefits—a sharp departure from the trends of the past decade. If all of these can be accomplished, a new model of course delivery will become viable; students and society will benefit from this cooperative effort. As Massy (2000) wrote, "Education process reengineering means challenging tried and true pedagogical methods, many of which have been in place for decades or even centuries."

Achieving Success with Instruction and Learning Technologies

The investment in course materials can become a barrier to widespread use of instruction and learning technology. As computer savvy, Internet using, computer game playing students become the new students, their expectations for the quality of instructional materials may increase their cost just as the cost of motion pictures increased—about 10 percent per year—to meet the expectations of the young audience. As more students work while attending college, the methods of instruction will have to accommodate these constraints, exactly as executive MBA programs have accommodated harried executives and as community colleges have turned to new forms of instruction that exploit the flexibility and effectiveness of learning technology.

To have a long, useful life, learning materials will have to be designed for the student of 2010 or 2015, not for what is acceptable or even new today. With more multimedia and adaptive learning designs, more internationalization of learning materials, and more implementation of remedial protocols, the costs of learning materials will continue to rise even though digital technologies are reducing the costs of current development. There are price constraints. The cost of learning materials and the associated networking infrastructure must have sufficient utilization—class size—to amortize the investment over a large number of users. The key to amortizing the high cost of multimedia learning materials for a large number of students is to standardize learning content and ensure it is interoperable with almost all learning management systems and virtual learning environments. If this were done, then the publishing industry or collaborations could play a major role in supplying learning content to colleges and universities at prices that yield cost of instruction comparable to the traditional classroom.

Some college presidents, especially at rural community colleges, are making the decision to employ instruction and learning technologies to provide access even though this requires internal subsidization from other programs. Some college presidents are also making the decision to employ these technologies solely to benefit students who otherwise could not attend the scheduled classes, again accepting higher costs in order to better serve the community.

To better understand the actions that need to be taken to achieve sustainable costs of instruction and the trade-off decisions that must be made both at the local level and at the state and federal level, it is useful to analyze what is known about these students and the experience in offering broadcast television, interactive instructional television, and Internet delivery. Some limited experience demonstrates the benefits of using multimedia learning materials in the traditional classroom.

Pat Suppes at Stanford University used CBT to teach Russian and mathematics. He reported that all students were able to complete the course satisfactorily. He observed that it took ten to thirteen times as much "terminal time" for the least-prepared student as for the most-prepared student. It appeared that CBT provided the opportunity for achieving competency over broad ranges of preparation and aptitude (Suppes and Stillinger 1999). Don Bitzer reported similar results from his work at the University of Illinois (Silberman 1997). Bitzer's work improved both the technology—becoming the source of today's plasma displays—and the learning materials. He introduced the idea of an online laboratory, using simulations of experiments typically done in early chemistry classes. His work, advanced by a major investment by Control Data Corporation, became the Plato system, which is still in use today. Plato was subsequently used by Chicago and Baltimore school districts and demonstrated similar successful results for students in K–12 schools.

With the support of the U.S. Department of Commerce's Interactive Instructional Television (IITV) program, colleges began installing microwave links providing two-way video and audio links between the source of the class and students at remote locations (Grobsmith and

Hurst 2004).[7] This approach was successfully used by Arizona community colleges to bring instruction to remote small towns throughout the state. Broadcast television was successfully used by Coast [California] Community College District and the Dallas County [Texas] Community College district to make courses available throughout a large urban area, and they became major suppliers of broadcast video courses. The University of Nebraska used broadcast television to bring classes to the rural areas. Policy makers funded such projects to make rich and varied academic programs available in areas where low population density could not support a college or university.

These projects often had external funding or succeeded because of unique circumstances. The unit cost of instruction was higher than traditional instruction. As mentioned earlier, in the early 1970s the California State Universities estimated the cost of an hour of terminal learning to be about $48. This meant that a typical three-unit course—45 hours of classroom work and study—would cost $2,160 for computer resources alone at a time when the average cost of a three-unit course was less than $300. But the computer industry assured higher education that unit cost would plummet, and it has—to less than $0.50 per hour in the typical college computer laboratory or only $24 for a course when the average direct cost of classroom course delivery is now about $450 and the fully allocated cost is $1,000.

The availability of the Internet has moved learning from the computer laboratory to learning at work and home. It has moved the source of learning from the nearby college or university to anywhere in the world. And it has sharply reduced the cost of networking.

With these early successes, what are the barriers to widespread use of instructional technology? Investment in learning materials—a major capital expense and computing infrastructure—is never really complete. And who will pay? Students—as they pay for books or special computing fees? Faculty—who have contributed to both textbooks and early e-learning materials? Or the colleges and universities—as part of education expenditures such as the library?

As with textbook publishing, the key to low unit costs will be the number of students who use the same learning material, not the cost of development. Funding for this effective method will be a combination of lowering unit costs—to make it economically viable—and some additional revenue reflecting the improved productivity. This will require several steps on the part of colleges and universities collectively, or ultimately the free-market, morphing from the training perspective, will extend the corporate training model into postsecondary education.

233

Technologies of Success

Several technologies have been successfully used in distance learning. One was the use of networked audio and video, which effectively increased class size and lowered unit costs. Several of the colleges became sources of video material that was licensed to other colleges, sharing the investment for their development. Typical license costs were $600 to $1,500 per semester course independent of the number of students. The costs of the broadcasts were generally contributed or subsidized as a "public service" required as a condition of having a broadcast license. This model was especially effective in urban areas that would have larger student enrollments within the area of broadcast reception. Another use of networked audio and video was the remote classroom, which increased the class size. Often the additional networking cost would still reduce unit costs as class size increased. This was particularly effective in community college districts that had several remote campuses in small cities or towns. Another, and more current, model is Internet delivery, a return to the CBT model using current technology.

Perhaps the most successful example is the British Open University that began using the broadcast technology model in 1975 and is continuing its transition to the Internet delivery model. The Open University succeeded where the U.S. publishing industry has failed because of one factor: it has demonstrated how a large investment in learning materials can be amortized over a large student enrollment to achieve low unit costs. The Open University's US$1 billion investment in its undergraduate curriculum is being amortized over an average class size of 11,000, with the lowest class size of 800.[8]

Rio Salado College, a Maricopa County [Phoenix] community college specializing in nontraditional instruction, has successfully developed and provides a large number of Internet courses. Courses are typically developed by their faculty. The college developed a teaching model that is effective and a business model that is viable, with course delivery costs comparable to or lower than other Maricopa community colleges.[9] Most of the college's distance learning now combines the features of all of the early models, and distance learning techniques have been added to many traditional courses to improve learning.

Effectiveness of Distance Learning

In general, distance learning instruction has been found to be as effective as, but perhaps no more effective than, classroom instruction.

Notwithstanding public opinion, as early as 1928 researchers have found "no difference in test scores of college classroom and correspondence study student enrollment in the same subjects" (Crump 1928), and in 1940 even found "correspondence study students performed as well as or better than their classroom counterparts" (Hanna 1940). Similar results were reported for interactive instructional television. Recent results show "no significant difference among the students taking distance education courses. . . . There really is no significant difference between the remote and nonremote groups" (McGreal 1994). More specifically, in 1994 researchers reported that "students learn equally well from lessons delivered with any medium, face-to-face or at a distance. . . . There is no inherent significant difference in the educational effectiveness of media" (Schlosser and Anderson 1994). And, in 1995 Sorenson reported, "There are generally no differences in achievement between students in traditional classes and those in distance-delivered classes, or between distance students at remote sites and those at origination sites where a teacher is present."

If this is true, then the focus can be on the costs rather than differences of effectiveness. Two observations suggest that there are differences that affect enrollment. Focus groups continue to report that students prefer classroom instruction. An unpublished study shows that students will commute farther to a traditional classroom than they will to an IITV classroom offering the same course.[10] This suggests that traditional student enrollments may be less affected by the choice of presentation media than by campus environment and institutional reputation. However, this observation may not be relevant, since distance learning is primarily used where students cannot conveniently be in a classroom either because of distance or because of schedule.[11]

Rio Salado College has observed that text-based Internet courses are enrolling a larger proportion of older students than other courses with multimedia. This suggests the use of instructional media may affect enrollment of younger students.[12]

Corporate Training and Instruction

Over the past decade, computer-based instruction (CBI) or computer-based learning (CBL) and computer-based training (CBT), all based on the same educational technologies, have taken on different meanings and different economics. The term "training" is typically used for corporate programs; the terms "instruction" or "learning," for colleges and universities.

As used here, training and instruction have sharply different economics. Employees are students of corporate training; their wages and travel expenses are part of the corporate "cost of instruction." For professionals such as airline pilots, these costs can be as high as $500 per hour of instruction.[13] And the number of students taking the same training tends to be much higher than the average class size in higher education. For this reason, the unit cost of instruction for corporate training tends to be insensitive to the investment cost of course materials.

Recent research summarizes the effective use of computer-based instruction by business: "Nucleus Research has found that many companies deploying e-learning solutions have achieved significant returns by reducing training-related costs and improving employee productivity" (Nucleus Research, Inc. 2002). We could add, "Increased productivity and reduced travel and training costs are the main benefits driving a positive ROI [return on investment] from e-learning."

Because the course content for training can be similar for a number of companies or agencies, commercial training materials are frequently used. Because of the quantity and low price sensitivity, an active market for corporate training materials exists for common subjects. Sophisticated learning materials that reduce student time are cost-effective for business. These economics are not available in higher education, where students bear the cost of their time and travel; and these costs are not included in the cost of instruction for the college or university. The students, their employers, and society—rather than the college or university—benefit from increased productivity.

The economic models of instructional technology and distance learning in this chapter use the cost of instruction as defined for colleges and universities. As the knowledge economy grows and the scope of corporate training expands, publishers of these courses are beginning to market them to traditional colleges and universities. The University of Phoenix has adopted some corporate training practices. Course content is determined and course materials are developed centrally; course and instructor evaluations are used continuously to revise both the course materials and teaching methods and to ensure the quality of course delivery at any location.[14]

Investing in Course Media Development

There are two significant differences between the cost of distance learning and that of the traditional classroom. Except for interactive in-

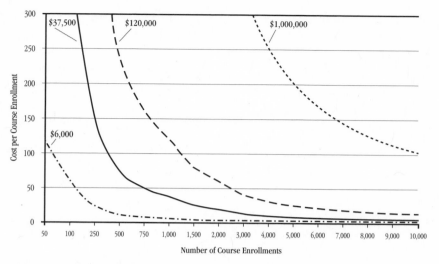

Figure 11.1. Average cost of instructional materials per course enrollment for various levels of course development cost.

structional television that uses an instructor teaching in a classroom, there are significant costs for the development of instructional media. In the past, the instructor had the responsibility for writing textbooks. These textbooks were in turn printed and sold to students. The cost of the textbook was principally the cost of printing, binding, and distribution. The professor wrote the text at no cost to the institution and for a small royalty from students who purchased the text. The professor "subsidized" the preparation of the instructional materials, and the cost of the professor's royalty, if any, was borne by the students, not the college.

The textbook business has changed. The textbook publisher now has responsibilities for contributing to the development of the content, choosing images such as charts and graphs that are included in the textbook, developing workbooks and other student materials, and producing multimedia instructional materials and instructor's guides that accompany the text. These costs are borne by the students in terms of higher costs for textbooks.[15] This investment is increased by the number of separate versions required to accommodate proprietary e-learning systems. For example, McGraw-Hill maintains at least twenty-four separate versions of its higher education course materials.[16] This leads to prices that students feel are exorbitant (see Fairchild 2005).

With new forms of instruction such as Internet courses, television courses (telecourses), and computer-based instruction courses, the costs

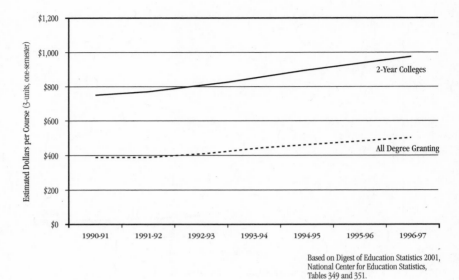

Based on Digest of Education Statistics 2001,
National Center for Education Statistics,
Tables 349 and 351.

Figure 11.2. Average national cost of course delivery.

for the development of the media are being borne by the college producing the materials or by the author—which may be someone other than the professor. When colleges bear these costs, they should be included in course costs and unit costs.

Some colleges have attempted to license course materials to others. This has been successful for telecourses used for broadcast television. Users pay a fixed fee plus an increment for each enrollment. Some Internet courses are being licensed for similar amounts, but it appears there is insufficient enrollment at this time to make this economically viable.[17] When media are licensed, then the cost of the license rather than the cost of media development is included in the course costs and unit costs.

Figure 11.1 illustrates the effect of development costs. The four levels of development cost represent a text-based three-unit Internet course, a multimedia-based Internet course, a commercially-developed CD-ROM course, and a television course.[18]

Typical costs of instruction range from several hundred dollars per course for low-tuition public colleges to several thousand dollars per course for private colleges and universities. National averages for two-year colleges and for all colleges is shown in figure 11.2. Figure 11.1 shows that it is difficult for any college to absorb the cost of development of television courses or even computer-based instruction courses.

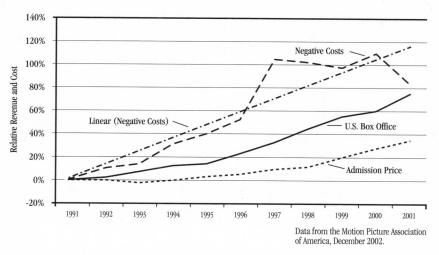

Figure 11.3. Average cost of motion picture development in the U.S.

Internet courses take several hundred enrollments over the life of the course to achieve costs per enrollment that are comparable to current costs of instruction or textbook costs.

The demand for multimedia courses of increasing complexity should cause the unit costs for instructional materials to escalate in a way that is similar to the cost of feature motion picture films. If so, this makes the cost of developing content even more difficult to absorb. This escalation is shown in figure 11.3 and averages about 10 percent per year. This also shows that the introduction of a new technology—digital editing and special effects—has an initial increase in cost but may subsequently lead to lower unit costs or higher quality or both. Although it is possible to achieve break-even enrollments for the most popular courses—much as telecourses do—significant issues will arise in developing multimedia materials for specialized courses.

In summary, although there are indications that multimedia course materials associated with instructional technology will increase enrollments and completions, these benefits are not sufficiently acknowledged to include in the analysis.[19] There are also indications that "screenager" students will prefer multimedia with their higher and increasing development costs. This will affect enrollments, but the effect of this has not yet been quantified.

The cost of course development appears to have passed from the instructor and student to the colleges and universities. Who will make this investment and how the investment will be recaptured is not known. It

239

could be the publishing industry if interoperability is achieved. It could be colleges and universities if they continue to work closely together on e-learning.[20]

Conclusions

The promise of technological change has been harder to realize in U.S. higher education than in the United Kingdom largely because structural differences between the two systems has made it easier for Britain to initiate the large-scale changes. Comparison with the film industry places the challenges facing U.S. higher education into perspective. Similarly, contract education has demonstrated that specialized content, delivery, and branding is attractive to businesses and their employees.

To achieve the goals of higher education, the priorities are

- Sharable learning content to encourage publishers to make the investment in multimedia learning materials and to make authoring learning materials viable at colleges and universities. This requires cooperation among the e-learning software suppliers.
- Convenient and effective methods of instruction for each learning market segment. This implies a transformation of the education process to accommodate the different methods of instructional delivery.
- Change at colleges and universities to accommodate this new diversity, especially specializations in teaching and learning to support faculty accommodating larger "classes." This includes specialists to support the student's use of technology—the new "help desk," for assessment and testing, and advisors on learning—the Open University's "tutors."
- Market segment pricing that takes advantage of "convenience" prices in some programs that can absorb a greater share of the infrastructure costs to reduce the price of instruction and research that is important to the college or university and its community but does not achieve economies of scale.

Notes

1. Completion rates increased from 60 percent to 85 percent in the sections where faculty had multimedia presentations. Analysis of simultaneous videos of both the instructor and class gave insight into the effectiveness of teaching techniques and uses of specific multimedia.

2. A series of Plato Learning "implementation stories" published in 2004 for Plato's algebra course show pass rates increasing from 45 percent to 60 percent at Northern

Oklahoma College, students completing two courses in a single term at Tarrant County College, and class size increasing at Rio Salado College from 35 to 100 with e-learning (Plato Learning 2004a, 2004b, 2004c).

3. From the author's experience as CIO of the California State University. This 1970 cost estimate was based on the use of computing terminals by architectural students at California Polytechnic University at San Luis Obispo and reported at a subsequent Educom meeting at Princeton University. The lower costs are based on estimates for Amarillo College made in 1996 and 1997 in an unpublished report.

4. Based on allocated instructional costs, including prorated academic and institutional expenses for U.S. fall 2002 enrollments and fiscal year 2002–2003 expenditures (National Center for Education Statistics 2003 [projected full-time enrollment], 2004 [financial data]). The full-time equivalent is assumed to be enrollment in 12 credit hours per term with three classroom hours per credit hour.

5. The Open University adopted the "talented team" approach to the development of its learning materials. Subject matter experts worked with education technologists, writers, graphic artists, and audio and video specialists to develop and test learning materials. The influence of BBC documentarians on the Open University came from the early form of delivery—television.

6. Thomas L. Russell (2005), Director Emeritus of Instructional Telecommunications at North Carolina State University, has listed conclusions of more than 200 studies from 1928 through 1996 showing that distance learning was at least as effective as classroom instruction. This has been true since early use of correspondence courses.

7. From the presentation slides of Liz Grobsmith and Fred Hurst, "Northern Arizona University: A University for the 21st Century," made to the NAU faculty on September 29, 2004, in a discussion of the university's strategic plan. NAU, a large recipient of U.S. Department of Commerce grants, offered IITV throughout rural Arizona, including reservations for Native Americans.

8. Based on an analysis of the Open University's financial statements, Justin E. Tilton and the author estimated this investment to be US$500 million. Subsequent discussions with Open University official Bob Masterson at a subsequent NCHELP conference corrected the investment to US$1 billion. The class sizes were estimated from enrollment data for the 1999–2000 academic year.

9. In a sense, the faculty are "subsidizing" course development since they were selected for their special interest in distance education and they work intensively on their course materials. As at the Open University, Rio Salado College faculty are continuously monitoring student performance and are adjusting their instruction to improve student retention and performance.

10. From an unpublished 1997 study by the author of the effect of distance on student enrollments of Pima Community College District.

11. The word "convenient" may have a new meaning when most students work, many at jobs that provide no schedule flexibility, or when traffic has increased commuting time.

12. The observation was made by Rio Salado College's Carol Wilson in 1996. Karen Mills confirmed this observation based on statistics from the student system. The needs and preference of "screenagers" was documented in an unpublished paper, "Screenagers and Learning," by John Kennel of instructional media + magic, inc., in 1997. This followed the 1996 publication of Douglas Rushkoff's *Playing the Future: How Kids' Culture Can Teach Us to Thrive in an Age of Chaos* (1996). Rushkoff used

the term "screenager" to refer to young people who use computers for entertainment rather than go to movies.

13. A planning estimate given by Rubin Siddique, Lufthansa Airlines, in response to a question at the May 4, 2000, meeting of the Aviation Industry CBT Committee Meeting in Frankfurt, Germany.

14. Personal conversations with Apollo Group Inc. chairman Dr. John G. Sperling in 1997 through 1998 while working with Rio Salado College and subsequent meetings with CEO Todd Nelson while working with the Arizona Board of Regents. According to the 2002 Annual Report of the Apollo Group, the University of Phoenix has 176 campuses in 37 states and the province of British Columbia and serves 157,800 students.

15. The cost of development of multimedia materials used in the classroom must be included in the cost of textbooks selected by faculty and purchased by students. The costs have also increased because of the growing number of color illustrations and photographs in the textbooks. This observation was confirmed by representatives of Mc-Graw-Hill at an August 16, 2004, meeting with Columbia University and New York University representatives in New York City, discussing the use of learning materials in the Sakai open source learning system.

16. From a 2004 meeting with representatives from McGraw Hill, New York University, and Columbia University. This includes four separate versions for Blackboard, the leading e-learning system in higher education.

17. Rio Salado College may be an exception because of its low cost of course development and the large number of enrollments.

18. These costs are reported costs from current community college course developments. The colleges and companies are considered to be low-cost producers.

19. One example is Yavapai College's experience. Professor Jon Freriks increased completion rates in his Biology 180 course and subsequent enrollments using a multimedia instructional presentation developed from his notes and images by Justin E. Tilton of instructional media + magic, inc. (Farmer 1996).

20. Several collaborative efforts, such as the Sakai Project, are emerging that produce software or course materials and implement them in the institutions.

References

Allen, I. E., and J. Seaman. 2004. *Entering the mainstream: The quality and extent of online education in the United States, 2003 and 2004.* Sloan Center for Online Education at Olin and Babson Colleges, The Sloan Consortium.

California Performance Review Commission. 2004. Education, training, and volunteerism, and recommendations on transfer from community colleges to the public universities. In *A government for the people for a change,* 497–688. Sacramento, Calif.: California Performance Review Commission.

Crump, R. E. 1928. Correspondence and class extension work in Oklahoma. Ph.D. diss., Teachers College, Columbia University.

Fairchild, M. 2005. *Ripoff 101: How the current practices of the textbook industry drive up the cost of textbooks.* Washington, D.C.: State PIRGs.

Farmer, J. 1996. Using technology. In *Handbook of the undergraduate curriculum: A comprehensive guide to purposes, structures, practices, and change,* ed. J. G. Gaff, J. L. Ratcliff, and associates. San Francisco: Jossey-Bass.

Grobsmith, L., and F. Hurst, F. 2004. Northern Arizona University: A university for the 21st century. Presentation on September 29 at Northern Arizona University.

Hanna, L. N. 1940. Achievement of high school students in supervised correspondence study. Master's thesis, University of Nebraska.

Massy, W. F. 2000. *Life on the wired campus: How information technology will shape institutional futures.* Palo Alto, Calif.: National Center for Postsecondary Improvement, Stanford University.

McGreal, R. (1994). Comparison of the attitudes of learners taking audiographic teleconferencing courses in secondary schools in Northern Ontario. *Interpersonal Computing and Technology: An Electronic Journal for the 21st Century* 2(4): 11–23.

National Center for Education Statistics. 2003. *Projections of education statistics to 2013.* NCES No. 2004–013. By D. E. Gerald and W. J. Hussar. Washington, D.C.: National Center for Education Statistics.

———. 2004. *Digest of education statistics, 2003.* NCES 2005–025. Washington, D.C.: National Center for Education Statistics.

Nucleus Research, Inc. 2002. *E-learning delivers consistent returns.* Research Note C49. Wellesley, Mass.: Nucleus Research, Inc.

Plato Learning, Inc. 2004a. *Diligent focus on results leads to soaring pass rates for students using interactive mathematics at Northern Oklahoma College.* Bloomington, Minn.: Plato Learning, Inc.

———. 2004b. *Profile: Rio Salado College, Tempe, Arizona, Interactive mathematics has helped Rio Salado College design cost-effective distance learning courses.* Bloomington, Minn.: Plato Learning, Inc.

———. 2004c. *Tarrant County College adds more interactive mathematics sections as student achievement rises.* Bloomington, Minn.: Plato Learning, Inc.

Russell, T. L. 2005. *The "No significant difference" phenomenon.* Available at http://nt. media.hku.hk/no_sig_diff/phenom1.html.

Rushkoff, D. 1996. *Playing the future: How kids' culture can teach us to thrive in an age of chaos.* New York: HarperCollins.

Schlosser, C.A., and M. L. Anderson. 1994. *Distance education: Review of the literature.* Ames: Research Institute for Studies in Education, Iowa State University.

Silberman, S. 1997, March 12. *PLATOfest to celebrate first online community.* Available at http://www.physics.uiuc.edu/General_Info/History/PLATOfest.htm.

Sorensen, C. K. 1995. *Evaluation of two-way interactive television for community college instruction.* Paper presented at conference of American Council of Engineering Companies, Ames, Iowa.

Suppes, P., and C. Stillinger. 1999. *Individual differences in gifted students' progress through computer-based algebra and pre-calculus courses.* Available at http://epgy. stanford.edu.

Tilton, J. E. 1995. Bio 180 instructor analysis. Report presented to Dr. Doreen Daily, president of Yavapai College, Prescott, Arizona, May 22.

IV
MAKING SENSE
OF CHANGE

CHAPTER TWELVE

Privatization and the
Public Interest

Edward P. St. John

The trend toward privatization of public higher education raises new questions about the public interest. If government shifts responsibility for funding higher education from taxpayers to students and lenders, then who has responsibility for the public good? More fundamentally, what is the public good in this new finance environment? Such questions must be asked—and some current policies must be altered—or the social progressive foundations of the U.S. system of higher education, now threatened, will be lost. Before rushing off to "reclaim the public interest," however, we must rebuild an understanding of the public interest in higher education and of the impact of privatization on higher education.

Privatization of public higher education can best be understood in its global context. Rizvi (chapter 3) illustrates quite clearly that the trend toward privatization is not uniquely American. Since the end of the Cold War, a new culture of corporate interest has emerged, one that argues that capitalism won the ideological war with socialism (Gilpin 2001; Stiglitz 2003). But to assume that the Cold War was won because of private enterprise overlooks the roles of social welfare and education: public investments in people may have been as important as massive investment in "Star Wars" technology and the military-industrial complex. However, regardless of the position one takes on the roles of economic and social progress, the importance of the public interest in higher education should not be overlooked.

The challenges facing higher education in the rapidly changing global economy are formidable. There is a push to raise the percentage of the population with at least some college education to about 80 percent in the United States. However, only 70 percent of each high school cohort graduates from high school, and only about half of the graduates go on to college (St. John, Chung, Musoba, and Simmons 2004), so capacity would have to more than double to meet this goal. The challenge of expanding access is also complicated by the growth of the traditional college-age cohort. It may be difficult to sustain the current enrollment rate for the traditional college-age population in the United States, given the emphasis on lowering tax rates in this country. Further privatization may be needed just to maintain the current level of access. Therefore, the responses to this new call for educational expansion may involve fundamental changes in both K–12 and higher education. Improvement in schools is needed both to enable more students to graduate and to better prepare students for higher education. The privatization of public higher education may be necessary to meet the goal of expanding access even if tax rates increase (St. John 2003). In other words, the tradeoff is not between investments by taxpayers or students in a static system, but it is between extent and intent of investment by both groups in an expanding system of higher education.

This chapter reviews the previous chapters in this volume and uses a historical perspective on the government role in financing higher education to explore the challenge of redefining and reclaiming the public interest in higher education. It focuses on the U.S. system of education as it emerges from the analyses in this volume and other recent literature. First, I consider the "covenant" that provided the basis for public funding in the twentieth century, reflect on how the tenets of the social contract have changed, and ponder the need to rethink the public interest. Second, I take a critical look at the ways public institutions have adapted to the new challenges and the emergence of a new market system and privatized, quasi-public institutions. Third, with this background, I reconsider the meaning of the public interest in the new market system of higher education. In the conclusion I briefly review critical issues that underlie the challenge of reclaiming the public interest.

The Broken Covenant

The Land Grant Acts of the mid- and late nineteenth century, which donated public lands to states for the establishment of colleges, epitomize the ethos of public investment in higher education in the United States. During the Civil War, Congress engaged in the debate about the future economic development of the country. A national system of public universities that focused on engineering and technical assistance for an essentially rural society became the strategy, and grants of land and other financial incentives were used to encourage states to build research universities in the young nation (Jencks and Reisman 1968; Johnson 1989). This strategy of federal incentives and state responsibility worked well for more than a century in efforts to build a strong national system of public higher education to complement the already-existing system of nonprofit, or private higher education.

There were debates in the late nineteenth century about financial strategies, with some economists arguing for more student grants and a market system rather than institutional funding (Marsden 1994). Even many of the early land grant colleges used some of their funding for student financial aid as a means of encouraging enrollment (Johnson 1989). According to historical accounts, there were not sufficient numbers of prepared students with sufficient financial means to fill available slots at both the original private colleges and the new state universities. It was necessary in this early period of transition to provide subsidies to the new public colleges as well as to students in both types of colleges. The financial aid was necessary to stimulate demand for the new system of higher education.

States' decisions to invest in a public system set in motion a sustained period of growth in public colleges, especially in the mid-twentieth century, when the United States entered a period of mass higher education (Trow 1974). But most private colleges were challenged and, many argued, their survival was threatened. By the early 1970s many groups began to question whether private colleges could survive the competition from the public sector, given the decline in size of the college-age cohort anticipated in the next few decades (Breneman, Finn, and Nelson 1978; Carnegie Commission on Higher Education 1973).

The views presented in this volume and other recent literature differ fundamentally from the forecasts of the 1970s. Not only is there a strong private sector of higher education in the early twenty-first century, but the public sector is undergoing changes that emulate the private not-for-profit sector. What explains the apparent contradictions between the vision of prognosticators of three decades past and the realities we now face? To untangle this question, we should consider the rationale for public funding, the role of public service, and the coordination of public systems.

Human Capital Theory and Public Funding

Human capital theory (Becker 1964) provided a theoretical explanation for public and private investment that could be empirically tested (Hansen and Weisbrod 1969; Paulsen 2001a, 2001b). Not only was the theory used as a rationale for public programs and funding (Slaughter 1991; Trammel 2004), but policymakers could use it to make their own judgments about the realities behind the claims for funding (St. John and Parsons 2004). There was an implied contract embedded in the human capital argument, as it evolved in the late nineteenth and early twentieth centuries, but it was broken as the funding rationales changed in the late twentieth century.

Human Capital Theory as Funding Rationale

As articulated by Gary Becker (1964), human capital theory argued that that both individuals and government make decisions based on their investment costs and expected benefits. In the context of education, the costs to individuals include direct expenses (i.e., tuition, room and board, and other costs of attending) and earnings forgone during the period of enrollment, while the expected returns include higher annual earnings and a better quality of life. Education costs to governments, according to human capital theory, take the form of spending on colleges (direct subsidies) and students (grants and other subsidies) and opportunity costs, or lost opportunities to invest in other enterprises. The benefits to government are thought to be economic development —gains in economic productivity and/or tax revenue in a progressive tax system.

The theory of human capital also provided an explanation for the efficacy of federal and state investments in colleges. Certainly, the intent of the land grant colleges related to the implied and measurable benefits of investment. Advocates of public funding for colleges (Honeyman and Bruhn 1996; McKeown 1996) and master planning for state systems (Halstead 1974) developed schemes that used this rationale. Over time, a close alignment evolved between economic theory and arguments for public investments, including lobbying for federal programs (Slaughter 1991).

The numeric ratios embedded in human capital theory held up well in economic research, given the correlations between state spending and state economic productivity (Paulsen 2001a, 2001b). However, if investment in higher education declined while the economy improved, then most of these ratios for public investment (the rate of return) actually improved. And that pattern evolved within states during the early

1990s—the cross-state correlations may have held up, but within states it became apparent that colleges could be maintained with less state funding per student because students could afford to pay more (St. John 2003). Individuals' and states' investments were not independent of each other; one could replace the other and the basic economic structure could be maintained. Individuals' returns from their investment provided an incentive for them to substitute their own spending to compensate for reductions in the public investment. The basic ratios of spending and returns seemed to hold up, but the source of investment shifted for the states' systems, moving toward the private college model. While human capital theory noted the elements of both individual and social investment, it was largely silent on the relative levels of the two forms of investment. Rational arguments about state funding simply did not hold up to the realities of market forces.

However, not all groups within the education system could afford to make the additional investments, especially at the level needed in four-year colleges (St. John and Wooden, chapter 2). In states with low grants and high tuitions, low-income students could not borrow enough from federally guaranteed loan programs to pay the costs of attending after receiving grants (St. John 2004). Thus, the breakdown of the old rationale had different implications for low-income students than for the majority, and inequalities were worse in some states than in others.

Breakdown of the Old Rationale

Advocates of privatization have essentially reinterpreted human capital theory to argue for shifting the investment decisions from society to individuals. In particular, the shift in emphasis from grants to self-help, especially to loans under the Reagan administration (Hearn 1993), was rationalized on the belief that grant recipients benefited disproportionately, an idea fostered by misguided analyses of the Pell Grant program (e.g., Hansen 1983; Kane 1995).[1] However, the cuts in need-based aid and funding for college have consequences that merit attention in the public discourse.

The real breakdown in the federal commitment to equalize opportunity, the explicit intent of the Higher Education Act (Gladieux and Wolanin 1976), came in the 1990s, with federal commitment to tax credits instead of reinvestment in Pell Grants. While both low-income and middle-income students had reasons for concern about rising prices, the Clinton administration chose to respond to the middle-income families through tax credits rather than to fix the system (St. John 2003). It may have seemed impossible to reinvest in Pell at the time, but there were alternatives, including expansions of State Student Incentive Grants (SSIG),[2] that would have addressed financial inequalities for students from low-income and lower-middle-income families (St. John 2003).

States, too, found that the institutional argument that public funding was needed to stimulate enrollment (McKeown 1996) did not hold up. Declining state spending per student on public colleges could be made up in one of two ways: through lower expenditures (including salaries) or higher tuition. State spending per student enrolled in state systems of public and private higher education declined in the 1980s and 1990s, while enrollment rates climbed, fueled by an increased rate of enrollment by traditional-age students and a sustained rate of enrollment by a growing nontraditional-age population (i.e., the baby-boom generation). The direct link between funding and enrollment, articulated in earlier government documents (e.g., Halstead 1974), did not hold up, however. Funding per student enrolled in public and private colleges went down nationally as enrollment rates went up (St. John 2003).

Institutions adapted to the breakdown of the state commitment to fund public colleges and the federal commitment to use need-based grants to equalize opportunity. Private colleges adapted the fastest and the best by redirecting funds from tuition revenue and other sources (gifts and endowment) to student grants, often using grants to raise prestige by attracting students with higher test scores (McPherson and Schapiro 1997). Public colleges are now adapting their pricing strategies as well, making choices about how to spend available dollars to improve enrollment, balancing the concerns of equity and prestige (Hossler 2004). But the shift to higher tuition in the public sector has unintended consequences for equal opportunity that cannot be fully addressed through these marginal adaptations in public colleges.

Students also have adapted to the new market system. As the cost after all grants rose, students borrowed more. In fact, debt per student rose faster than tuition in the 1990s (St. John, Hu, and Weber 2000, 2001; Wei, Li, and Berkner 2004). However, not all students could make these adaptations. Even with the increased loan limits of the 1992 reauthorization of the Higher Education Act, low-income students couldn't borrow enough through subsidized loan programs to pay the burden after grants. In 1999–2000, that burden for the average low-income student in a public four-year college was $9,100 (National Center for Education Statistics 2004; St. John 2004). Even if this level of borrowing were possible, the cumulative debt could cause serious long-term problems. Many of the mid-skill fields that required some technical postsecondary education simply did not pay enough to pay off the debt (Grubb 1996), and some middle-class professions, like teaching, were not much better off.

Public Service

Public service, another important element of the Land Grant Acts, is often overlooked in the current discourse over public finance. Teaching, research, *and* service have long been integral to the American image of academic responsibility (Paulsen and Feldman 1995). Typically, internal service to universities was distinguished from external service—service to community. Historically, service to community was valued in research universities, especially service to public and nonprofit organizations. In fact, as an integral part of their mission, land grant colleges provided extension services to support the rural economy.

While the helping hand that universities provided to communities was once integral to the concept of service, it is less so now. Like large-scale research projects, service projects by universities have become a mode of economic enterprise—an important revenue source. Not only are revenues generated on grants, rather than as service per se, and used as an indicator of success in promotion, but these funds are part of what it takes to keep some universities afloat in the incentive-budgeting world of public universities (Priest and Boon, chapter 8).

Applied fields like business, law, and even education have become akin to consulting businesses, with faculty earning extra revenue from their services as independent contractors. Whereas faculty were once given a day per week of service time to support their local communities, this day has becomes a faculty "right" to earn extra income. Faculty experts often become paid experts for business, government, education, and the nonprofit enterprise. With the growth in the professional services industry, the faculty privilege to consult has become part of the income calculations of many academic families.

As these developments are part of the movement toward a market system in general, these observations are not intended as a negative critique of faculty or institutional behavior. Rather, the point here is to note that the nature of the academic enterprise is changing. The change in economic incentives in universities has been toward taxation of service activities in the form of overhead for funded projects. It is little wonder that many faculty view their consulting privilege as a part of service and are right to charge fees for their expertise. The behavior of faculty mirrors their treatment within the academy. The introduction of these market forces into universities not only changes the public image of universities, but it undermines to some extent the social contract between public higher education and citizens in states. It is little wonder that some voters don't support the use of tax dollars for universities.

Autonomy and Coordination

Another complicated aspect of the older implied social contract between universities and states has been the notion of institutional autonomy. As states took a more active role in coordination of the higher education enterprise in the 1960s and 1970s, research universities claimed their independence from regulation. During the last period of expansion, the often constitutional autonomy of public universities was respected, as states used coordinating councils to collaborate on major planning (Glenny 1959, 1971).

In the 1972 reauthorization of the Higher Education Act, the federal government provided funding for "1202 commissions,"[3] and all states soon formed some type of state agency to conduct statewide planning. However, as the federal funding incentives for structured state planning faded, and as these funding provisions disappeared, some states dropped their coordinating boards and higher education commissions or folded the function into other state agencies. Now, as we enter a new period of structural constraints on access, there is a clear need for states to coordinate funding strategies with plans for system development.

As state universities have responded to the new market incentives, a new generation of analysts have argued for accountability systems that would provide extra funding to increase graduation rates and other practices thought to be in the state and federal interest (Ewell 2004; Hauptman 2004; Longanecker 2004). The risks in such a scheme are great: while they may yield more money for elite public universities that serve mostly wealthy students (Weerts 2002), they could also structurally reinforce inequalities created by inadequate grant aid (St. John, Kline, and Asker 2001). It is difficult to adjust any such funding scheme to deal adequately with the inequalities that are increasingly evident in college access. It is evident from the reanalysis of the NCES longitudinal study of the 1992 cohort that, controlling for preparation, low-income students were more likely to be still enrolled after eight years (in 2000), while wealthier students were more likely to have attained degrees (St. John and associates, in preparation). Clearly, the current system has embedded inequalities that probably cannot be corrected by providing additional dollars to colleges with higher completion rates, a strategy that would inevitably add to inequalities.

Is It Time to Rethink the Public Interest?

The emergence of market mechanisms has fundamentally changed the public role in financing higher education, creating new incentives for states, institutions, and students. In many respects the adaptation to the market has gone well. In the 1970s few experts, if any, would have predicted that reduced funding for student grants and public colleges, increased tuition charges, and an expansion of loans would provide a formula that could expand the rate of college enrollment for traditional-age students over the next three decades; yet it happened. However, there are some serious problems with the new model of public finance.

First, structural inequalities in educational opportunities have worsened. As noted in previous chapters (Heller, chapter 1; St. John and Wooden, chapter 2), there is growing inequality in the opportunity for low-income students to enroll in public four-year colleges. While the expansion of loans and the creation of tax credits shielded the middle class from the rising costs of attendance, these remedies were unworkable for the poor. Given the expected growth in the size of the college-age cohort of the next decade or two, it will be exceedingly difficult to remedy these inequalities.

Second, we are entering a period of growth with limited enrollment capacity, especially in four-year colleges. Throughout the 1990s, planning groups called for the founding of new public campuses in the western United States, the part of the country with expanding college-age populations. Yet the responses were too late and far below the levels recommended. Although the nation's rate of college enrollment by high school graduates increased substantially between 1992 and 2000, five western states actually had decreased enrollment rates (St. John 2004). Now the country as a whole faces a similar challenge: During the next two decades we can expect an increase in demand for enrollment due to growth in the college-age population (NCES 2003). But enrollment rates could decline in the United States unless there are further adjustments to financing strategies enabling more students to enroll. Will the current market method of public finance stimulate sufficient growth of four-year colleges? Will it be possible to equalize opportunity for prepared students while expanding under the current model? The past may not be a good basis for future prediction, but there are ample reasons for concern.

Third, the public trust—the covenant that once provided the basis of public support for higher education—has been broken. The argument once used for public funding—the human capital rationale—has been reconstructed. Institutions have adapted the rationale to argue for specific investments, including research (Trammell 2004) and technology (Farmer 2004, chapter 11). However, the general argument for public funding has not held up well. The transformation of public service— from a support for states and communities to paid services—also erodes the public will to invest. Public coordination has been weakening, while calls for public accountability have been on the upswing. Do we have the capacity or the will to respond to the new challenges?

Responding to Market Challenges

Institutional responses to market forces provide insight into changes in the public good. The chapters in this volume give us an opportunity to examine how well institutional adaptations respond to the public interest. The major lessons learned about adaptation to the market model are summarized below, along with critical review of the emergent market model.

Lessons Learned about Institutional Strategy

Lesson 1: It has proven possible to generate additional revenues to replace the loss of state funding, but alternative revenue sources do not replace the need for educational revenue to support instruction. Several of the chapters in this volume illustrate the ways public colleges have adapted their enterprise to generate additional revenue, as states and the federal government withdraw traditional funding sources.

First, Hearn (chapter 4) provides an overview of alternative revenue sources and their growth in recent decades. Second, Conley and Tempel (chapter 7) describe the ways public colleges have begun to catch up with private nonprofit colleges in the donor game. Through concerted efforts, public research universities have climbed in the rankings of colleges with large endowment campaigns. However, like their nonprofit peers, most public universities face constraints on the use of endowment funds and private gifts. Private funding can enhance the educational enterprise, but seldom does it replace the need for tuition and/or government support as the primary source of revenue for education and related purposes. Endowments can support professorships and other "named" features of the educational enterprise and, as a consequence, can marginally reduce the percentage of costs covered by the combination of tuition and state subsidies.

The notion that public colleges and universities will suddenly find other profitable enterprises that will subsidize college costs for state residents is a pipe dream. Certainly, the quality of education can be enhanced by private giving. However, increasing revenue from government funding can reduce the portion of total costs borne by students, just as funding reductions had increased those costs. There is no escaping the fact that tuition and state subsidies must pay most of the direct costs of instruction. The question is: Who pays what share of these costs?

Lesson 2: Public colleges and universities are learning difficult lessons from technology integration, but improved use of technology has not substantially reduced the cost of education delivery or driven down the prices students are charged. The two chapters dealing with technology help illuminate the difficult path toward technology integration, while acknowledging the financial challenges facing public systems of higher education.

After decades of promise, technology finally appears to be making inroads in the delivery of higher education. However, as Farmer (2004) has argued, in most cases technology can be used to deliver a college course at a slightly higher cost than the traditional method, but it is difficult to do so in a way that reduces costs. In chapter 11, Farmer provides further insights into the reasons why the adaptation process has been slower and less efficient than initially imagined. Simply put, in the American system of higher education, colleges and universities lack the monopoly power some national education systems have had in building technology-based programs.

Farmer argues that the British Open University was a success in finding means to deliver college courses at lower costs because they had the class size necessary to realize a return on investment. However, the competitive market in the United States has led to false hopes as well. As Bok (2003) has so aptly described, under present conditions it is difficult for colleges and universities to realize profit on very substantial investments in new instructional technologies. Farmer (chapter 11) argues that major adaptations are necessary in related industries, including publishing, before lower delivery costs will be realized.

Second, Hossler and Gorr (chapter 10) illuminate the complexity of implementation of the new enterprise systems. While some senior administrators may have sold their boards on the idea that these large-scale investments in administrative systems would save money, the reality has been quite different. While the early efforts to develop administrative software were oriented toward economizing people's time, the newest wave of systems seem oriented toward changing the way administrative business is done, not the cost of doing business. Very often, modernizing means people spend time working in new ways; the medium of exchange—the practices of admissions, registration, and student aid—may change, but the new systems do not appear to reduce the time required by students, faculty, or administrators to complete the administrative process. They spend their time differently, engaging with technology, but there does not appear be great gains in the amount of time people have available for the educational side of the enterprise. "Bells and whistles" may help improve an institution's competitiveness by modernizing administrative activities, but such enhancements are unlikely to reduce the costs of education.

Lesson 3: The development of commercial enterprises at institutions of higher education may improve revenue at the margin and in the long run, but such innovations can be risky and do not replace the need for educational revenue. Analyses of entrepreneurial activities and auxiliary enterprises reveal a pattern of more responsible action but not "gold mines" capable of replacing tuition or tax dollars.

As Powers (chapter 6) so aptly observes, the extent of commercial activity, as measured by patents, has grown substantially in public higher education. However, the revenue from this growth has not kept pace with creative activity. Whether or not colleges and universities have been too quick to patent their new intellectual capital, most start-ups and most inventions don't lead to profitability.

The chances are good that research universities will generate revenue from patents on new technologies and medical products. This type of activity is not only fundamentally different from the older notion of public service in land grant colleges (which supported the introduction of technologies for economic development rather than for profits), but it also adds to the complexity of technology integration. Rather than putting products into the marketplace for industry to adapt, the new model places universities in partnership with specific corporations, sharing some of the capital risk on new ventures.

There are also lessons to learn from decades of experimentation with housing and other auxiliary enterprises (Priest, Jacobs, and Boon, chapter 9). The bottom line is that business enterprises need to be run well, managing costs to provide a good product for students. In addition, housing may become a place of academic innovation, providing supplemental support to the academic enterprise either through revenues generated from off-season activities or through educational gains from learning communities placed in dormitory settings.

Lesson 4: Integrating incentive-based budgeting enables public universities to adapt to the new market environment, but it does not add to efficiency. Priest and Boon (chapter 8) add to the literature on incentive-based budgeting. The experience of Indiana University and others that have ventured into and adapted the model reveals a tighter link between financial strategies and academic strategies in incentive-based budgeting models. In decentralized budgeting systems, individual programs must make decisions on investing in faculty stars as well as on recouping the investment. For example, at Indiana University, the School of Business and the School of Music, both highly rated enterprises, balance the costs of star faculty with other instructional strategies that constrain education costs. The decisions about where and how to invest as well as when to economize are appropriately made within academic units. Incentive budgeting makes this possible.

Institutional Responsibility in a Market System

The picture that emerges from these lessons reveals that public colleges and universities, like their nonprofit counterparts, are becoming fiscally proactive and, in the process, are learning new forms of responsibility in the new marketplace. However, the major policy lesson learned is that *the new strategies do not replace the need for revenue that directly supports the educational side of the academic enterprise.* The new market environment also has lessons to teach us about how to make a market system work better.

Two theories have been used to explain the patterns of revenue substitution evident in public colleges and universities. Slaughter and Leslie (1997) used resource dependency theory to explain why colleges would generate revenue from tuition and other sources as substitutes for the decline in state funding. In addition, Bowen's revenue theory—the argument that institutions raise all the money they can in pursuit of their goals for excellence (Bowen 1980)—has been used to explain resource substitution (Hossler 2004). However, while the phenomenon of revenue substitution is clearly evident and appears related to both theories, neither theory explains the role of market adaptation.

Another possibility is that educational organizations change strategies through innovation in response to market changes, an argument that has been used in support of vouchers (Chub and Moe 1990, 1991). An examination of adaptations to the voucher scheme in urban settings reveals that system administrators and principals (St. John and Ridenour 2001, 2002) adapted their thinking about innovations and markets when the finance scheme changed, but teachers in public schools were slower to adapt because of regulatory constraints on their teaching behavior (Ridenour and St. John 2003). Qualitative studies of organizational adaptation to changes resulting from market forces in higher education can help build an understanding of governance and finance.

Clearly, public universities have responded to changes in external markets by seeking alternative revenue sources, as is evident from the chapters of this volume, but the core functions seem slower to change. For example, Farmer (chapter 11) argues that technologies and industries must adapt to the structure of colleges to achieve the goals of e-learning, rather than the reverse. Since the current market precludes imposition of monopoly status for a distance learning organization like the British Open University in this country, more adaptive strategies are needed both within universities and in related industries like publishing.

In addition, the constraints on the uses of revenue from research, commercialization, gifts, and endowment limit the use of these alternative revenue sources for the support of the core teaching function. Rather, revenue accrued for educational purposes remains the primary source of funds for expenditures for educational purposes (St. John 2003). So while a pattern of seeking new revenue sources is evident in academe as a response to the decline in state funding, the new revenue has not been used to subsidize teaching. Instead, there are increased incentives for faculty to engage in alternative revenue-generating activities. To the extent that revenues from research and service projects buy out faculty teaching time, talented teachers focus on activities other than teaching. Lower-cost part-time teachers may be used in their stead, creating microprofit centers, potentially eroding the quality of instruction. So adapting to market forces alone is unlikely to generate the revenue needed to expand educational opportunity or reduce students' costs of higher education, an axiom illustrated by the history of private, nonprofit colleges.

The introduction of responsibility-centered management and other incentive budgeting schemes, on the other hand, brings internal market incentives into universities, enabling these large, complex organizations to adapt through strategic resource reallocation across units. The internal competition for educational revenues creates incentives for improving teaching (Becker and Theobald 2002; Paulsen and St. John 2002). Introducing new, market-based incentive structures into research universities may create more incentive to innovate on the educational side of the enterprise.

Whether we hold to the revenue theory or the resource theory, it does not appear that alternative revenue sources and the introduction of market forces will solve the equity problems facing higher education. As long as the majority of students can afford the cost of attendance at public four-year universities, there is room for further adaptation. Institutions will probably continue to raise tuition to compensate for the loss of state funding as institutional severance protection. However, the introduction of market forces saves taxpayer dollars, reducing taxpayer funding per student by shifting the cost to students (St. John 2003). It also introduces a new set of barriers to realization of the public interest.

As a consequence of the market forces—the rise in cost of attendance plus expansion of loans—public colleges and universities have become more responsible participants in the privatizing educational market. There is a fairer form of competition for students between public and private colleges than was envisioned three decades ago (e.g., Breneman, Finn, and Nelson 1978). Research universities have seized the opportunity to raise revenues from a wider range of sources as a means of strengthening their core missions.

While the notion of resource substitution clearly holds up a partial explanation for the behaviors described in the preceding chapter, this idea alone does not fully deal with the market adaptation process. In a sense, the older model of finance in public universities was more linear, but it was dependent on state funding as the dominant avenue for securing funding for educational operations. Enrollments drove state funding, and tuition was a relatively modest concern in the old model. The shift to dependence on tuition revenue as a more central portion of educational revenues has meant that public colleges must consider tuition as well as student grants when trying to gain balance in revenues for educational purposes (Hossler 2004). Not only is it harder to estimate revenues in this more dynamic environment, but new incentives for change and improvement are introduced, especially when internal markets are used along with the new finance models.

In sum, the process of privatizing public higher education is well under way, but it is far from complete. Public colleges clearly have adapted to the new environment, taking on more revenue-generating activities to diversify, but these diverse funding sources do not decrease dependency on enrollment for educational revenues. Rather than appealing to their states for educational revenues, institutions are forced to make sure their programs appeal to students who can pay the cost of attending. If the institutions must use tuition revenue to support operations, then they have limited room to use tuition as a leveraging process

261

to increase enrollment. In this context, it could be argued that at least some public universities are starting to behave more responsibly, as least as fiscal agents. They are less dependent on states and may become more responsive to students as they become more dependent on student choices for their educational revenues.

Reclaiming the Public Interest

Adapting public financial strategies to assure that the public interest is met in this emergent market system of higher education represents a formidable challenge for states and the federal government. If public institutions are forced to raise tuition, then it is not reasonable to expect them also to take on state and federal responsibilities for equalizing postsecondary opportunity.

While the equal right to higher education, unlike the equal right to K–12 education, may not be protected under state and federal constitutions (St. John and Chung 2004), there are other strong arguments in its defense. Specifically, the basic educational standard required for economic citizenship—the ability to contribute economically to family and society—has risen, probably to a level that includes at least some college education. If such a standard is emerging, as appears to be the case in the policy literature (St. John and associates, in preparation), then the government obligation to provide equal educational opportunity merits reconsideration. The failure to equalize opportunity could destine many to substandard livelihoods, if not dependence on the public for basic subsistence. Furthermore, the standards we use to judge whether equal opportunity exists are intertwined with both the level of academic preparation provided by K–12 education and the use of market strategies to finance higher education opportunity.

Since the theory of human capital lacks the value basis needed for determining the government fiduciary responsibility for promoting equal opportunity in the new market system, we turned to the literature on just societies for a new basis for such a standard. After presenting the logical basis for such a standard, we review the evidence in this text relative to the standard.

Just Societies in Perspective

When setting a standard for government involvement in the market system of higher education, it is important to consider a standard of jus-

262

tice that considers all citizens. John Rawls's theory of justice (1971, 1999) provides a starting point for this task but must be anchored in the practical realities of pluralistic democratic societies such as the United States. Rawls proposes two principles of justice, along with a "just savings principle" that relates to the role of tax support:

- Principle 1 relates to basic rights, which all individuals have in a democratic society. The rights to an education are nearly universally accepted (Nussbaum 1999; Sen 1999), and in the United States equal access to college should be a right for those who qualify academically.
- Principle 2 relates to equal opportunity, holding that if there is an inequality, it should favor the most disadvantaged. School desegregation and student aid are just two of many areas of education policy where there has been a historic emphasis on equal opportunity.
- The just savings principle relates to cross-generation equity, which includes the use of taxation to support education. In the current context of majority concern about tax rates, it is important to balance taxpayer costs with concerns about equity and basic rights in education.

These three principles can provide a way of thinking about the balance achieved in K–12 education policies and higher education finance (St. John 2003; St. John and associates, in preparation). The first principle relates to the rights to a basic education through K–12 preparation for higher education and/or employment. The second principle relates to (a) whether that basic right is open to all and (b) whether, if available, the privilege to enter higher education is equal for equally prepared students regardless of income. In contrast, the just savings principle relates to whether citizens are willing to be taxed to provide opportunities for higher education.

Since the implementation of the market model of public finance evolved in response to voter concerns about tax rates, among other concerns, it is important that the use of these or other principles of justice consider this constraint. In his critique of Rawls's theory, Walzer (1988) argues that alternatives such as vouchers must be considered in democratic societies, but that equal opportunity still merits attention. Therefore, there is sound reason to consider how equity can be maintained as an explicit intention of government during the transition to a market system. Thus, rather than argue for a reversal of this trend, our approach is to consider ways of achieving equity within this context.

There are two ways that the equity standard applies to the transition to a market system of finance. First, it is crucial to provide basic education at the level that allows all citizens to achieve full citizenship—a right that extends to all women and men (Nussbaum 1999). In the United States it is apparent that there is unequal opportunity to prepare for higher education. This is in part a consequence of the failure of education reforms in the 1980s and 1990s, because implementation of these reforms increased rather than decreased inequalities (Miron and St. John 2003; St. John and associates, in preparation). The apparent failure of school reform merits consideration in admissions offices and retention programs. It is important to ensure that academic support is provided where appropriate and as needed to admitted students. However, assuming relatively equal rights to prepare, then we must consider the equal right to enroll in higher education for students who are equally prepared. As a minimum standard, *students who are equally prepared for four-year colleges should have equal rights to enroll.*

The federal government claims that this standard is currently being met (e.g., NCES 1997; see also St. John and Wooden, chapter 2). Yet several reanalyses of national studies indicate that hundreds of thousands of low-income, college-prepared students are being denied opportunity to enroll in four-year colleges each year (Advisory Committee on Student Financial Assistance 2002; Fitzgerald 2004; Lee 2004; St. John 2002, 2003; St. John and associates, in preparation). Equitable financing of higher education provides the best means for equalizing opportunity for prepared students.

Reclaiming the Public Interest

Just as the higher education community has not completed the adjustment to a market system, government agencies also face challenges. Perhaps the biggest challenges for states and the federal government are

- Readjusting K–12 reform to improve the opportunities for low-income students to attain a college preparatory high school education to ensure that equity is maintained in a period of rising educational standards and expectations.
- Adapting the new market strategies to ensure equal opportunity for students who have prepared academically.

The fact is that high schools have been widely criticized for failing to meet the necessary standards (Kazis, Vargas, and Hoffman 2004; St. John and associates, in preparation). For decades the federal government and states have tried to raise standards through accountability, a strategy that appears to have failed, especially in minority-serving high schools (St. John and associates, in preparation). Through outreach and technical assistance to high schools, public colleges and universities have roles to play in testing better approaches to the reform of high schools. In addition, the admission standards for public higher education should be adjusted to recognize differences in high schools, using a method that enhances rather than detracts from academic success (e.g., Goggin 1999; Sedlacek 2004; St. John, Simmons, and Musoba 2002).

The issue of equalizing opportunity for college enrollment of prepared students also merits more attention from states. There are two major ways this can be achieved: (1) doubling the size of the Pell Grant maximum (St. John, Chung, Musoba, Simmons, Wooden, and Mendez 2004); and (2) expanding the state-federal partnership in the second-tier grant programs (St. John 2003; St. John et al. 2004). The second option involves less total cost for taxpayers and relies on both states and the federal government to adapt their policies. However, it is abundantly evident that it is possible to correct the financial inequalities created by the new market system of higher education finance.

The Underlying Challenge

A shift is under way from the public funding of colleges and universities as a means of providing access to the new market system with a reduced level of public funding per student. Public colleges and universities have only partially adapted to the new direction of policy, but they demonstrate a responsible pattern of change, at least with respect to the generation of alternative sources of revenues. However, while colleges and universities may become more directly responsive to external markets through their new finance strategies, it is unlikely that these new strategies will substantially reduce students' costs of higher education. The final chapter of this book further considers the institutional adaptation process.

The challenge for states and the federal government in this shift is to make the adjustments necessary to ensure that low-income students who prepare for college have the financial opportunity to enroll. Very few states have met a reasonable equity standard in recent decades (National Center for Public Policy and Higher Education 2004; St. John 2004). Yet there is a strong link between funding for state grant programs and improvement—or decline—in college enrollment rates within states (St. John 2004; St. John, Chung, Musoba, and Simmons 2004). Therefore, states should be part of the solution.

What is remarkable and should not be overlooked in the critiques of the market system (e.g., Slaughter and Leslie 1997; St. John 2003) is that college enrollment rates have improved in spite of a decline in funding. This is a prima facie indicator that institutions have responded to the changing conditions—including the decline in the size of the traditional-age cohort in the 1990s—by increasing opportunity. However, these adaptive strategies have also accentuated inequalities, increasing the gap in opportunity between low-income students and similarly prepared peers.

Racial and financial inequalities in higher education are now greater than at any period since the early 1960s. States and institutions, along with the federal government, need to be part of the solution, just as they were part of the problem. It is in the public interest in the United States —as a society that espouses the principles of justice—to adapt by equalizing opportunity. If the market approach to higher education finance continues to predominate, then the challenge of ensuring equal opportunity will become more, not less, urgent.

Notes

1. These analyses essentially constructed ratios of spending on Pell in relation to enrollment rates. However, they ignored the large decline in other federal grants, including social security and veterans' benefits (St. John 1994, 2003). When these other government investments are considered, it is evident that (a) public spending on grants declined after Pell was implemented, and (b) enrollment rates were maintained and equity was improved as a consequence of targeting aid dollars on low-income students (St. John 2003).

2. SSIG, part of the Leveraging Educational Assistance Partnership (LEAP) authorized under Title IV of the Higher Education Act (HEA), funds grants with one-third federal and two-thirds state funding.

3. Authorized under Section 1202 of the education amendments of 1972.

References

Advisory Committee on Student Financial Assistance. 2002. *Empty promises: The myth of college access in America.* Washington, D.C.: Author.

Becker, G. S. 1964. *Human capital: A theoretical and empirical analysis, with special reference to education.* New York: Columbia University Press.

Becker, W. E., and N. D. Theobald. 2002. Reward structures and faculty behavior under responsibility-centered management. In *Incentive-based budgeting systems in public universities,* ed. D. M. Priest, W. E. Becker, D. Hossler, and E. P. St. John. Northampton, Mass.: Edward Elgar.

Bok, D. 2003. *Universities in the marketplace: The commercialization of higher education.* Princeton, N.J.: Princeton University Press.

Bowen, H. R. 1980. *The cost of higher education: How much do colleges and universities spend per student and how much should they spend?* San Francisco: Jossey-Bass.

Breneman, D. W., C. E. Finn, and S. Nelson, eds. 1978. *Public policy and private higher education.* Washington, D.C.: The Brookings Institution.

Carnegie Commission on Higher Education. 1973. *Priorities for action: Final report.* New York: McGraw-Hill.

Chubb, J. E., and T. M. Moe. 1990. *Politics, markets, and America's schools.* Washington, D.C.: The Brookings Institution.

———. 1991. Schools in a marketplace: Chubb and Moe argue their bold proposal. *The School Administrator* 48(1): 18, 20, 22, 25.

Ewell, P. T. 2004. An accountability system for "doubling the numbers." In *Double the numbers: Increasing postsecondary credentials for underrepresented youth,* ed. R. Kazis, J. Vargas, and N. Hoffman, 101–11. Cambridge, Mass.: Harvard Education Press.

Farmer, J. 2004. Financing instructional technology and distance education: Reviewing costs and outcomes. In *Public funding of higher education: Changing contexts and new rationales,* ed. E. P. St. John and M. D. Parsons. Baltimore, Md.: Johns Hopkins University Press.

Fitzgerald, B. 2004. Federal financial aid and college access. In *Public policy and college access: Investigating the federal and state roles in equalizing postsecondary opportunity,* Vol. 19 of *Readings on equal education,* ed. E. P. St. John, 1–28. New York: AMS Press.

Gilpin, R. 2001. *Global political economy: Understanding the international economic order.* Princeton, N.J.: Princeton University Press.

Gladieux, L. E., and T. Wolanin. 1976. *Congress and the colleges: The national politics of higher education.* Lexington, Mass.: Lexington Books.

Glenny, L. A. 1959. *Autonomy of public colleges: The challenge of coordination.* New York: McGraw-Hill.

———. 1971. *Coordinating higher education for the 70s: Multi-campus and statewide guidelines for practice.* Berkeley, Calif.: Center for Research and Development in Higher Education.

Goggin, W. J. 1999. A "merit-aware" model for college admissions and affirmative action. *Postsecondary Education Opportunity Newsletter* (May): 6–12. The Mortenson Research Seminar on Public Policy Analysis of Opportunity for Postsecondary Education.

Grubb, W. N. 1996. *Working in the middle: Strengthening education and training for the mid-skilled labor force.* San Francisco: Jossey-Bass.

Halstead, D. K. 1974. *Statewide planning in higher education.* Washington, D.C.: U.S. Government Printing Office.

Hansen, W. L. 1983. The impact of student financial aid on access. In *The crisis in higher education,* ed. J. Froomkin. New York: Academy of Political Science.

Hansen, W. L., and A. B. Weisbrod. 1969. *Benefits, costs, and finance of public higher education.* Chicago: Markham Publishing Co.

Hauptman, A. M. 2004. Using institutional incentives to improve student performance. In *Double the numbers: Increasing postsecondary credentials for underrepresented youth,* ed. R. Kazis, J. Vargas, and N. Hoffman, 121–33. Cambridge, Mass.: Harvard University Press.

Hearn, J. C. 1993. The paradox of growth in federal aid for college students, 1965–1990. In *Higher education: Handbook of theory and research,* ed. J. C. Smart, 9:94–153. New York: Agathon Press.

Honeyman, D. S., and M. Bruhn. 1996. The financing of higher education. In *A struggle to survive: Funding higher education in the next century*, ed. D. S. Honeyman, J. L. Wattenbarger, and K. C. Westbrook, 1–28. Thousand Oaks, Calif.: Corwin.

Hossler, D. 2004. Refinancing public universities: Student enrollments, incentive-base budgeting and incremental revenue. In *Public funding of higher education: Changing contexts and new rationales*, ed. E. P. St. John and M. P. Parsons, 145–163. Baltimore, Md.: Johns Hopkins University Press.

Jencks, C., and D. Reisman. 1968. *The academic revolution.* Chicago: Doubleday Press.

Johnson, E. L. 1989. Misconceptions about early land-grant colleges. In *ASHE reader on the history of higher education*, ed. L. F. Goodchild and H. S. Wechsler, 222–33. Needham Heights, Mass.: Ginn Press.

Kane, T. J. 1995. *Rising public college tuition and college entry: How well do public subsidies promote access to college?* Working paper series, No. 5146. Cambridge, Mass.: National Bureau of Economic Research.

Kazis, R., J. Vargas, and N. Hoffman, eds. 2004. *Double the numbers: Increasing postsecondary credentials for underrepresented youth.* Cambridge, Mass.: Harvard Education Press.

Lee, J. B. 2004. Access revisited: A preliminary reanalysis of NELS. In *Public policy and college access: Investigating the federal and state roles in equalizing postsecondary opportunity*, Vol. 19 of *Readings on equal education*, ed. E. P. St. John, 87–96. New York: AMS Press.

Longanecker, D. A. 2004. Financing tied to postsecondary outcomes: Examples from states. In *Double the numbers: Increasing postsecondary credentials for underrepresented youth*, ed. R. Kazis, J. Vargas, and N. Hoffman, 113–22. Cambridge, Mass.: Harvard University Press.

Marsden, G. M. 1994. *The soul of the American university: From Protestant establishment to established nonbelief.* New York: Oxford University Press.

McKeown, M. P. 1996. State funding formulas: Promise fulfilled? In *A struggle to survive: Funding higher education in the next century*, ed. D. S. Honeyman, J. L. Wattenbarger, and K. C. Westbrook. Thousand Oaks, Calif.: Corwin Press.

McPherson, M. S., and M. O. Schapiro. 1997. *The student aid game: Meeting need and rewarding talent in American higher education.* Princeton, N.J.: Princeton University Press.

Miron, L. F., and E. P. St. John. 2003. Implications of the new global context for urban reform. In *Reinterpreting urban school reform: Have urban schools failed, or has the reform movement failed urban schools?* ed. L. F. Miron and E. P. St. John, 299–11. Albany: State University of New York Press.

National Center for Education Statistics (NCES). 1997. *Access to higher postsecondary education for the 1992 high school graduates.* NCES 98–105. By L. Berkner and L. Chavez. Project Officer: C. D. Carroll. Washington, D.C.: National Center for Education Statistics.

———. 2003. *Projections of education statistics to 2013.* NCES 2004–013. By D. E. Gerald and W. J. Hussar. Washington, D.C.: National Center for Education Statistics.

———. 2004. *A decade of undergraduate student aid: 1989–90 to 1999–2000.* [NCES 2004–158]. By C. C. Wei, X. Li, and L. K. Berkner. Washington, D.C.: National Center for Education Statistics.

National Center for Public Policy and Higher Education. 2004. *Measuring up 2004: The state-by-state report card on higher education.* [Report No. 04–6]. San Jose, Calif.: National Center for Public Policy and Higher Education.

Nussbaum, M. C. 1999. *Sex and social justice.* Oxford, UK: Oxford University Press.

Paulsen, M. B. 2001a. The economics of human capital and investment in higher education. In *The finance of higher education: Theory, research, policy and practice,* ed. M. B. Paulsen and J. C. Smart, 55–94. New York: Agathon Press.

———. 2001b. The economics of the public sector: The nature and role of public policy in higher education finance. In *The finance of higher education: Theory, research, policy and practice,* ed. M. B. Paulsen and J. C. Smart, 95–132. New York: Agathon Press.

Paulsen, M. B., and K. A. Feldman. 1995. Toward a reconceptualization of scholarship: A human action system with functional imperatives. *Journal of Higher Education* 66(6): 615–40.

Paulsen, M. B., and E. P. St. John. 2002. Budget incentive structures and the improvement of college teaching. In *Incentive-based budgeting systems in public universities,* ed. D. M. Priest et al., 161–84. Northampton, Mass.: Edward Elgar.

Rawls, J. 1971. *A theory of justice.* Cambridge, Mass.: Belknap Press of Harvard University Press.

———. 1999. *The law of peoples.* Cambridge, Mass.: Harvard University Press.

Ridenour, C. S., and E. P. St. John. 2003. Private scholarships and school choice: Innovation or class reproduction? In *Reinterpreting urban schools reform: Have urban schools failed, or has the reform movement failed urban schools?* ed. L. F. Miron and E. P. St. John. Albany: State University of New York Press.

Sedlacek, W. E. 2004. *Beyond the big test: Noncognitive assessment in higher education.* San Francisco: Jossey-Bass.

Sen, A. 1999. *Development as freedom.* New York: Anchor Press.

Slaughter, S. 1991. The official "ideology" of higher education: Ironies and inconsistencies. In *Culture and ideology in higher education: Advancing a critical agenda,* ed. W. G. Tierney, 59–86. New York: Praeger.

Slaughter, S., and L. L. Leslie. 1997. *Academic capitalism: Politics, policies, and the entrepreneurial university.* Baltimore, Md.: Johns Hopkins University Press.

Stiglitz, J. E. 2003. *Globalization and its discontents.* New York: Norton.

St. John, E. P. 1994. *Prices, productivity, and investment.* ASHE/ERIC monograph, No. 3. San Francisco: Jossey-Bass.

———. 2002. *The access challenge: Rethinking the causes of the new inequality.* Policy Issue Report No. 2002–01. Bloomington: Indiana Education Policy Center.

———. 2003. *Refinancing the college dream: Access, equal opportunity, and justice for taxpayers.* Baltimore, Md.: Johns Hopkins University Press.

———. 2004. *Unequal financial access to postsecondary education.* Prepared for Renewing Our Schools, Securing Our Future, National Task Force on Public Education.

St. John, E. P., and associates. (in review). *Education and the public interest: School reform, public finance, and access to college.* Dordrecht: Springer.

St. John, E. P., and C. G. Chung. 2004. Merit and equity: Rethinking award criteria in the Michigan scholarship program. In *Public funding of higher education: Changing contexts and new rationales,* ed. E. P. St. John and M. D. Parsons, 124–40. Baltimore, Md.: Johns Hopkins University Press.

St. John, E. P., C. G. Chung, G. D. Musoba, and A. B. Simmons. 2004. Financial access: The impact of state financial strategies. In *Public policy and college access: Investigating the federal and state roles in equalizing postsecondary opportunity,* Vol. 19 of *Readings on equal education,* ed. E. P. St. John, 109–29. New York: AMS Press.

St. John, E. P., C. G. Chung, G. D. Musoba, A. B. Simmons, O. S. Wooden, and J. Mendez. 2004. *Expanding college access: The impact of state finance strategies.* Indianapolis, Ind.: The Lumina Foundation for Education.

St. John, E. P., S. Hu, and J. Weber. 2000. Keeping public colleges affordable: A study of persistence in Indiana's public colleges and universities. *Journal of Student Financial Aid* 30(1): 21–32.

———. (2001). State policy and the affordability of public higher education: The influence of state grants on persistence in Indiana. *Research in Higher Education* 42: 401–28.

St. John, E. P., K. A. Kline, and E. H. Asker. 2001. The call for public accountability: Rethinking the linkages to student outcomes. In *The states and public higher education: Affordability, access, and accountability,* ed. D. E. Heller, 219–42. Baltimore, Md.: Johns Hopkins University Press.

St. John, E. P., and M. D. Parsons. 2004. Introduction to *Public funding of higher education: Changing contexts and new rationales,* ed. E. P. St. John and M. D. Parsons, 1–16. Baltimore, Md.: Johns Hopkins University Press.

St. John, E. P., and C. S. Ridenour. 2001. Market forces and strategic adaptation: The influence of private scholarships on planning in urban school systems. *The Urban Review* 33: 269–90.

———. 2002. School leadership in a market setting: The influence of private scholarships on education leadership in urban schools. *Leadership and Policy in Schools* 1(4): 317–44.

St. John, E. P., A. B. Simmons, and G. D. Musoba. 2002. Merit-aware admissions in public universities: Increasing diversity. *Thought and Action* 27(2): 35–46.

Trammell, M. L. 2004. Reconstructing rationales for research funding. In *Public funding of higher education: Changing contexts and new rationales,* ed. E. P. St. John and M. D. Parsons, 164–85. Baltimore, Md.: Johns Hopkins University Press.

Trow, M. 1974. *Problems in the transition from elite to mass higher education.* New York: McGraw-Hill.

Walzer, M. 1988. *The company of critics: Social criticism and political commitment in the twentieth century.* New York: Basic Books.

Weerts, D. J. 2002. *State governments and research universities: A framework for a renewal partnership.* New York: RoutledgeFalmer.

Wei, C. C., X. Li, and L. K. Berkner. 2004. *A decade of undergraduate student aid: 1989–90 to 1999–2000.* NCES 2004–158. Washington, D.C.: National Center for Education Statistics.

CHAPTER THIRTEEN

Privatization in
Public Universities

Edward P. St. John and Douglas M. Priest

The shifting concepts of the public interest in higher education are important for policy makers, university administrators and faculty, and the public as well. The economic value of the public investment (Paulsen 2001a) supported one rationale for funding, but is no longer a sufficient basis for rationalizing public funding. The investment in colleges and universities is constructed in recurrent government budgets based on beliefs about the value of and returns from this investment. The privatization of state colleges and universities involves the withdrawal of some state funding per FTE from institutions with some fund replacement from other revenue sources and, where possible, effective use of available resources. The source most directly related to student instruction is tuition revenue, but the shift from general funding for universities has implications for research and service as well. The review of these developments in relation to a workable standard of the public interest (chapter 12) suggests that the transition has enabled the public system to accommodate unexpected enrollment—given that enrollment was consistently higher than predictions in the late twentieth century—but that adjustments are vitally needed to contend with the inequalities created by the new system of public finance.

With this reconstructed understanding of the public interest, along with the review of changes in public finance and organizational adaptation in public universities, it is possible to reconsider strategies for adaptation. The process of transition in public systems of higher education

271

in student charges and targeted state funding has proceeded unevenly across the states. Of course, there is substantial reason for critique of privatization (Rizvi, chapter 3). In fact, in their latest book on academic capitalism, Slaughter and Rhoades (2004) reframed this theory to argue that the older notion of the public good has given way to a capitalist image of the university. We stop short of taking such a critical view in this volume and instead focus on constructive steps that can be taken to reclaim the common good in the midst of the transition to a privatized system of public higher education in the states (chapter 12). This final chapter returns to the themes of the book to build a better understanding of the critical challenges facing voters, policy makers, and university officials as they make strategic decisions in this period of adaptation.

Rebuilding Government Relationships

The relationships between state governments and public universities are inherently uneasy. From the beginning of the progressive period in the late eighteenth century, state and the federal governments funded universities based on the idea that they promote the economic and social development in their states. While this assumption placed universities in inherent leadership roles within states, state funding also included obligations to the states and sometimes even direct controls. Placing controls on institutions that are by their very mission and purpose supposed to play a leadership role creates ambiguity. In the middle of the twentieth century, state coordinating boards and commissions were formed, and although many have since been dismantled, the ambiguity continues. At the current time, the notion of accountability prevails among many policy makers (Ewell 2004; Hauptman 2004; Longanecker 2004) as the preferred means of contending with this underlying ambiguity. Before turning to the notion of accountability per se, it is important to consider how the relationships between universities and states are evolving with respect to the core functions of universities.

Teaching and Educational Attainment

The teaching function of public universities contributes directly to educational attainment of state residents and indirectly to the economic development of states through the economic contributions of educated citizens. There is clearly a shift underway in the share of instruction paid for by states. In practice, it is difficult to subtract out funding for the other missions—research and service—from the teaching mission because state funding has typically been analyzed on a per-FTE basis. Theoretically, state funding contributes to the research and service mission as well. For simplicity's sake, we focus first on the role of public funding for teaching.

Given the market system of higher education finance that has evolved, it is appropriate to shift from the older notion of providing funding directly to colleges for each student (i.e., state funding formulae) to coordinating finance strategies (student aid, grants, and subsidies to colleges) to optimize educational attainment. Direct funding per student placed the primary focus on funding for public institutions, adding to the inherent conflict between public and private colleges within states. Since the 1970s most states have had some form of need-based grant aid. But few states have fully shifted to appropriate funding strategies that balance state funding for institutions with tuition charges and student grant aid—the approach needed to focus on optimizing educational attainment as an outcome of education policy.

Minnesota continues to be a good example of coordinated state funding to promote educational attainment of citizens. For more than twenty years the state has balanced funding for public institutions with tuition charges to ensure adequate funding, while maintaining an adequate grant program to ensure equitable access to public and private colleges (Berg and Hoenack 1987; Hearn and Anderson 1989, 1995; Hearn and Longanecker 1985; St. John 2005). The Minnesota strategy explicitly considers the state and student shares of per-FTE revenues and sees funding for students and institutions as part of the same budget process. The per-FTE revenue targets for education at each type of public institution—two-year college, state and regional institution, and research campus—are set in relation to their peers. In this model the percentage of costs paid by students increases, and so does funding for grants. The new grant dollars stimulate market forces in the state (i.e., expansion of private colleges). In addition, the state grants are calculated based on the expected award through the federal Pell Grant program, thus coordinating state student grants with federal grants.

Focusing on balanced funding strategies that promote education attainment provides a means of addressing the three primary interests in state finance: expanding overall enrollment through balanced support (justice principle 1); equalizing opportunity for equally prepared students across income groups (justice principle 2); and finding an appropriate level of taxpayer support for the state system of public and private colleges (just savings principle). Using this approach, it may be possible

273

to reduce the costs to taxpayers per student enrolled, expand college access, and maintain equity. In the past two decades two of these goals—expanding access and saving tax dollars—have been emphasized in most states at the expense of the third goal—equity (St. John 2003, 2005). However, given the expected enrollment growth in the next decade (Heller, chapter 1; NCES 2003), the current structure of public finance requires change.

There should be little remaining doubt that this coordination of funding mechanisms provides a workable approach to financing educational attainment through this period of shift toward privatization, yet this alternative has not been very attractive to advocates of public colleges. Lobbyists for state colleges and universities typically press for direct funding and treat funding for state student grants as a loss of revenue. Thus, the shift toward the strategic use of state funding to promote education attainment provides a means of promoting the collective good of citizens in the state. Most states are long overdue for changes in government relationships with universities. Reforming the budget process may help reconstruct the relationship between institutions and their states by better coordinating the basic interests of different types of colleges providing two-year and four-year programs in public and private universities. In some states student grants and loan forgiveness are used to stimulate the supply of professionals in fields like education and nursing. In addition to these state mechanisms, federal funding for Pell Grants and the state-federal partnership are obviously important (see chapter 12).

Research, Service, and Economic Development

Historically, state funding for state universities has included some subsidy for faculty time for research and service as integral parts of state funding formulae. The embedded funding from research related to faculty time has benefits to states through higher quality of education and contributions to economic development, as traditionally argued in the human-capital rationale (Paulsen 2001a, 2001b). This type of embedded funding differs from external funding for research, which is our focus here. In the evolving market model of public finance, there is also increasing pressure on university faculty to generate revenue from research and service. In fact, the incentives for these mechanisms are often explicitly considered within the newer university budgeting systems according to Priest and Boon (chapter 8) and may be increasingly considered integral internal budgeting.

We would be remiss, however, if we did not note that the privatization of public higher education changes the funding relationship for research and service activities that can be thought of as state projects. In the older land-grant model, funding was provided for research and service in direct support of agriculture and related areas, support that was thought to promote economic development. In other fields, however, this type of general funding for research and development seldom became routine unless there were line items in state and federal governments for these mechanisms.

Accountability Reconsidered

Many states have tried out different types of incentive funding using accountability criteria (Zumeta 2001). Typically these schemes use completion rates and other target goals as a basis for providing supplemental funding. However, since these strategies generally overlook state responsibility for equity funding (chapter 12), they add to inequalities. Funding incentives coupled with accountability schemes are a poor substitute for the development of workable, well-coordinated approaches to state funding for higher education.

Generating Revenue to Support Missions

Hearn (chapter 4) clearly articulates the importance of aligning revenue-generating strategies with the strategic decision process within universities. The primary challenge facing universities as they adjust to the privatization process is to substitute tuition revenue for the loss of direct state funding (Heller, chapter 1). Seeking alternative revenue sources can have different sorts of outcomes, from enriching them through building endowments (Conley and Tempel, chapter 7) to putting them at financial risk and undermining access (Bok 2003; Powers, chapter 6). We conclude that explicit consideration of mission is central to the revenue substitution function of tuition and the revenue mission enhancement function of alternative revenue sources.

Tuition as Substitute for Direct State Funding

Hossler (chapter 5) examined the implications of using tuition revenue as a substitute for state funding. At a minimum, this shift involves viewing students and their families as a revenue source. While private nonprofit colleges have historically had this type of fiduciary relationship with students and families, these developments represent a fundamental shift in the roles of admissions and student aid in public universities. As tuition has risen, enrollment management has become an important mechanism for promoting and ensuring financial stability. Two issues raised in Hossler's chapter merit further attention in relation to the reconstructed understanding of the public interest.

The first issue relates to the state obligation for maintaining equitable opportunity for equally prepared students across income groups. As Hossler articulates, state institutions cannot afford to assume this obligation as they privatize. The majority of private colleges use aid leveraging, a process that combines merit and need in the strategic use of student aid (McPherson and Schapiro 1997; Heller, chapter 1) as a means of generating tuition revenue. While this process undermines the equity goals of the general public, it is an appropriate adaptation to the inadequacy of state and federal aid (St. John 2003, 2005).

Over the past two decades there has been a substantial shift in the philosophies used to package student financial aid. In the 1970s, when federal student financial aid was more substantial on a per-FTE basis (St. John and Wooden, chapter 2), it was easier for public and private colleges to meet the remaining need after state and federal grants. In this context, public and private colleges could aim to meet the unmet need with modest institutional grants for students who met admission criteria. In the 1980s, private colleges began to allocate larger shares of tuition revenues to grants as a means of substituting for the loss of federal grant dollars. As a consequence of competition for high-achieving undergraduates, the practice of using aid to attract admitted students became linked to academic ability even more explicitly than to financial need. Now public colleges are going through a similar sort of transition. For example, Hossler (2004; also chapter 5) documents the ways public colleges have used aid leveraging to attract out-of-state students who pay higher tuition.

Using resident tuition as a substitute for federal or state grant dollars would be highly problematic, however. It would put public universities in the position of taxing students from upper-income families to pay for enrollment of students from low-income families. Therefore, the goal of maintaining a just system of public finance (St. John, chapter 12) necessitates that states not abdicate their responsibility to equalize opportunity. The previous chapter advocates changes in public funding that would enable states to reassume this responsibility.

Other Revenue and Mission Enhancement

Conley and Tempel (chapter 7) document the progress public universities have made in their efforts to raise endowments and other revenue from gifts and philanthropy. An appropriate response to privatization, building endowments directly aligned with mission and strategic plans enables public colleges to enhance their offerings. However, few private universities use their endowments as a substitute for tuition. In the few cases where this has been done (e.g., Rice University), it has been the intent of donors to subsidize student costs. In the current context, both public and private colleges raise gift and endowment support for scholarships, another means of aligning mission and endowment.

Strategic investment decisions are obviously complex, but they remain important because of the costs associated with endowment initiatives, technology transfer offices, and the like (Hearn, chapter 4). It can take many years to gain revenue from patents and joint ventures with private companies, and many universities do not realize substantial revenue from these efforts (Powers, chapter 6). Therefore, it is important that institutions treat these decisions as investments with appropriate risk assessment. We suggest that these investment decisions be guided by strategic planning and goals for mission enhancement, given the limits on financial resources for discretionary investment.

Similarly, decisions about privatizing services (Priest, Jacobs, and Boon, chapter 9) and about technology (Bok 2003; Farmer, chapter 11; Hossler and Gorr, chapter 10) should be carefully assessed because they may generate supplemental revenues. Therefore, we view these areas of adaptation as decisions about how best to modernize, rather than decisions about revenue generation per se.

Reframing Revenue Generation in Privatization

There is a literature on higher education finance that extols the virtues of privatization as being more efficient and rational than traditional forms of higher education finance (Goldstein, Kempner, Rush, and Bookman 1993). Such arguments are appropriately viewed as rationales that must be tested against evidence (St. John and Paulsen 2001). The analysis of auxiliary services (Priest, Jacobs, and Boon, chapter 9) illustrates that there are times when discretionary resources can be generated from privatization of services, but these changes in the locus of control do not mean lower costs for students. The example of updating laundry services through replacement and privatization of machines (chapter 9) illustrates that even small-scale outsourcing can have hidden costs for students. Raising living costs in dorms can constrain the ability to raise tuition costs if a student population is highly price sensitive. Therefore it is appropriate to consider decisions about both the investment in new revenue-generating ventures, such as patent and endowment offices, and decisions about privatization as being related to the fiduciary responsibility of the institutions. Thus, rather than viewing privatization and revenue generation as a goal, these practices should add to the arsenal of strategies university administrators can use to manage their universities in fiscally responsible ways.

We recommend that privatization be viewed in relation to the core mission of universities. The transition to strategic enrollment management that uses financial aid to leverage enrollment will be an unfortunate consequence of privatization if its eventual effect is to further increase inequalities in access. As public institutions wrestle with the complexities of pricing decisions, an inevitable stumbling block on the pathway to privatization, they must be concerned about sticker prices as well as price subsidies for low-income students. Not all students receive need-based aid or merit aid. There is a risk that some students paying the full cost of attending will not be able to handle the cost and will drop out as a result. The process of passing higher costs of services on to students does not mitigate these risks. Therefore, it is important to consider whether privatization of services actually raises or lowers costs to students when making decisions about outsourcing, just as it is necessary to consider budgets when setting tuition. Since many states constrain the use of tuition dollars for grants, it is crucial to encourage states to be partners in this process of assessing costs and risks of outsourcing.

Finally, revenue-generating strategies are appropriately viewed as being part of the mission enhancement process. Typically, colleges and universities use mission-oriented planning as the basis for developing endowment campaigns. This provides an appropriate method of aligning decisions to invest in development activities with enhancement of teaching and other mission-related functions.

Modernizing Universities

The massive changes in communications and information technologies have transformed the business enterprise, creating global connectivity in industries of all types. Such changes transform the structure of private corporations, moving from centralized strategic decision making to more complex organizational models that use technology and incentive structures to build appropriate governance and collaboration strategies. In addition to facing a shift in the locus of funding, public universities are facing demands to respond to these changes in technology and incentive structures in professional activities.

In this context it is crucial to distinguish mission-related and mission-supporting activities from centralization and control mechanisms. In our discussion of revenue generation, we argued that the mission of the institution should guide investment decisions. However, we also recognize that in contemporary universities these investment decisions are often made in decentralized ways within departments and colleges. In other words, within universities with decentralized incentive budgeting systems, it is important to provide the core units with the capability to make their own investment decisions. This means that schools, departments, and colleges should not only be engaged in identifying targets for university-wide endowment agendas, but they also need to be involved in the construction and execution of their own agendas. In other words, the alignment process should happen within the core academic units.

Thus, twenty-first-century universities need a dynamic, decentralized capacity for decision and action, but the system itself requires coordination, refinement, and alignment where appropriate. This dynamic organizational change process, now under way, contextualizes the need for technology integration and the evolution of market-based systems within universities.

Technology Integration

The complexities of technology integration are well documented by Hossler and Gorr for administrative support (chapter 10) and by Farmer (chapter 11) for e-learning. Both processes merit brief reconsideration relative to the challenges of changing government relationships and revenue generation.

Hossler and Gorr document that technology modernization does not save money; it changes operations. Clearly, there are monetary and human costs associated with building modern decentralized information systems that use the current technology in the business enterprise. The drive to build these systems is no longer to reduce administrative costs, although that will probably remain an elusive goal, but rather to enable university systems as enterprises—and their various subsidiary units—to work better and faster. Prospective students expect nearly instant responses when they contact an admissions office, just as admitted students expect to be able to file their forms and check and update records at their own convenience. The older system resulting in long lines for student services has vanished within many universities. To be competitive, universities must respond to these challenges.

However, the process of building these new systems is complex and costly. Each of the pathways the authors document—from patching together locally developed systems to purchasing new integrated systems—requires adaptation, modification, and refinement to get the parts to work together. There is currently no turnkey administrative system that universities can purchase. Instead, universities are faced with choosing a path toward enterprise modernization, and each alternative path has relatively high costs.

In addition, the efforts to integrate technology into the academic side of the educational enterprise are slowed by the rigidities of related industries. In the United Kingdom, the British Open University has had the capacity to evolve its own electronic publications capacity. In the U.S. market system, where many universities make independent decisions about the use of technologies in curriculum, universities must rationalize their conversion costs based on their own expected enrollment. In addition, the publishing industry is largely independent of the university enterprise, so it has been more difficult in the United States to evolve information technology that is compatible with curriculum. Publishers control reproduction of texts, which can limit their availability through automated systems. Recently, however, there is evidence of change. For example, the University of Michigan and Harvard University have announced agreements with Google to provide electronic access to their entire library collections. However, there is a six-year time line for the collaborative project. Even when rapid changes are technologically possible, organizational and cultural barriers impede change.

Thus, while the implied promise of technology—to modernize the way people work and learn in universities—may seem closer than ever with recent technological breakthroughs, the process of change is complex, costly, and often slow. Public colleges and universities face critical decisions about modernizing their administrative and academic practices at the same time that they are adjusting to privatization, which means major changes in their revenue sources.

Incentive-Based Budgeting Reconsidered

Budgeting systems come and go in higher education. However, the process of change from systems with strong central control to decentralized systems with embedded incentive structures is well under way.

As Priest and Boon describe (chapter 8), the early decentralized budget models started in private universities but are now widely used in major research universities. These models increase the complexity of budgeting for academic units. Some units of a university that have good enrollments may reap economic benefits, while other units in the same institution may face reductions in staff and erosion of support structures due to declining resources. These newer decentralized budgeting systems provide opportunities for academic units to manage their own enterprises, but their ability to provide technology to students and faculty could be impaired during periods of volatility.

Decisions about privatization of activities within universities may be appropriately made within academic units. Some academic units may decide to use contract personnel to build administrative systems, while others may choose to invest in permanent staff. In addition, the innovations in knowledge and uses of technology across academic and professional fields require increasingly specialized staff to support automation on the academic side. Faculty within the same academic department and program often have radically different software requirements to support their research. Thus, not only has technology become a necessary enhancement of the academic enterprise, but budgeting systems must be adapted to meet these diverse demands.

Privatization has evolved as a result of incremental political decisions made over time, rather than as a result of a new consensus. Public universities are not alone among institutions in facing pressure to decentralize their strategies, operations, and budgeting. Public hospitals, social service agencies, schools, and many other enterprises face similar challenges. But the process has been made more complex for public universities by the lack of stability in state funding.

Privatization in Context

There is ample reason to be critical of privatization and to mourn the loss of the public good (e.g., Slaughter and Leslie 1997; St. John and Parsons 2004). However, our goal in this volume has been to go beyond mere criticism to place these changes in a broad, understandable context. Three major themes have emerged from this examination of privatization. Each illustrates a challenge that requires both better understanding and new forms of action.

First, the tale of privatization of public higher education in the United States started with government actions that forced a transition from dependence on public subsidies to reliance on tuition and other revenue sources. This transition has enabled an expansion of higher education during a period of restricted tax revenue but has amplified inequalities, creating a need for universities and public officials to build better and more equitable approaches to public funding. It is unlikely that states will return to old levels of financial support to expand opportunity. However, it is possible to reframe public strategies, from subsidizing students in the public sector to providing an adequate and equitable approach to financing the expansion of attainment. The crucial issue is to ensure adequate state support for need-based grants as tuition charges climb. This new covenant has emerged in only a few states.

Second, the privatization process has led to transformation in resource acquisition within public colleges and universities. Students and their families have become an increasingly important revenue source for the core teaching function of the university. States still subsidize a portion of instructional costs, but the reliance on student tuition and fees creates a different relationship between colleges and students and their families. Paying more, they expect more, increasing the pressures to change. Seeking alternative revenue sources by adopting new organizational strategies is a possible path toward enhancement of operations, but these revenue sources generally do not decrease tuition dependence. Given that there are risks and rewards associated with efforts to raise external revenues, we recommend that colleges and universities take steps to align revenue generation with institutional missions, possibly through decentralized educational and budgeting systems.

This process of change in universities' financial mechanisms comes at the same time when universities are racing to achieve greater and better technology integration. Technology has become integral to operations at modern universities, but building new enterprise systems that use the technology has been costly and has had uneven results. Indeed, there are serious risks that efforts to modernize both administrative and academic systems could undermine the core teaching function. However, given the tighter linkages between technology and knowledge within fields, it is appropriate that many of the decisions about where and how to invest in technology be made within academic units, adding substantially to the complexity of governing the academic enterprise.

Both understanding and patience are required, therefore, as public colleges and universities speed down the road toward their new status as partially private—or quasi-public—institutions. In this concluding chapter we have focused on building a practical understanding of these changes, rather than trying to add to criticism or to redefine the problems. There is not a new crisis, but rather a set of challenges—to adapt the financing mechanisms, to change the operations to embrace the new technologies, and to improve public understanding of universities. If universities are to make it through this period of change and dwindling public financial support, they must become more valued as vital public resources that not only educate students but also contribute to social and economic development.

References

Berg, D. J., and S. A. Hoenack. 1987. The concept of cost-related tuition and its implications at the University of Minnesota. *Journal of Higher Education* 58(3): 276–305.

Bok, D. 2003. *Universities in the marketplace: The commercialization of higher education.* Princeton, N.J.: Princeton University Press.

Ewell, P. T. 2004. An accountability system for "doubling the numbers." In *Double the numbers: Increasing postsecondary credentials for underrepresented youth,* ed. R. Kazis, J. Vargas, and N. Hoffman, 101–11. Cambridge, Mass.: Harvard Education Press.

Goldstein, P. J., D. E. Kempner, S. C. Rush, and M. Bookman. 1993. *Contract management of self-operation: A decision-making guide for higher education.* Alexandria, Va.: Association of Higher Education Facilities Officers.

Hauptman, A. M. 2004. Using institutional incentives to improve student performance. In *Double the numbers: Increasing postsecondary credentials for underrepresented youth,* ed. R. Kazis, J. Vargas, and N. Hoffman, 121–33. Cambridge, Mass.: Harvard University Press.

Hearn, J. C., and M. S. Anderson. 1989. Integrating postsecondary education financing policies: The Minnesota model. In *Studying the impact of student aid on institutions,* ed. R. H. Fenske, 55–74. New Directions for Higher Education, No. 62. San Francisco: Jossey-Bass.

———. 1995. The Minnesota finance experiment. In *Rethinking tuition and student aid strategies,* ed. E. P. St. John, 5–26. New Directions for Higher Education, No. 89. San Francisco: Jossey-Bass.

Hearn, J. C., and D. Longanecker. 1985. Enrollment effects of alternative post-secondary pricing policies. *Journal of Higher Education* 56(5): 485–508.

Hossler, D. 2004. Refinancing public universities: Student enrollments, incentive-based budgeting and incremental revenue. In *Public funding of higher education: Changing contexts and new rationales,* ed. E. P. St. John and M. P. Parsons, 145–63. Baltimore, Md.: Johns Hopkins University Press.

Longanecker, D. A. 2004. Financing tied to postsecondary outcomes: Examples from states. In *Double the numbers: Increasing postsecondary credentials for underrepresented youth,* ed. R. Kazis, J. Vargas, and N. Hoffman, 113–22. Cambridge, Mass.: Harvard University Press.

McPherson, M. S., and M. O. Schapiro. 1997. *The student aid game: Meeting need and rewarding talent in American higher education.* Princeton, N.J.: Princeton University Press.

National Center for Education Statistics. 2003. *Projections of education statistics to 2013.* NCES No. 2004–013. By D. E. Gerald and W. J. Hussar. Washington, D.C.: National Center for Education Statistics.

Paulsen, M. B. 2001a. The economics of human capital and investment in higher education. In *The finance of higher education: Theory, research, policy and practice*, ed. M. B. Paulsen and J. C. Smart, 55–94. New York: Agathon Press.

———. 2001b. The economics of the public sector: The nature and role of public policy in higher education finance. In *The finance of higher education: Theory, research, policy and practice*, ed. M. B. Paulsen and J. C. Smart, 95–132. New York: Agathon Press.

Slaughter, S., and L. L. Leslie. 1997. *Academic capitalism: Politics, policies, and the entrepreneurial university*. Baltimore, Md.: Johns Hopkins University Press.

Slaughter, S., and G. Rhoades. 2004. *Academic capitalism and the new economy: Markets, state, and higher education*. Baltimore, Md.: Johns Hopkins University Press.

St. John, E. P. 2003. *Refinancing the college dream: Access, equal opportunity, and justice for taxpayers*. Baltimore, Md.: Johns Hopkins University Press.

———. 2005. *Affordability of postsecondary education: Equity and adequacy across the 50 states*. Prepared for Renewing Our Schools, Securing Our Future, National Task Force on Public Education, Center for American Progress.

St. John, E. P., and M. D. Parsons, eds. 2004. *Public funding of higher education: Changing contexts and new rationales*. Baltimore, Md.: Johns Hopkins University Press.

St. John, E. P., and M. B. Paulsen. 2001. The finance of higher education: Implications for theory, research, policy and practice. In *The finance of higher education: Theory, research, policy and practice*, ed. M. B. Paulsen and J. C. Smart, 11–38. New York: Agathon Press.

Zumeta, W. 2001. Public policy and accountability in higher education: Lessons from the past and present for the new millennium. In *The states and public higher education policy: Affordability, access and accountability*, ed. D. E. Heller, 155–97. Baltimore, Md.: Johns Hopkins University Press.

Contributors

Rachel Dykstra Boon is Research Analyst in the Chancellor's Office at Indiana University Bloomington. She is a doctoral student in education policy studies. Her research interests include state K–16 policies, higher education access and financing, and policy organization interactions.

Aaron Conley is Executive Director for Development and Alumni Relations with the School of Engineering at the University of Pittsburgh. He earned an Ed.D. in higher education and philanthropic studies from Indiana University Bloomington in 1999.

James Farmer is CEO of instructional media and magic, inc. He previously taught the Information Systems and Strategy Planning modules at Harvard University's Graduate School of Education. He graduated from the University of Oklahoma with a B.S. in mathematics, from Harvard University with an S.M. in applied mathematics, and from UCLA with an M.B.A. He has also done graduate work in economics at UCLA on the value of information.

William P. Gorr is a doctoral candidate in higher education at Indiana University. He served for twenty-three years in the U.S. Air Force, where he led software development and software migration projects for the Department of Defense and NATO. Presently, he serves as the Training Coordinator for the Department of Homeland Security in Indianapolis, Indiana.

James C. Hearn is Professor of Public Policy and Higher Education, Peabody College, Vanderbilt University. He holds an M.A. in sociology and a Ph.D. in the sociology of education from Stanford University, as well as an M.B.A. in finance from the University of Pennsylvania (Wharton) and an A.B. from Duke University. Professor Hearn's research and teaching focus on higher education policy, organization, and finance. He is a past recipient of the Distinguished Research Award of Division J of the American Educational Research Association.

Donald E. Heller is Associate Professor and Senior Research Associate at the Center for the Study of Higher Education at Penn State University. His research centers on higher education economics, public policy, and finance, with a primary focus on issues of access, choice, and persistence in postsecondary education. He received the 2002 Promising Scholar/Early Career Achievement Award from the Association for the Study of Higher Education and the 2001 Robert P. Huff Golden Quill Award from the National Association of Student Financial Aid Administrators.

Don Hossler is Professor of Educational Leadership and Policy Studies, Professor of Philanthropic Studies, and Vice Chancellor for Enrollment Services for Indiana University Bloomington. His areas of specialization include college choice, student financial aid policy, enrollment management, and higher education finance. Hossler is the author, or co-author, of twelve books and monographs and more than sixty-five articles and book chapters.

Bruce A. Jacobs serves as Vice Chancellor of Auxiliary Services and Programs at Indiana University. He believes that campus auxiliaries should function as an academic support and student development unit. He also holds an adjunct assistant professor appointment in the Higher Education and Student Affairs program in the School of Education. He is currently involved with the National Survey of Student Engagement Project DEEP (Documenting Effective Educational Practices).

Joshua B. Powers is Assistant Professor and Coordinator of the Higher Education Leadership Program at Indiana State University. His research focuses on university technology transfer performance as well as the emergent ethical implications of its practice.

Douglas M. Priest is Associate Professor of Educational Leadership and Policy Studies at Indiana University Bloomington. He has published in the areas of higher education finance and planning. He consults both within the United States and internationally in the areas of higher education administration, finance, and planning.

Fazal Rizvi has been Professor in Educational Policy Studies at the University of Illinois at Urbana-Champaign since August 2001, having previously held academic and administrative positions in a number of Australian univer-

286

sities, including Pro Vice Chancellor (International) at RMIT University in Melbourne. He is currently researching issues of student mobility and the uses international students make of their higher education abroad in the formation of global networks for both social and economic purposes.

Edward P. St. John is the Algo D. Henderson Collegiate Professor in Education at the Center for the Study of Higher and Postsecondary Education at the University of Michigan. He is author of numerous books, book chapters, and articles on topics related to student financial aid, the financing of higher education, and educational reform. He has served on the editorial boards of *The Journal of Higher Education* and *Research in Higher Education* and is series editor for *Readings on Equal Education*.

Eugene R. Tempel is Executive Director of the Center on Philanthropy at Indiana University and Professor of Philanthropic Studies, Public Administration, and Higher Education at Indiana University–Purdue University Indianapolis. A nationally recognized expert in the study and practice of philanthropy and nonprofit management, his professional experience includes teaching, training, and consulting nationally and internationally.

Ontario S. Wooden is Director of the Honors Program and Academic Success Initiatives and Assistant Professor of Education at Albany State University, Georgia. He serves on the editorial board of the National Association of Student Affairs Professionals Journal. His research interests include urban schooling, teacher preparation, and higher education access issues.

Index